ARCHITECTURE, LIBERTY AND CIVIC ORDER

Architecture, Liberty and Civic Order

Architectural Theories from Vitruvius to Jefferson and Beyond

Carroll William Westfall
University of Notre Dame, USA

Routledge
Taylor & Francis Group

LONDON AND NEW YORK

First published 2015 by Ashgate Publishing

Published 2016 by Routledge
2 Park Square, Milton Park, Abingdon, Oxon OX14 4RN
711 Third Avenue, New York, NY 10017, USA

Routledge is an imprint of the Taylor & Francis Group, an informa business

Copyright © Carroll William Westfall 2015

Carroll William Westfall has asserted his right under the Copyright, Designs and Patents Act, 1988, to be identified as the author of this work.

All rights reserved. No part of this book may be reprinted or reproduced or utilised in any form or by any electronic, mechanical, or other means, now known or hereafter invented, including photocopying and recording, or in any information storage or retrieval system, without permission in writing from the publishers.

Notice:
Product or corporate names may be trademarks or registered trademarks, and are used only for identification and explanation without intent to infringe.

British Library Cataloguing in Publication Data
A catalogue record for this book is available from the British Library.

Library of Congress Cataloging-in-Publication Data
Westfall, Carroll William.
  Architecture, liberty and civic order : architectural theories from Vitruvius to Jefferson and beyond / By Carroll William Westfall.
    pages cm
  Includes bibliographical references and index.
    ISBN 978-1-4724-5653-3 (hardback : alk. paper)—ISBN 978-1-4724-5654-0 (ebook)—ISBN 978-1-4724-5655-7 (epub)
  1. Architecture and history. 2. Architecture—Philosophy. I. Title.
    NA2543.H55W47 2015
    720.1—dc23
                                                                            2015004202

ISBN 13: 978-1-4724-5653-3 (hbk)

Contents

List of Figures — *vii*
Preface — *ix*
Acknowledgements — *xiii*

1. Imitation in General — 1
2. Vitruvius — 13
3. Alberti on the Art of Building — 25
4. Alberti, Architect and Urbanist — 39
5. Vitruvianism and Palladio — 61
6. Events in the Classical Tradition on the Continent — 77
7. The Classical Tradition's Fate West of the Channel — 97
8. Jefferson, Architect, and the Classical Tradition — 119
9. Imitation and Architecture's Restoration — 147
10. The Beautiful and Good City — 167

Bibliography — *183*
Index — *201*

List of Figures

1.1 Sir Banister Fletcher, "The Tree of Architecture"

1.2 Columns, trees, and men as models of resistance to nature's forces, at the University of Virginia

4.1 Leon Battista Alberti, façade, Santa Maria Novella, Florence, begun 1458

4.2 View of Florence with a Chain, c.1480? c.1510? Woodcut, in the Staatliche Museen Pruessischer Kulturbesitz in Berlin

5.1 Francesco di Giorgio Martini, "Man, Church, and Proportions"

5.2 Sebastiano Serlio, Temple of Vesta, Tivoli

5.3 Sebastiano Serlio, Bramante's Dome, Basilica of Saint Peter

5.4 Sebastiano Serlio, The Five Orders

5.5 Giacomo Barozzi da Vignola, Doric at the Theater of Marcello

5.6 Andrea Palladio, Villa Capra, la Rotonda

6.1 Claude Perrault, The Five Orders

6.2 Gianbattista Piranesi, *Carcere di inventione* 14, c.1749/50–c.1761

6.3 Claude-Nicolas Ledoux, Barrière de la Villette, Paris, 1788, by an unknown artist in 1810

7.1 Roland Freart Sieur de Chambray, Palladio and Scamozzi, Ionic Order

8.1 Maison Carrée, Nîmes

8.2 Thomas Jefferson, Capitol, Richmond, 1786, engraving, c.1840

8.3 Richmond, Virginia, seen from the James River in 1817. Drawn by C. Fraser; printed by Hill

8.4 Thomas Jefferson, sketch plan for national capital, made between March 10 and 21, 1791

8.5 Central section of Jefferson's 1791 sketch superimposed on the Washington/ L'Enfant scheme

8.6 Thomas Jefferson, Poplar Forest, view of the site, 1806f

8.7   Thomas Jefferson, Poplar Forest, from the garden, 1806f

8.8   Thomas Jefferson, University of Virginia, Charlottesville, 1817–25

9.1   Léon Krier, Civitas: res publica and res private; monuments without streets and squares, streets and squares without monuments

9.2   Images of the seven building idea types: 1, tholos; 2, temple; 3, theater; 4, regia; 5, domus; 6, taberna; 7, hypostyle

Preface

> *A civilization is said to be a large society, but we are not told clearly what kind of society it is. If we inquire how one can tell one civilization from another, we are informed that the most obvious and least misleading mark is the difference in artistic styles. This means that civilizations are societies which are characterized by something which is never in the focus of interest of large societies as such: societies do not go to war with one another on account of differences of artistic styles.[1]*

This book is about the most important thing people make, which is the city. We build it to assist our pursuit of happiness, which each of us defines according to our own lights. To serve that pursuit the city must be a community that preserves and protects the liberty of each citizen. In a well-ordered and well-built city the good that its citizens seek is served by buildings whose beauty is the counterpart to the good.

The good city and the beautiful building have a common source. It is nature, and imitating nature as it has been understood in the classical tradition has always connected the aspiration for the good and the beautiful.

That is what the classic treatises on architecture teach. Their authors are few: Vitruvius, an ancient Roman, then Leon Battista Alberti and Andrea Palladio, the Renaissance architect–theorists who modernized Vitruvius, and finally Thomas Jefferson, the American Founder who left only snippets of theory. This narrative will review what they wrote supplemented by what they built and other ancillary material.

This book will immerse architecture within the political life that it has served from antiquity down to the present when the civil order has come to preserve and protect liberty and justice. The narrative will stress the continuity within the classical, western tradition of the innovative changes that have made architecture the servant of liberty and present the resistance and threats to that service.

A common thread will be the obvious truth that buildings, the cities they make, and the rural countryside express the purposes their builders expect them to serve.

This truth is much more profound than the banal slogan that form follows function or the common sentiment that cities are expressions of their civilizations, and it has largely been ignored in earlier interpretations of this material. Architects build only what the civil order allows them to build, and the good city can be built only by citizens who recognize that the city is the means of preserving and protecting the liberty of all of its citizens to pursue their happiness.

The topic here is the modern city within the classical tradition that runs back almost three millennia. In this tradition the good city imitates the order, harmony, and proportionality of nature, which is the same source that is imitated by an architecture that seeks beauty as a complement to the good and understands that architecture is a civic art.

Today architecture is considered a Fine Art and the architect a creative artist who obeys the irresistible influences of the *Zeitgeist* to make a building that is "of its time" while fulfilling the demands of the client. This scheme absolves the architect of responsibility for what he produces. Not so when the architect imitates nature. She must apply reason, judgment, and knowledge to wrest from nature that which makes beauty perceptible and serves the quest for the good that unites individuals into a civil order. The architect receives praise or blame according to her success in rendering this service just as every other citizen does for their service. Explanations based on influences and those on imitation are antithetical. If the one is the cause that the building turned out as it did the other cannot be. One purpose of this book is to describe the neglected role of imitation in building the good city.

The civil order exercises authority over architecture, and it uses architecture to build an urban place where that authority resides, which points to two inescapable facts: architecture and urbanism are indissolubly bonded, and architecture is inescapably a civic art. Those facts reside at the center of the classical tradition in which the American nation is a recent and illustrious chapter. Our language is redolent with words from that tradition: architecture, political, polite, city, civil, civility, urban, rural, and so on. In earlier eras cities were relatively small communities of individuals who assisted one another in pursuit of what Aristotle called the "good life" and we refer to as happiness. The history of civilization (there's that word again) is the narrative of that pursuit that extends into the modern era when cities encompass a wide range of communities from intimate to national in scope, but they all call on architecture and urbanism to serve that pursuit.

The current culture of architecture, which embraces most architects as well as those who approve and build what they design, teach them and write about them, and hire them, neglects the truth that one day tells its tale to another, and one night imparts knowledge to another. They treat buildings as cultural products of an irreversible sequence of disconnected civilizations in much the same way that Henry Ford and his fellow mechanics treated automobiles. In the early years each new mechanical improvement made the old models obsolete, but then the style of the outside became more important than what was under the hood, which led to tweaking the style to make old models unfashionable and therefore undesirable and eventually obsolete except for the very few best among them. While the rest went to the junkyard, they were recognized as classics and went to museums and classic car enthusiasts.

A similar treatment of the history of architecture has caused every new building to make every previous building unfashionable and obsolete. This is the very definition of Modernist architecture, and it denigrates anything that values tradition or the classical and adds insult to injury by treating old buildings as examples of obsolete styles. Every Modernist building must be of its time, which makes it unsuitable for any other time and turns Modernist histories into stories about the inevitable obsolescence of every new style.

Here the narrative will be about the continuity of architecture within the classical or western tradition (they are synonymous) and the innovations that each new generation introduces that have kept, and still keep, tradition alive, instructive, and striving for the classical. We are accustomed to referring to buildings as modern, traditional, or classical with finer differentiations given by the names of the periods when they were built, for example Roman, Gothic, medieval, Renaissance, neo classical, Beaux Arts, Modern, Bauhaus, Corbusian, and so on. These terms are useful for sorting but not for evaluating. They are the equivalent of shelving books as fiction and nonfiction and then according to spy or romance novels, or biography, war, history, art, and so, categories that identify their genre but do not assess them as examples of literature. For non-Modernist buildings the two commonly used catch-all terms are traditional and classical, which are especially reductionist and limiting because traditional buildings are always nourished by many traditions and the classical refers to the best in the kind of thing it is, whether an automobile, a novel, a thought, or a Gothic building with indifference to whether it is very old or very new or from some moment in between. Our interest is in the role of tradition as a guide for achieving the classical.

This approach runs counter to the currently dominant culture of architecture, which follows a narrative of an irreversible sequence of distinctive styles culminating in Modernism. This narrative has shielded us from the knowledge that traditional and classical buildings were being built, and are still built, despite the claim of Modernism's hegemony, and it has habituated us to using the terms Modernist, Modern, and contemporary interchangeably.[2] This raises the problem of what to call all those non-Modernist buildings. The term that will be used here occasionally is "Other Modern" but not as the name of a style; there is no "Other Modern Style." The now-standard narrative has also presented the body of pre Modernist theory as a prelude to Modernism and buildings as expressions of the *Zeitgeist*'s influences. This book's narrative will treat buildings as responses by architects to the changing demands of the civil orders that command what is built and the service the city they build renders to individual liberty.

Carroll William Westfall
Richmond, Virginia

NOTES

1 Leo Strauss, *Natural Right and History* (Chicago and London: University of Chicago Press, 1953), 138.

2 For Other Modern buildings see, among others, Alireza Sagharchi and Lucien Steil, ed., *Traditional Architecture: Timeless Building for the Twentieth-Century* (New York et al.: Rizzoli, 2013), with important essays by Samir Younés, "Modern Traditional Architecture," and Richard M. Economacis, "From Apologia to Praxis."

Acknowledgements

Only a few of the many who should be acknowledged are named here. Five individuals will find their contributions on nearly every page: Daniel N. Robinson, Hadley Arkes, Samir Younés, Norman Crowe, and my quite tolerant and generous Dean at Notre Dame, Michael Lykoudis. Allan Greenberg and Jaquelin Robertson were important mentors when I shifted from Italian to American topics. Others responded to questions, made valuable suggestions, and provided insightful conversations: Rafael De Clercq, Mary Campbell Gallagher, Bryan Clark Green, Paul Hardin Kapp, Oscar Machado, Denis MacNamara, Ralph Muldrow, Ingrid Rowland, Roger Scruton, Marie Tanner, Gibson Worsham, and innumerable students who over the years have tolerated my thinking aloud with them. All of these people helped me get things right, but where I went wrong I did so on my own. The unsurpassed resources in books and personal assistance in the School of Architecture Library at the University of Notre Dame presided over by Jennifer Parker were invaluable. I gratefully acknowledge the generosity of Mr and Mrs. Fritz Duda Sr to the University of Notre Dame.

I conclude with a dedication to my wife Relling and our sons Nicholas William and John Salvatore who gave me the room to wrangle this material into its pen.

1

Imitation in General

We must begin with imitation. In the full body of the classical tradition everyone understands that it is the method used to make a building, painting, or sculpture, but now it needs to be explained. "One way of interpreting the critical relevance of the ancient and Renaissance fixation on imitation is to see it as the equivalent in those times to the modern critic's and historian's fixation on *influence*."[1] Another historian called influence an "astrological metaphor."[2] Influence is so deeply entrenched in the culture of architecture that the profession's accrediting board requires students to know the influences that they must obey as they shape their works.[3]

Imitation is the most natural and effective way people learn to do and to make things. Aristotle called it one of humankind's "advantages over the lower animals." The human person "is the most imitative creature in the world, and learns at first by imitation. And it is also natural for all to delight in works of imitation" (*Poetics* 1448b, trans. Bywater here and below). Ever since people began pondering their human nature and its relationship to the cosmic natural world they recognized imitation as their most valuable tool for knowing, doing, and making. It remained a fixture in theories of art and architecture down to the cusp of the modern era when it began to face challenges from other methods that explained how to know, to do, and to make. Gradually architects began disparagingly to identify imitating with copying, and a century or so ago both imitating and copying were shown the door and barred from the shrine to creativity and the obeisance to the *Zeitgeist* that Modernism was erecting.[4]

The culture of architecture interviewed a diverse range of potential replacements for imitation, and by the end of the nineteenth century the canonic narrative of the history of architecture had hired one: the influences of the *Zeitgeist* that G.W.F. Hegel had formulated. The influences were the stars in the many editions of a book that has always been immensely popular among English readers ever since it first appeared in 1896. Colloquially called simply "Fletcher," it is *A History of Architecture for the Student, Craftsman, and Amateur being a Comparative View of the Historical Styles from the Earliest Period*.[5] David Watkin has noted that it put Hegelianism

1.1 Sir Banister Fletcher, "The Tree of Architecture"
Source: Banister Fletcher, *A History of Architecture on the Comparative Method*, 8th edn (New York: Scribner, 1928), courtesy of the RIBA. Image provided by the University of Notre Dame's Architecture Library.

"in conveniently potted form at the feet of the twentieth-century architectural student."[6] An image that first appeared in its 1901 edition carried the story so well the narrative could be ignored. It portrays "THE TREE OF ARCHITECTURE" with each of the sequential styles of architecture rising to the top with the six "influences" portrayed as maidens clothed in ancient robes intertwined in the tree's roots: Geography, Geology, Climate, Religion, Social, and History.[7]

Influences will not help us build beautiful buildings that are the visible counterpart to the good purposes that they serve in the civil order. Imitation will, and it has done so ever since the ancient Greeks used imitating nature to serve the enduring, human quest for the beautiful in things made, the good in things done, and the true in things known.

The word imitate (and imitating and imitation) comes with a host of relatives: image, mimic, mime, copy, counterfeit, facsimile, replica, replication, reproduction, transcription, likeness, and so on. The core meaning is to make something new based on a model but different from it, a meaning distinct from copy which is to reproduce or replicate a model. People learn by imitating, not by copying, although copying may precede imitating. "Show me how to do that and let me try"—to pronounce a foreign word, to play the French horn, to cook, to drive, to detail a building's cavity wall, to draw a classical columnar order. First copy or do as I do or as the canonic model demonstrates, and when you have mastered that by understanding the principles that are involved, innovate in order to possess the act as your own. Dullards stop at copying; the able move on to imitating and thereby making an original example of the thing.

The copying of models teaches us how to make new versions of old models but only when using them to imitate their source in nature. In this way imitating allows us to make new things that serve us now. Consider speech: copying teaches us the mechanics of speech involving vocabulary, syntax, grammar, and pronunciation, and models teach us how to make various forms or genre of the *types* of speech such as poetry, prayer, prose, narrative, panegyric, political oratory, and so on. Thorough mastery of those mechanics and media allow us to reach into the nature of the rules and *principles* of speech and its genre so that we can make speech our own. The result can range from a civil servant's recitation of bureaucratic rules to the skillful distillation of insight and wisdom found in the 273 words Abraham Lincoln uttered in Gettysburg.

Two italicized terms in those last sentences, types and principles, play important roles in imitation. The word type refers to the most generalized similarities in things that allow us to group together various examples that we identify with one another. A song is not a speech; songs and speeches use words, but they are different types of things. Similarly, a speech is not a city, a city is not a building, a building is not a sculpture, and no sane person would mistake any of those for another. But each of these has different characteristics that allow us to establish finer categories or genre within the type: hymns, operatic arias, national anthems, dance music, and symphonic songs without words. Examples of these different genres use the principles unique to the type, in this case song, governed by the rules of the various genres to produce examples of hymns, arias, and so on.

That is, different types of things are generated by different principles whose rules are capable of producing a variety of examples that are both like one another (they are typical) and different from one another in the same way (they are characteristic of certain genres). Imitation involves using those principles to make unique and characteristic examples of things, whether songs or anything else. When the principles that belong to the type are honored we will know it is a song, a speech, a city, a building, or a sculpture, and we will enjoy what style that is unique to it.

We find the word character a handy way to refer to the specific qualities that are intermediary between the generality of the type and the example's unique specificity. On one level all songs sound alike in their contrast to traffic noise. On another level all hymns and arias sound alike because they have the characteristics of hymns and arias, but yet no two hymns or arias sound alike because each one has its own manner or style, whether it is that of a composer, a performer, or both. To make a hymn or an aria the composer must follow the rules for hymns and arias while honoring the principles of song, and so must the person giving a unique performance of it.

This differentiation between the typical, the characteristic, and the unique provides the nexus running from the principles that are imitated through the rules that define the character to the inventions that produce the style or manner that is unique to every example. When we hear another person speak or we hear a song or we see and use a building we establish our knowledge of it and a rapport with it by discerning its type, character, and style based on our experience with other examples of things said, sung, or built. We will have more to say about type, character, and style in Chapter 9.

This sequence leads not to a copy but to a representation of the type of thing being imitated. The word representation is a useful, general term that covers the various meanings that imitation carried among the ancients. These meanings embraced a varying cluster of ideas about how to extract the best example of an action or thing by imitating a model. The doctrines of imitation that Plato and Aristotle forged had the greatest longevity. Although neither philosopher discussed how it applied to architecture it is important to review what they said about imitation. The greatest interest for us is where the maker of something finds the type to imitate.

Plato's familiar doctrine made the heavens the ultimate source of the ideas, or types, that the maker of things imitates whether they are shoes or civil justice. One familiar example occurs in the image of the good city in his conclusion to *The Republic*: "... [P]erhaps there is a pattern of it laid up in heaven for him who wishes to contemplate it and so beholding to constitute himself its citizen" (592b). But it was, and is, difficult to bring that city down to earth.

Aristotle's ideas about imitation are less familiar but offer greater and longer service. He began with the examination of things that nature and men had made in order to discover what the various individual examples had in common with one another. Doing so required going beyond knowledge of their appearance or physical qualities to discover what they possessed by virtue of their nature as exemplified in their types and the principles of their making. The physical qualities that they revealed were of two sorts, active and passive, terms that Jan Białostocki introduced. The active kinds were disclosed by empirical investigation and reason and concerned the means nature used in producing them. The passive ones were the properties that presented themselves to the senses.[8] Aristotle's imitating did not produce an inferior copy of an idea of a thing, as Plato's did, but an improved representation of the thing, one that was perhaps even superior to nature's production. "Greek thought," Erwin Panofsky stated, "was thoroughly familiar with the notion that the artist's relation to nature is not only that of an obedient copyist but also that of an independent rival, who by his creative ability freely improves on her necessary imperfections."[9]

The improvements are always made for a good reason. Aristotle explains one of them in his *Poetics*. It points to a fundamental property of the classical tradition in which an imitation that makes a representation always carries moral content. He presents several comparisons between tragedy, the highest form of drama, and painting, which gives pleasure by representing the moral content of actions or persons (1448a). "[T]he first essential, the life and soul, so to speak, of Tragedy is the Plot; and that the Character come second—compare the parallel in painting, where the most beautiful colors laid on without order will not give one the same pleasure as a simple black-and-white sketch of a portrait" (1450a). Aristotle is not justifying unalloyed realism. On the contrary, good portrait painters "reproduce the distinctive features of a man, and at the same time, without losing the likeness, make him handsomer than he is" (1454b).

A second reason for making improvements is found in a much-cited story that Cicero and others tell. It also makes the point that imitation requires judgment. Zeuxis, one of Greece's recognized master painters, was asked in Croton to paint Helen of Troy. To do so he selected five young women from among several in the city and fused them into a whole, "He chose five because he did not think all the qualities which he sought to combine in a portrayal of beauty could be found in one person, because in no single case has Nature made anything perfect and finished in every part."[10] Zeuxis exercised judgment in making the selection and composing the whole. Elsewhere Cicero explained more about judgment. "The criterion of truth arose indeed from the senses, yet was not in the senses: the judge of things was, they [i.e., "some Platonists"] held, the mind. ... The thing they call the *Idea*, a name already given it by Plato; we can correctly term it *form (speciem)*."[11] Here Cicero quite masterfully fuses Plato and Aristotle and finds the content of the truth in cognition, not in mere visibility.

A painting's representation can be compared to the things present elsewhere than in it. Zeuxis the painter made a representation based on the five women serving as models. When a person looks at Zeuxis' painting of Helen he sees the identifiable characteristics of maidens, perhaps even particular maidens. Perhaps the maiden's parents were proud when they recognized their daughters in the painting. Painting, an art of representation, is easily recognized as an imitative art, but in the twentieth century the avant-garde painters abandoned imitation and representation and began making things that lacked a counterpart external to the painting. Paintings that could be called realist or naturalistic or objective were joined by those that are called abstract, nonrepresentational, and subjective.

Architecture did not attract a commentary by ancient authors about its role for imitation with the clarity we found in Aristotle or Cicero. The first comprehensive treatise on architecture appeared in the last years of the first century BC. Its author, Vitruvius, uses the term much as Zeuxis did in Croton, although he does not mention fusing several models into one example as Zeuxis did, and neither did he give imitation the same representational role it had for painters. He states that the Corinthian order "imitates the slenderness of a young girl."[12] And he launches the enduring idea that stone construction imitates construction in wood when he states, "the mutules are shaped by slanted cutting, because they are an imitation of the rafters. ... Thus, for Doric works the principle underlying the triglyphs and mutules was derived from these imitations" (4.2.3).

We will find Vitruvius giving imitation a much more profound role in our Chapter 2, just as we will in the treatise that Leon Battista Alberti wrote 1,500 years later and discussed in Chapters 3 and 4. As a preliminary we can note that unlike Vitruvius, Alberti used the word quite generously, and he gave it several different meanings.

One of these referred to the relatively humdrum achievement of establishing visual similarity or analogy to nature's creations within the Great Chain of Being, as when he likened a column's entasis to a belly, and it is not necessarily the belly of a human figure.[13] In another a column is like a bone in a body (10.15.359/991; 10.17.361/995). And again, "who would not criticize a body for having excessively swollen limbs?" he asks, in criticizing those who think that "extremely thick walls lend a temple dignity" (7.10.219/605). Other simpler uses point to a mere visual resemblance to things in nature.[14] There is also "do as" and "don't do as" the famous and infamous have done.[15] Imitating can carry more content as when he states, "we should imitate the moderation shown by nature" (1.9.24/67). Imitation can translate form from one material to another, as in the tree-to-column trope he used early and which resembles Vitruvius' maiden-column analogy (1.10.25–6/71). There is imitating the "ingenuity of Nature" (14.86/247). And he would have masons imitate carpenters to achieve grace (9.10.316/857).

A more important role for imitation concerns his instruction for using examples to understand types and principles. The architect must diligently explore and measure the work of his predecessors.

> [S]hould he find anything anywhere of which he approves, he should adopt and imitate it; yet anything that he considers can be greatly refined, he should use his artistry and imagination to correct and put it right; and anything that is otherwise not too bad, he should strive, to the best of his ability, to improve. (9.10.316/857)

Imitation's assistant is invention, and this pair always appears at work with tradition where innovation reinforces tradition's authority and makes improvements available for his successors.[16]

Imitating the works of predecessors is like Zeuxis at work in Croton. The imitation results from making a representation of a model external to the product of the imitation and which it resembles. Alberti makes it clear that the examples that existing buildings offer are to be corrected by judgment and find their way into new buildings, which would exemplify Białostocki's passive imitation.

THE SPECIAL CASE OF ARCHITECTURE

Białostocki's active imitation offers to architecture a more profound role for imitation. It makes imitation possible in this nonrepresentational art, a characteristic that is too rarely noted. Both Aristotle and Cicero recognized that imitation can make visible content that has no model. We will find that in classical or traditional architecture that content is the order, harmony, and proportionality of nature or of the cosmos that govern the natural laws that control the actions of material nature and are the qualities of the beauty that is the counterpart to the justice whose source is nature's moral order.

Architecture has its beginnings in the vernacular art of building. The building that that art produces is elevated to architecture by using reason and judgment to guide handicraft to imitate nature. Art cultivates what nature offers or, as Cicero put, "In fine, by means of our hands we essay to bring into being as it were a second world within the world of nature," or a second nature, a term that has a long afterlife.[17]

Demetri Porphyrios has modernized this ancient idea in his emphasis on architecture as archi-tectonics, that is, the handling of the building's physical materials. He summarizes the point by stating that architecture is "the product of artistic intention, whereas building is the product of necessity."[18] Architecture "is the imitative celebration of construction and shelter qualified by the myths and ideas of a given culture."[19] Its basis, in short, involves the passive review of the art of building to discover the active principles of nature at work and making visible their imitation to elevate building to architecture. The traditions of the art of building, such as the "Classical, Gothic, Chinese, or Romanesque tectonics," transmit the knowhow of the art of building and are more important to architecture than putative "influences" or a succession of formal styles. Each tradition has its own "fictional images" that allow architecture to raise "itself above the mere contingencies of building" that are resident in the qualities of materials and the means of using natural forces to resist the forces of nature's actions. And it offers "symbols for recognition. These symbols are composed, varied and recomposed in an ever-changing chain of transformations. Yet always the aim is to make man come to terms with the world."[20]

Essential to imitation is the distance between the thing being imitated and the imitation's product. This involves changing the material and having a fictionalized image mediate between the thing being imitated and that thing's resemblance in imitation's product. When that image is the same as the representation, the result is a copy, not an imitation. When fiction is not at work the result is kitsch, not imitation. Fiction plays its best role when it reveals the truth in the facts. As Porphyrios writes of the architect, "*Mimesis* (imitation) discloses the way in which the world is true for him. If, or when, we find such truth relevant to ourselves, we rejoice and call the work beautiful."[21]

Nature is always the source of that truth and its counterpart, beauty. Fiction is a means of truth-telling, as we all know when we use stories to illustrate truths. Consider the role of the vernacular lintel that sustains its load and a canonic architectural element that assures us that it does so. "The form of the classical architrave makes us recognize the universal law of gravity and stability."[22]

1.2 Columns, trees, and men as models of resistance to nature's forces, at the University of Virginia
Source: Photo by author.

Imitation has the stone temple allude to its beginning in the wooden hut. Applying and drafting stucco on an irregular ashlar wall to represent regular ashlar is not deceit (pace, Ruskin) but an improvement that architecture brings to the art of building. A tree and a well-formed human figure are truth-telling models of their capacity to resist the facts that abound in the forces of nature. Architecture imitates the truths of nature that these reveal not by imitating them but by imitating the truths of nature that they model. When they become a column the tree or figure remains but as image not as representation.

The occasional stone column equipped with lobbed branches reminds us of this, as do Caryatids. Molded bricks beneath stucco-clad columns, or a steel post inside a wooden or terra cotta sheathing when properly proportioned and detailed in no way interfere with the column's fictive image.

Truth and beauty are prominent in three characteristics of tectonics, in "the finite nature and formal properties of constructional materials … the procedures of jointing, which is the way that elements of construction are put together. … [and] the visual statics of form, that is the way by which the eye is satisfied about stability, unity and balance and their variations and opposites."[23] Imitation in architecture is easily lured away into copying, especially when we forget, as Porphyrios reminds us, "Buildings can only be made out of other buildings." That is, to imitate nature requires an intense and learned knowledge of the art of architecture and the traditions of fictive imagery that will allow a new building to take its proper place among others in its own time. And it is nature, not something else, that architecture imitates. "Architecture shapes itself. Its forms can no more exist outside architecture than the form of a sonata can exist outside music." Nor can it be made from a sonata, a narrative, a functional program, an inner welling up of emotion, or a technology. The classical always speaks with a modern voice as it reaches across time and makes the enduring and the timeless visible.[24] Those with eyes that can see and a discerning and perceptive mind will find pleasure in architecture's beauty that in the classical tradition is most visibly signaled by the columnar orders. Others may be blind to that and see them only as copies of an obsolete architecture.

Beauty has always been a challenging term. In the ancient world and in the classical tradition its meaning is as protean a term as imitation. It is the quality experienced in things that opens perception to the deepest rapport with nature's order, harmony, and proportionality. That quality is found in things that are made as the best imitations of those qualities in nature. Its relatives are the true in things known and the good in things done. In the classical tradition that trinity encompasses different manifestations of the same thing: justice, or the Good, or God in the Christian tradition, and so on. We can imagine their separateness and their interdependence by imagining them inscribed equally distant from one another on a ball. The three cannot be seen at the same time, and when concentrating on one of them the other two are in nearby zones with no sharp distinctions between it and them. We can move from one to the other by turning the ball this way and that. This illustrates a point to be made throughout this book, that the good of morality and of the truth in knowledge are aspects of the beautiful in things that are made. We will find these ideas in the Scottish philosophers in the eighteenth century when others elsewhere were differentiating between the three and denying their existence because they lacked quantifiable empirical evidence for their presence. We will touch on those developments in Chapters 6 and 7.

The best and most accessible model in the classical tradition for the good and the beautiful has always been in the heavens viewed from earth. Modern mathematics and empirical science have vastly enlarged and radically altered what we see and the laws we use to explain it all, but it remains as law abiding now as it was when men first began finding wonder in that order and imitating it in the things they made, they did, and they found to be true. The canonic formulation for many centuries was in the textbook written well after Cicero and Vitruvius by Claudius Ptolemy (90–168) that formulated earlier research and interpretations into mathematical, geometric, and proportionate explanations for the regular changes observed in the cosmic order.[25] The truths never fully corresponded to the observable facts any better than the current scientific explanations provide the whole truth about the facts we gather from the cosmos, but those truths were embodied in the inaudible music produced by the movements of the crystalline spheres and were paradigmatic of the beauty perceived in the things men made. The paradigmatic model of the heavens was brought down to earth in the acts of people who sought to serve the good and by artisans who sought to reveal the beautiful while knowing full well that perfect goodness and beauty are impossible to achieve in our mortal lives.

Pagans believed that this cosmos was complete at creation; it held all that had ever existed at any moment, and the qualities of the types of all those things would exist unchanged as long as time existed. Christianity absorbed this natural history, or lack thereof, with only one important change: "In the beginning God created the heaven and the earth." The cosmos now had a beginning, and it and mankind whom God made to dwell in it had a history that would run to an end. The radical skepticism and empiricism that emerged in the seventeenth century began to challenge the entire legacy of natural and human science that tradition transmitted to it, and over the next few centuries new facts were used to challenge that legacy. Physical nature was given a new history that ignored its role as the home of mankind, and Darwin's theories inserted evolution into history to produce a narrative in which humankind no longer occupied the favored pinnacle of the Great Chain of Being. Meanwhile astronomy and astrophysics gave the cosmos a new narrative history. Modernism allied itself with all this new science and found it could substitute influences for imitation. But as Porphyrios' ideas suggest, imitation, truth, and beauty remain vital in architecture and only await expansion and renewal to return their service to the good and the beautiful, as this book will explain.

NOTES

1. James S. Ackerman, "Imitation," in *Origins, Imitation, Conventions* (Cambridge, Mass. and London: MIT Press, 2002), 135; original emphasis. See also Rudolf Wittkower, "Imitation, Eclecticism, and Genius," in Earl R. Wasserman, ed., *Aspects of the Eighteenth Century* (Baltimore: Johns Hopkins Press, 1965), 143–61; Martin Kemp, "From 'Mimesis' to 'Fantasia': The Quattrocento Vocabulary of Creation, Inspiration and Genius in the Visual Arts," *Viator*, 8 (1977), 347–98; and Alina A. Payne, *The Architectural Treatise in the Italian Renaissance* (Cambridge: Cambridge University Press, 1999), 36, 82, and passim, which is marred by projecting sixteenth-century ideas into antiquity and the fifteenth century.

2. David Summers, *The Judgment of Sense: Renaissance Naturalism and the Rise of Aesthetics* (Cambridge: Cambridge University Press, 1987), 15.

3. See Carroll William Westfall, "Toward the End of Architecture," *Journal of Architectural Education*, 64:2 (2011), 149–57.

4. See for example Anthony Blunt, *Artistic Theory in Italy, 1450–1600* (1940) (8th impression, Oxford and New York: Oxford University Press, 1985), where in Chapter 1 imitating is copying and inferior to inventing.

5. (London: B.T. Batsford; New York: Charles Scribner's Sons). Before the fourth, 1901 edition the title page included his father, Banister F[light]. Fletcher (1833–99). See also W. Hanneford-Smith, *The Architectural Work of Sir Banister Fletcher* (London: Batsford, 1934).

6. David Watkin, *The Rise of Architectural History* (Chicago: University of Chicago Press, 1980), 87.

7. The tree first appeared in the fifth edition in 1905 and the maidens arrived in the eighth edition of 1928 and remained unchanged down into the sixteenth edition in 1954. Gwendolyn Wright, "History for Architects," in Gwendolyn Wright and Janet Parks, eds, *The History of History in American Schools of Architecture 1865–1975* (New York: Temple Hoyne Buell Center for the Study of American Architecture and Princeton Architectural Press, 1990), Figure 11 mistakenly dates it and the example of Fletcher's distinctive drawings in her Figure 12 to 1896.

8 Jan Białostocki, "The Renaissance Concept of Nature and Antiquity," in *The Renaissance and Mannerism: Studies in Western Art, Acts of the Twentieth International Congress of the History of Art*, ed. Millard Miess et al. (Princeton: Princeton University Press, 1963), 2: 19–30.

9 Erwin Panofsky, *Idea: A Concept in Art Theory*, trans. Joseph J.S. Peake (Columbia: University of South Carolina Press, 1968), 15. See also Władysław Tatarkiewicz, *History of Aesthetics*, ed. J Harrell and trans. Adam and Ann Czerniawski. (Mouton: The Hague and Paris; and Warsaw: PWN—Polish Scientific Publishers, 1970-74), 1: 16–17; 23–4.

10 Cicero, *De inventione*, trans. H.M. Hubbell, (Cambridge, Mass. and London: Harvard University Press: 1976), II.1.1.

11 Cicero, *Academica*, trans. H. Rackham, revised edition (Cambridge, Mass. and London: Harvard University Press: 1951), I, viii, 30. We will encounter this meaning of *speciem* in later chapters.

12 Marcus Vitruvius Pollio, *Ten Books on Architecture*, trans. Ingrid D. Rowland (Cambridge: Cambridge University Press, 1999), book IV, chapter 1, section 8; hereafter citations will be given in that order in Arabic numbers within textual parentheses and notes. I have occasionally amended the translation.

13 Leon Battista Alberti, *On the Art of Building in Ten Books*, trans. Joseph Rykwert et al. (Cambridge, Mass. and London: MIT Press, 1988), book 6, chapter 13, 186; Alberti, *L'architettura (de re aedificatoria)*, Latin text and Italian trans. Giovanni Orlandi, 2 vols, (Milan: Polifilo, 1966), Book 6, Chapter 13, 523. Henceforth the translation's reference will be in Arabic numbers in the order just given with a slash preceding Orlandi's translation. I have occasionally amended the translation. See also Arthur O. Lovejoy, *The Great Chain of Being: A Study in the History of an Idea* (Cambridge, Mass.: Harvard University Press, 1936).

14 7.8.209/583; 6.10.178/509; twice; 7.16.238/657; 7.7.204/575; 7.9.213/599; 8.4.256/697; 8.7.270/729; 8.7.274/743; 7.6.201/565; 3.5.67/191; 3.16.90/259; 6.9.177/503; 9.8.311/843.

15 6.4.160/461; 8.1.245/669; 7.17.242/649; 7.16.239/651; 7.17.241–2/659.

16 Contrast the negative assessment in the otherwise very well argued chapter by Christine Smith, "Originality and Cultural Progress: Brunelleschi's Dome and a Letter by Alberti," in *Architecture in the Culture of Early Humanism* (New York and Oxford: Oxford University Press, 1992), 26.

17 Cicero, *De natura deorum*, trans. H. Rackham, (Cambridge, Mass.: Harvard University Press, 1979), 2.60. For second nature see Norman Crowe, *Nature and the Idea of a Man-Made World* (Cambridge, Mass.: MIT Press, 1995), 3 and throughout.

18 Demetri Porphyrios, *Classical Architecture* (London: Academy Editions, 1991), 41.

19 Demetri Porphyrios, "The Relevance of Classical Architecture," *Architectural Design* 59:9–10 (1989), 53–6; from the reprint, Kate Nesbitt, ed., *Theorizing a New Agenda for Architecture* (New York: Princeton Architectural Press, 1996), 95.

20 Porphyrios, *Classical Architecture*, 38, 26.

21 Porphyrios, *Classical Architecture*, 19.

22 Porphyrios, *Classical Architecture*, 2.

23 Porphyrios, *Classical Architecture*, 37.

24 Porphyrios, *Classical Architecture*, 98–100.

25 Liba Chaia Taub, *Ptolemy's Universe: The Natural Philosophical and Ethical Foundations of Ptolemy's Astronomy* (Chicago and LaSalle, Ill.: Open Court, 1993), esp. 138ff.

2

Vitruvius

Marcus Vitruvius Pollio (b. c.80; d. after c.15BC) wrote the oldest surviving comprehensive treatise on architecture. Like so many other Roman things it has for ever after permeated our thought and actions.

What little we know about this retired architect comes from the treatise itself. He describes one building that he designed, he enjoyed a pension for his service to Julius Caesar, and he transferred his allegiance to Caesar's adopted son Octavian after he became the Emperor Augustus. The treatise is now honored more for its survival than for its clarity, although the Renaissance enthusiasm for all things ancient led to mining it for insight into architecture and made its author a model for architects serving princes. Today Other Modern architects value many of its topics, and every architect knows him as the author of the three conditions that a building must satisfy: usefulness, structural stability, and pleasantness, or, in architects' argot, the Vitruvian trilogy of commodity, firmness, and delight. No one accepts less from a building; these three conditions are valid for the art of building in all times and places. But there is more to Vitruvius than his trilogy, and here we will give it a closer look and review the role he gave imitation.

THE ARTS OF BUILDING AND OF ARCHITECTURE

In Chapter 1 we found Vitruvius' explicit references to imitation, but here we will ferret out its more important implicit presence. Our first step is to clarify what Vitruvius means by architecture; it is not the same as the art of building. Consider the euphonious translation of Sir Henry Wotton in 1624, slightly modernized here: "Well-building has three conditions: commodity, firmness, and delight."[1] Sir Henry accurately identified these as the conditions of well-*building*. They must be satisfied to make the art of architecture possible. They are necessary but not sufficient conditions for architecture. Here is how Vitruvius put it in Ingrid Rowland's translation: "The divisions of *architecture* itself are three: *construction* [i.e., building], gnomonics (the making of sundials), and mechanics. *Construction* in turn is divided into two parts . ... All these works should be executed so that they exhibit the principles of soundness, utility, and attractiveness."[2] Vitruvius' Latin was *utilitas, firmitas,* and *venustas*. We will usually use Wotton's terms but often substitute *venustas* for delight.

Neither sundials (Book 9) nor mechanics (Book 10, principally about war machines) found lasting footholds in later treatises. The art of building's handling of physical material is the focus of Book 2 with the focus shifting to architecture in Book 3. The only substantial treatment of theory appears in the first parts of Books 3 and 6 and in Book 1 where we find the Vitruvian trilogy and these criteria for the art of architecture: "Architecture consists of ordering, which is called *taxis* in Greek, and of design—the Greeks call this *diathesis*—and eurhythmy and symmetry and correctness and allocation, which is called *oikonomia* in Greek."[3] These terms call out for commentaries. Vitruvius supplied his, and before the eighteenth century lost interest in them the commentators concentrated on these criteria rather than on the conditions of the Vitruvian trilogy. Here is how they will be translated here:

Ordering; *ordinatione*; *taxis* in Greek
Composition; *dispositione*; *diathesis* in Greek[4]
Eurhythmy; *eurythmia*
Symmetry; *symmetria*
Decorum; *decore*
Allocation; *distributione*; Greek *oikonomia*.[5]

A common sorting out of these six criteria, the one followed here, puts them into two classes.[6] Those that are commonly called technical or *operative procedures* are ordering, composition, and allocation. The others compose an aesthetic category with formal *criteria* that must be satisfied, namely symmetry, eurhythmy, and decorum.

Imitation is not at work among the operative criteria of ordering, composition, and allocation. These are fully occupied in other work, which they do on the building site where the art of building is busy satisfying the three conditions of well-building. They need only brief comments here.

Allocation: Rowland's translation captures the meaning quite well: "Allocation is the efficient management of resources and site and the frugal, principled supervision of working expenses" or, quite simply, job management (1.2.8).

Ordering and composition engage the architect in the actual fabrication and assembling of the building's members as they labor at the intersection of two words that play a very large role in all theories of architecture, namely, the hand and the head or the workman and the directing mind. Vitruvius names them *fabrica* and ratiocination. *Fabrica* refers to the operations of the workmen who affect the actual physical, material building. Ratiocination takes us to the role of the intellect and its reasoning, which involves two tasks. One is to conceive the building to be built and direct the work of the three operative terms. The other is to provide the basis for the architect's explanation of how the building takes its place as a member of the whole body of knowledge that he had catalogued in the early pages of Book 1 where he described the education of the architect.

The architect's ratiocination directs the ordering and composition that occur on the building site. Vitruvius defines ordering as "the proportion to scale of the work's individual components taken separately, as well as their correspondence to an overall proportional scheme of symmetry."[7] (More will be said about these terms shortly.) In ordering the architect does more than place the members in their proper places. He also shapes the members into canonic, proportionate, material building components and passes them on to the next task among the operative criteria, composition, which puts them in the places that are specified by the canonic requirements for each particular species of building.

Here we meet appearance or, more properly its aspect, which is Vitruvius' word that refers to the visible form that a temple or any other kind of building must satisfy, a conventional appearance that everyone knew, an appearance that identified the use of the building, a building that had to look like the kind of building that it is. In the building's aspect nothing, he states, must be "wanting."[8] The required aspect of any particular temple will not be achieved by following only the guidance of what we mean by a formal type as when we refer, for example, to a "temple type" or "Doric temple type." Vitruvius' conventions are predetermined compositions that are then manipulated to achieve the character that expresses the content. This is perhaps most clearly explained when he turns to residences. The conventions will guide the architect to the aspect that will express the resident's status. These include "five types" of interiors, Tuscan, Corinthian, tetrastyle, displuviate, and covered, that describe the tectonic structure for the "three types" of atria, each with its normative proportions (6.3.1–3).

More is required of temples, the houses of gods, which Vitruvius discussed before he moved down to residences. "Temples should not be made according to the same principles for every god, because each has its own particular procedure for sacred rituals" (4.8.6). The sites of the various gods must be chosen according to the roles they play. Juno, Jupiter, and Minerva, the Capitoline gods, should occupy the "very highest place, the vantage from which to see the greatest possible extent of the city walls. Temples to Mercury should be located in the Forum, or, as with Isis and Serapis, in the marketplace," and so on (2.7.1). He does not discuss how to express a god's character in its temple's aspect, although he does describe the Doric Order as masculine, the Ionic as matronly, and the Corinthian as maidenly (4.1.4–10). Instead he stressed two qualities that will determine the convention's particular aspect. The "first principle" concerns the plan's composition, which is governed by the columns' ordering relative to the enclosed chamber or cella with collocations identified as in antis, prostyle, amphiprostyle, and so on (3.2). The convention's other quality concerns the particular kinds (*species*) of intercolumniations, for example, pycnostyle, systyle, eustyle, and so on, that are established by multiples of the diameter of the column shafts' base, or its module (3.3. 1–11).

The module not only proportions the columns' spacing but also controls the assemblage of all the members, for example the podium, the steps, and so on, to produce a whole, proportionate body that satisfies and honors the three aesthetic criteria.

Whole numbers in proportionate ratios measured as modules and their divisions, and not dimensional units such as feet and inches, establish the size of the footprint and other principal elements of the plan and elevations and the various details of Roman buildings.[9] Ordering with modules rather than with dimensional units enables the workmen using dividers, compasses, and strings to carry out the technical or operative procedures and satisfy the aesthetic categories of symmetry and eurhythmy.

The aesthetic twosome of symmetry and eurhythmy work in tandem. Symmetry refers to the proportional relationship of the parts to one another. "Nothing should be of greater concern to the architect than that, in the proportions of each individual element, buildings have an exact correspondence among their sets of principles" (6.2.1). The gifted architect will satisfy "use and appearance (here *speciem*, not *aspectus*)" that the contingent conditions require by making dimensional adjustments to the symmetries, a quality that the criterion of eurhythmy satisfies. For example, corner columns need to be thickened so that the circumambient light does not make them appear to be too thin.[10]

IMITATION IN VITRUVIUS

In English symmetry and proportion have long been linked and are sometimes made synonymous. But Vitruvius gave them a very different relationship, as in this well-known passage:

> *The composition of a temple is based on symmetry, whose principles architects should take the greatest care to master. Symmetry derives from proportion, which is called analogia in Greek. Proportion is the mutual calibration of each element of the work and of the whole, from which the proportional system is achieved. No temple can have any system of composition without symmetry and proportion, unless, as it were, its elements have precisely calculated relationships like those of a well-proportioned man.*
> *For Nature composed the human body in such a way [etc.]. ...* [11]

Here is the anthropomorphic analogy that is second only to the Vitruvian trilogy as the treatise's most familiar theoretical proposition. The passage goes on to describe the proportional relationships between the various important parts of the human figure that nature has composed and describes it as supine with arms and legs extended and enclosed within a circle and square. Later theorists had him stand as the famous "Vitruvian man." The passage then turns to statements by philosophers and mathematicians about the so-called perfect numbers of 6, 10, and 16, the variations they yield, and their validation in the human figure and in their interior reason. His next topic concerns temples: "With temples, the first principles are those that determine the appearance of the plans," followed by his descriptions of the qualities of their collocation discussed a moment ago.

Here is where we find imitation. Vitruvius used a discussion of proportions and the perfect numbers that pervade the cosmos and microcosmic man as the introduction to his discussion of the ordering and composition of temples. He also gave an important prompt in his singular note that the Greeks call proportion *analogia*. Here Vitruvius explains how to use the method of imitation in composing a temple: "The composition of a temple is based on symmetry … Symmetry derives from proportion. … " Proportions are the content of symmetry, and as Indra Kagis McEwan puts it simply, "Symmetry is the condition of coherence."[12] Symmetry found in the proportions of the human figure and the other sources of the perfect numbers and ratios will establish a precisely calculated relationship between the parts and the whole of the building, the parts and whole of the well-formed human figure, and the numbers and geometry contributed by philosophers and mathematicians. These are the qualities of the cosmos's enduring proportionality and of man's as microcosm, and they are found where the heavens and the earth intersect. "[T]he cosmos," Vitruvius noted, "is the all-encompassing system of everything in nature and also the firmament, which is formed of its constellations and the courses of the stars" (9.1.2). Here he is in line with the main content of the classical tradition. The proportions found in the symmetries of those various sources are transferred to the ordering and composition of a building, most notably and importantly those that are in the most important building, the temple, to invest it with symmetry that eurhythmy will refine to give it the required aspect. We can say that proportion is the workman that transfers the symmetry extracted from the cosmos and the microcosmic human figure to the temple. *Proportion is the hired hand of the architect engaged in the work called imitation.* It is worth noting that as a hired hand proportion is unworthy of a place among the six criteria where we might have expected to have found it, although as with any good hireling, without it those criteria cannot be satisfied.

Here three comments are called for. First, the thing that is imitated is not a type in the sense that we introduced in Chapter 1 but the proportions of models which are the human figure and various harmonic ratios that model the proportions of the cosmos.

Second, those proportions embody the symmetry that is the content of beauty. Its perception is "both intellectual and sensory; it comes from the combination of actual quantitative 'modular' symmetry and the appearance of such symmetry to the human eye." It binds all things into an ordered, beautiful whole. It is the analogue in architecture to the unity of knowledge that Vitruvius presents as the body of knowledge that the architect must command. In both Platonic and Aristotelian terms, Vitruvius is presenting what is true of the cosmos, and that truth is beauty itself.[13]

And third, in ancient aesthetic doctrine imitating that symmetry which imitates truth and beauty produces the delight of encountering visual pleasantness, charm, and attractiveness, which are synonyms for Vitruvius' word *venustas*. Eurhythmy makes that visual delight more evident: it is "an attractive appearance (*venustas*) and a coherent appearance (*aspectus*) in the composition of the elements."[14]

We may usefully pause here to note that Vitruvius does not use the richer ancient term for beauty, *pulcher* (pulchritude) that carried moral content in ancient aesthetic doctrines and will find an important place in the theoretical treatments of his successors. It is not as if, like imitation, the concept is present but the word is missing. The concept itself is absent. The pleasure of delight in *venustas* is enough for architecture to offer, and it is found in the art of building's coherent relationship to the cosmic order. The word, after all, is one that connects us with one of Rome's foremost gods, Venus, and her pleasures and beyond that with the city that venerates her. Shortly we will encounter the *venustas* that decorum offers.

McEwan's comments shed additional light on delight. "The built analogue for a man's well-shapedness, the *appearance* of symmetry, is what Vitruvius called eurhythmy ... the utterly convincing *visible* coherence of form that an architect must strive for by adjusting or 'tempering' proportions so as to flatter the eye of the beholder."[15] *Venustas* provides delight as a condition of well-building; we delight in seeing how well built the temple is. As eurhythmy *venustas* becomes an attribute of architecture and, in McEwan's reckoning, "a sign of virtue[,] and without it ... there was no love or friendship—nor any city."[16] And neither were any of these present without the god-like care and attention of the Emperor Augustus, Vitruvius' patron.

That relationship is one of the first things Vitruvius mentions in his first Preface, which is worth quoting at length.

> So long as your divinely inspired intelligence and your godly presence Imperator Caesar, were engaged in taking possession of the world, ... [and] the Roman People and Senate, freed from fear, were piloted by your far-reaching deliberations and plans, I dared not ... publish my writings on architecture, ...
>
> When, however, I perceived that you were solicitous not only for the establishment of community life and of the body politic, but also for the construction of suitable public buildings, so that by your agency not only had the state been rendered more august by the annexation of entire provinces, but indeed the majesty of the Empire had found conspicuous proof in its public works—then I thought that I should not miss the opportunity to publish on these matters ... [W]hen the council of the Olympians consecrated him [Julius Caesar] among the abodes of immortality and passed his sovereignty into your own jurisdiction, this same devotion of mine, ... naturally transferred allegiance to you ... .
>
> For I perceived that you had already built extensively, were building now and would be doing so in the future: public as well as private constructions, all scaled to the amplitude of your own achievements so that these would be handed down to future generations. I have set down these instructions ... so that by observing them you could teach yourself how to evaluate the works already brought into being and those yet to be. (1. Pre. 1–3)

Here is the standard relationship between patron and client, this time in a social and political order in which every person was the subservient client rendering service to a superior patron who assumed responsibility for the well-being of his clients. In the Roman world the emperor was the patron of all the Romans all of whom were his clients. We find a glimpse of this relationship farther down the hierarchy when Vitruvius notes that the private residences of the wealthy must have public areas where "even uninvited members of the public may ... come by right" while for "those of moderate income, magnificent vestibules, tablina, and atria are unnecessary because they perform their duties by making the rounds visiting others rather than having others make the rounds visiting them" (6.5.1).

The terminology has been reversed now, but this superior–inferior relationship remains the common model of practice in architecture. The architect is hired by a client, perhaps one who is a patron of the arts, who commands or controls the land and resources required to build, and the architect's professional obligation is to fulfill the client's purpose. That purpose unfolds within the framework of the law that gives him the authority to build, and the building will express his purpose and that authority. Here is the inescapable role of a building: to serve and express the purposes of the authority that sanctions its construction. Vitruvius' architect built for the Emperor, and Augustus' "divinely inspired intelligence and … godly presence" gave him the authority to build and thereby serve and express his purpose of restoring Rome's legal and civil order. The claims made for the authority of clients have changed over time as their titles have changed, running to pope, king, prince, nation state, and so on, but the architect's role of satisfying and expressing the client's authority endures.

Clear all through this explanation is the role of buildings as parts of cities and the role of cities to serve and express the purposes of the civil order they house. Buildings, cities, and the political life of the civil order are coordinated with one another. Briefly put, politics, or the activities that transpire to maintain and defend the civil order, is more important than architecture because architecture serves the ends of politics by building cities. We find this when Vitruvius described construction, or the art of building:

> Construction … is divided into two parts, one of which is the placement of the city walls, and public works in public places, the other is the erection of private buildings. The allocation of public works are three, of which the first is defense, the second religion, and the third service. (1.3.1)

The inseparability of architecture and urbanism is inescapable in what we encounter in the rest of Book 1, which concerns urbanism. Vitruvius covers defensive walls and topography, the role of the site's suitability for protecting the residents' health and offering them convenience, and how to address those ends by accounting for the various winds, the movement of the sun, and the elements, or "humors," in the environment that directly influence physiology and psychology. This required locating the urban place in its proper relationship to the cosmos, which required drawing on the skill of experts, in this case the Etruscan seers, the augurs who would use traditional rites in matters concerning selecting the site, laying out the walls and the lanes and broad streets, and siting the public buildings.[17]

Here we encounter imitation in a new role. In the art of architecture imitation provides the method for producing a building with the symmetry and eurhythmy that makes visible the order, harmony, and proportionality of the cosmos that is available only to perception. Here in the art of augury and the attention to the orientation of the urbanism we find the city's and the buildings' sites being given their proper alignment with that cosmic order. This alignment provides the basis for Roman urbanism and connects Roman architecture and urbanism with the foundations of its political order, which, like the architecture and the urban order, imitates the cosmic order.

A name for what they imitate is natural law, which is the bedrock of the classical tradition. From it reason and experience extract enduring and unchanging principles that take particular form in the civil law. Aristotle wrote,

> *Particular [that is, civil] law is that which each community lays down and applies to its own members: this is partly written [that is, positive (statutory) law] and partly unwritten [that is, embedded in custom and tradition]. Universal law is the law of nature. For there really is, as every one to some extent divines, a natural justice and injustice that is binding on all men, even on those who have no association or covenant with each other.*[18]

The Romans were notoriously attentive to law and, except for Cicero, were uninterested in philosophy. Here he explains natural law in the epistolary defense of a friend:

> *There does exist, gentlemen, a law which is a law not of the statute-book, but of nature; a law which we possess not by instruction, tradition, or reading, but which we have caught, imbibed, and sucked in at Nature's own breast; a law which comes to us not by education but by constitution, not by training but by intuition—the law, I mean, that should our life have fallen into any snare, into the violence and the weapons of robbers or foes, every method of willing a way to safety would be morally justifiable.*[19]

True law, he explains elsewhere,

> *is right reason in agreement with nature; it is of universal application, unchanging and everlasting; it summons to duty by its commands, and averts from wrong-doing by its prohibitions ... God ... is the author of this law, its promulgator, and its enforcing judge.*[20]

Natural law cannot be fully known or put into practice universally and eternally. It varies among different communities, and formulating its civil law precepts is a communal enterprise, the very essence of the political life of citizens. A civil order that strives for justice revises those civil law precepts whenever it believes the change would bring it closer to the natural law, which sometimes requires war, as it did in America in 1861–5.

The civil order and the political life it governed were the lifeblood of Rome and the Romans, and they were not indifferent to its origins. It was embedded in the traditions that defined the Romans as Romans that they understood was validated by natural law and the law that imitation could pull down from Heaven to give form to the civil order of a people in a particular urban place. Romans believed that their civil order occupied the head and navel of the world. The Forum was the center of its civil life, and the Capitol rising above it protected the various talismans that provided visible proof of heaven's benevolence to Rome. As Rome pushed its empire to the boundaries of the known or conquerable world Roman law followed with a civil law tailored to each place. Eventually Roman citizenship, formerly the possession only of free residents of Rome, followed.

Romans imitated the order of the cosmic heavens when they made an urban site for the civil law. The Etruscan augurs "set aside and limited" certain places "by certain formulaic words for the purpose of augury or the taking of the auspices" and thereby connected heaven and earth by planting the heaven's quarters on the urban site.[21] Their elaborate ceremonies traced the plan of the city's walls and established the north-south axis that defined the *cardo* or sun's path and the *decumanus* at right angles to it. Their rites also defined a place called a *templum* for the Capitoline temple from which the eyes can gaze upon and contemplate a replication of heaven's order, and they defined the various precincts dedicated to the gods and places for various civil acts that would please the gods inside the city or beyond its boundaries where the civil law of the urban center provided the law for the surrounding districts.

In these Roman usages we find the words and meanings still familiar to us. The city occupies the urbanism of a definite place, and beyond it are cultivated fields (*ager cultus*), meadowland (*prata*) that was "'prepared' without labor," and *rura* or "country-lands" where "the same operations must be done every year" to obtain their fruits (Varro, V.36.40). Many rural areas in Europe still display the long, narrow fields that were defined for distribution to colonists, who were normally army veterans. These constituted centuriated rural districts each of which, like each *urbs*, was a separate precinct with its own cardinal axis orienting it to the heavens. For the Romans the land was not a spatially homogeneous continuum and so, unlike the great American grid of the Northwest Ordinance, the axes of contiguous districts and of the urban sites they surrounded were discontinuous.

DECORUM

Maintaining and expressing this relationship between heaven and earth was the task of decorum, the third aesthetic criterion. Here is Vitruvius' definition of decorum, which is often translated as correctness (Rowland) or appropriateness (Schofield). It is "the refined appearance of a project that has been composed of proven elements and with authority. It is achieved with respect to function … or tradition, or nature" (1.2.5). This large mouthful requires identifying where the "proven elements," the "authority," the "function," the "tradition," and "nature" are found. Unlike the knowledge, skill, and ratiocination of the architect who imitates nature to get the aspect right, all of these lie outside the architect's control. Vitruvius told the Emperor, the restorer of Rome and the patron of all patrons and the client of none, that buildings are to be "scaled to the amplitude of your own achievements so that these would be handed down to future generations" (1.Pre.3). The aspect of each building must lodge it at its proper place within the hierarchy of duties or purposes that buildings are to serve and express within the civil order.

The duty of a building is the same as that of a citizen: to fulfill its purpose in the civil order and thereby make public a character that is worthy of receiving fame. A citizen does this by fulfilling his office, and when he does so exceptionally well he is rewarded with ascent in the social and political hierarchy and even enduring fame. A building does this by fulfilling the functions required to serve its purpose and by making visible a character that expresses its purpose within the civil order.

Symmetry and eurhythmy guide the architect in imitating the cosmic order to make that order visible in the building. Decorum identifies the role and status of that purpose within the civil order. It makes visible the concord between the things of heaven and of earth. It is not the architect's control of symmetry and eurhythmy that makes this visible. Instead, it is the "proven elements," the "authority," the "function," the "tradition," and "nature" that have authority over him.

This authority controls decorum. It makes decorum the only one of the six criteria of architecture whose control lies outside the architect's art and that he uses his art to make manifest in the building's aspect. It takes control in the first steps leading to the final building when it lays out the architect's brief. From there on the architect keeps decorum in mind as he satisfies the other five criteria of architecture (and the three conditions of the Vitruvian trilogy) with eurhythmy serving the architect in a role analogous to that of the statesman who sets and trims his sails according to the wind that is blowing on the ship of state. In both building and governing, achieving the end that is sought requires making adjustments to deal with ever-changing contingencies, and here, at decorum, where patron and client meet, the patron's honoring of his duty exercises the final authority. In the final outcome, the politics that transpires within the civil order is more important than what the architect can do on the building site.

Getting the decorum right will allow Vitruvius, the client, to fulfill that purpose of his patron. Discussing how to honor decorum is the closest Vitruvius came to addressing the moral content of architecture. Decorum, as John Onians explained, is, "a Greek idea, formulated as a means of ensuring that people followed the pattern of nature." It figured in Greek and especially Roman doctrines of rhetoric, the supreme political art, and Vitruvius imported it into architecture.[22] With this importation Vitruvius made explicit the alliance everyone knew about, the alliance of architecture with governing.

In the classical tradition the end of the statesman's purposeful activity is the good and that of the architect is the beautiful. As Władysław Tatarkiewicz noted, symmetry "signified an accord with the general laws of beauty" while decorum was "individual beauty, adjusted to fit the specific character of each object, human being or situation."[23] Cicero linked decorum with beauty in civil conduct when he described how public men should conduct themselves:

> For, as physical beauty (pulchritudo) with harmonious composition of the limbs engages the attention and delights the eye, for the very reason that all the parts combine in harmony and grace, so this propriety (decorum), which shines out in our conduct, engages the approbation of our fellow-men by the order, consistency, and self-control it imposes upon every word and deed.[24]

Elsewhere Cicero wrote, "In an oration, as in life, nothing is harder than to determine what is appropriate. The Greeks call it *prepon*; let us call it *decorum* or 'propriety.' … This depends on the subject under discussion, and on the character of both the speaker and the audience."[25]

Presenting an appearance with proper decorum and proportionality is the purpose and fulfillment of the art of building and the end of architecture.

They are the final criteria brought to bear on the design, and they are the final criteria used to assess the architect's success. What decorum demands is also the point of departure for any project. The architect's starting point is not invention but knowledge of the composition, membrature, ornamentation, and appearance poised within the triple framework of what Rowland glosses as "(1) formal cultural rules, (2) that which is tacitly accepted in a culture, and (3) that which is clearly prescribed by nature."[26] The temple that the architect completes must be proportionate to the aspect of a temple and to the sacred purpose it serves within the civil and urban order. The same obtains for the other two kinds of buildings he discusses extensively, the theater and the private residence. It hardly needs saying that these are places where the gods dwell, in public temples for the gods of the Romans, in the theater with its presiding divinities, and in the private dwellings with the household's *penates* and *lares*. And neither do we need reminding that these are the building blocks of the urban realm that serves the religious–civil order. The commanding position of decorum and proportionality in the classical tradition is here and is quite simply put: no decorum and no proportionality, no architecture.

NOTES

1 Henry Wotton, *The Elements of Architecture*, facsimile, (Charlottesville: University Press of Virginia, 1968), 1. The passage is in Vitruvius at 1.3.2.

2 1.3.1; emphasis added. Władysław Tatarkiewicz, *History of Aesthetics*, 1: 270–71 mentions the fourth division of architecture, ship building, in antiquity; Vitruvius does not discuss it.

3 I.2.1; substituting eurhythmy for Rowland's shapeliness and decorum for her correctness. Subsequent references are to this translation, with alterations noted. References to the Lain are from Frank Granger, ed., 2 vols (Cambridge, Mass,: Harvard University Press; and London: William Heinemann, 1933–35). The chapter divisions were added by Fra Giocondo in 1511. For symmetry, which does not yet refer to bilateral quality across an axis, see Giora Hon and Bernard R. Goldstein, *From Summetria to Symmetry: The Making of a Revolutionary Scientific Concept* (n.p., Springer, 2008).

4 Here translating *dispositione* as composition is usually preferable to using the word design.

5 The six translators cited in the Bibliography provide several variations.

6 I have followed most closely those of the following, all listed in the Bibliography: Danielle Barbaro; Tatarkiewicz, *History of Aesthetics*; Roger Scruton, *The Aesthetics of Architecture*; Hanno-Walter Kruft; most importantly Herman Geertman; Payne, *The Architectural Treatise*; Mark Wilson Jones; and Indra Kagis McEwen, *Vitruvius*.

7 1.2.2; this modifies Rowland's translation.

8 6.2.1; Rowland's commentary in "Introduction," in Vitruvius, *Ten Books*, 15, is useful.

9 See Mark Wilson Jones, *Principles of Roman Architecture* (New Haven and London: Yale University Press, 2000).

10 See Alexander Tzonis and Liane Lefaivre, *Classical Architecture: The Poetics of Order* (Cambridge, Mass.: MIT Press, 1986).

11 3.1.1; the last clause of the complete sentence is based on Schofield; see also Rowland's commentary, 188–9.

12 Indra Kagis McEwen, *Vitruvius: Writing the Body of Architecture* (Cambridge, Mass., and London: MIT, 2003), 195.

13 See Robert E. Proctor, "Beauty as Symmetry: The Education of Vitruvius' Architect," *American Arts Quarterly*, 27:1 (2010), 8–16.

14 1.2.3, with some modification in the translation. See also Rowland's commentary, 188–9.

15 1.4.5; with some modification in the translation. McEwen, *Vitruvius*, quoting 198 (original emphasis); see also 210–12. Léon Krier, *The Architecture of Community*, ed. Dhiru A. Thadani and Peter J. Hetzel (Washington, etc.: Island Press, 2009), section IX, has developed tempering as tuning.

16 McEwen, *Vitruvius*, 212.

17 See Joseph Rykwert, *The Idea of a Town: The Anthropology of Urban Form in Rome, Italy and the Ancient World* (Princeton: Princeton University Press, 1976).

18 *Rhetorica* 1737b (W. Rys Roberts). See also *Nicomachean Ethics* 1135a, trans. R.C. Bartlett and Susan D. Collins.

19 Cicero, *Pro Milone*, trans. N.H. Watts (revised edn, Cambridge, Mass., and London: Harvard University Press: 1953), ¶10, 17. Daniel N. Robinson brought this source to my attention.

20 *De Republica*, III.xxii.33, quoted in A.P. d'Entrèves, *Natural Law: An Historical Survey* (London: Hutchinson, 1951; reprinted New York: Harper Torchbook, 1965), 20–21.

21 Varro, *On the Latin Language*, trans. Roland G. Kent, revised edn (Cambridge, Mass., and London: 1951), VII, 7–11. See also V.143; VI.53–4; VII.13. The fundamental study is Rykwert, *Idea of a Town*.

22 John Onians, *Bearers of Meaning* (Princeton: Princeton University Press, 1988), 37.

23 Tatarkiewicz, *History of Aesthetics*, 1: 189.

24 Cicero, *De officiis*, trans. Walter Miller (Cambridge, Mass., and London: Harvard University Press and William Heinemann, 1925), I.28, 98.

25 Cicero, *Orator*, trans. H.M. Hubbell, revised edn (Cambridge, Mass., and London: Harvard University Press, 1962), xxi.70–71. Tatarkiewicz, *History of Aesthetics*, 1: 196–7, gives other, similar instances.

26 Rowland commentary, in her translation, 151.

3

Alberti on the Art of Building

In the middle of the fifteenth century Leon Battista Alberti (1404–72), a leading figure in the second generation of the Italians' recovery of all things antique, wrote the second comprehensive treatment of the theory of classical architecture.[1] For good reason in 1860 Jacob Burckhardt, in the book that defined the Renaissance for us, identified Alberti as the universal Renaissance man in the period in which he found the first born of modern men.[2] The Renaissance rejection of medieval Christianity and its return to pagan antiquity was the overture to the modern era. But overlooking its Christian content is as egregious an error as ignoring the continued role of imitation in making things from God's creation.

It goes without saying that Alberti was a Christian, and probably not a nominal one. He spent the greatest portion of his life in service to the Church, although perhaps financial necessity and worldly companionship were as important as any sacred roles. His doctorate in canon and civil law in Bologna was followed by a visit to France and the Low Countries in the train of Cardinal Biagio Molin. Sometime before 1432 Pope Eugenius IV removed his bastard status and he could take holy orders. He joined the papal Curia, gained the income from a priory in the Diocese of Florence, and later became a canon of Florence cathedral. He enjoyed long periods of residence in Florence and Rome interrupted occasionally by activities in various princely courts.[3]

In the fifth century Saint Augustine had developed Christ's question to the Pharisees ("Whose is this image and inscription" on the tribute money? [Matt. 22:20]) to give doctrinal form to the relationship between the city of man and the City of God. Their cohabitation permeated the profoundly Christian cities of fifteenth-century Italy that were alive with reasoned discourse about civil and theological issues and man's place in the world of nature.[4] Alberti, his peers, and his colleagues admired the ancients but were not neo pagans. The world was God's finished, stable, and enduring creation where individuals were to exert their wills to honor His commandments and achieve their earthly fame and heavenly glory through the grace that was vouchsafed to the Church, and they were committed to its reform. Renaissance leaders looked back to find guidance for moving forward, which is central to the classical tradition.[5] Alberti found in ancient architecture an instrument of reform, and it drew on two principal sources. One was in the massive, mostly ruinous ancient buildings in Rome and elsewhere in Italy; these he energetically and enthusiastically measured and delineated. The other was Vitruvius' treatise. It had been consulted occasionally throughout the medieval period, but the discovery of a fair copy in 1415 had excited Florentines. A generation later Alberti, an excellent Latinist, would write that Vitruvius' "very text is evidence that … he might just as well not have written at all, rather than write something that we cannot understand"[6] (6.1.154/441).

FROM LINES TO BUILDINGS

Vitruvius' text was surely at his elbow when he wrote his own.[7] The division into 10 books and the order in which he presents his material begs for comparison, but modern studies have largely missed his originality in transforming and modernizing the treatise's content. The difference is conspicuous when Alberti offers a striking revision to Vitruvius' definition of the art of building.

> [T]he whole matter of building is composed of lineaments (lineamentis) and structure (structura). All the intent and purpose of lineaments lies in finding the correct, infallible way of joining and fitting together those lines and angles which define and enclose the surfaces of the building. It is the function and duty of lineaments, then, to prescribe an appropriate place, exact numbers, a proper scale, and a graceful order for whole buildings and for each of their constituent parts, so that the whole form and appearance of the building may depend on the lineaments alone. … Since that is the case, let lineaments be the precise and correct outline, conceived in the mind, made up of lines and angles, and perfected in the learned intellect and imagination. (1.1.7/19–21)

In his treatise Vitruvius had introduced ratiocination and *fabrica* in this same position. Alberti has *fabrica* become *structura*, ratiocination becomes lineaments, and their order has been reversed. We saw that Vitruvius' ratiocination directs the work of fashioning, placing, and refining the appearance of the building's members so that the aspect (*aspectus*) will be right, and it explains why the building's material reality is as it is. In Alberti's pairing the second term, *structura*, is unproblematic. It is Vitruvius' *fabrica* but with an emphasis on the tectonic role of the building's material reality. But the term lineaments carries a much greater load than ratiocination, which earned it first place in Alberti's pairing.[8]

We read that lineaments are "made up of lines and angles," a statement that, in conjunction with their use throughout the treatise, makes it clear that they are the intellectual concepts that render the geometric and proportional order that imitates those qualities in the cosmos. "It is quite possible," he tells us, "to project whole forms in the mind without any recourse to the material, by designating and determining a fixed orientation and conjunction for the various lines and angles" (1.1.7/21). Later he writes, "I have often conceived of projects in the mind" that then require extensive revisions as they find their way into the building's material (9.10.317/861). The lineaments are the "forms in the mind" that put reason or intellect in charge of every step from extracting raw material from nature and fabricating the elements of the building's structure out of them to the building's completion as an ornament in a city.

There are four of these steps presented in the following order in the treatise. First comes the fabrication of the individual pieces from nature's raw materials to furnish three of the six elements of building, namely, walls, roofs, and openings. Second is making and assembling the pieces to form canonic motifs that will become the building's material membrature. Third comes the role of the other three elements of building, locality [or region], *area* [or footprint], and compartition [or plan], that deal with where these components of the membrature are to be placed in the compartition's volumetric configuration to produce the whole body of the building (1.2.8–9/23–5). So far he has concentrated on the art of building that will produce delight or Vitruvius' *venustas*. The present chapter covers these three steps. The next chapter will present the fourth and final step, which involves making the adjustments to the parts and to the whole body that will elevate the building to the status of architecture, equip it to serve the civil order, and invest it with beauty.

Each step puts into play the three components of beautiful objects that give pleasure, namely, the "invention and the working of the intellect," the "hand of the craftsman," and the qualities of the materials themselves (6.4.159/459). Directing the steps is the classical triplet of reason, judgment, and nature: the reason that the architect shares with the order of nature, the judgment that allows knowledge to mediate between the universal and contingent in nature, and the craftsman's hand that elevates nature's material to the material of culture. Their coordination requires "true knowledge rather than ... a mindless set of rules."[9] It directs the hand in doing the physical work that involves the weight, lightness, density, and so on of nature's raw materials by cutting, joining, and polishing to give "the work grace" in the pieces, elements, and motifs assembled to make the building.

The architect's knowledge comes from the tradition of the art of architecture that began with the vernacular art of building that innovation constantly improved. Like the arts of medicine and sailing, Alberti writes, architecture "was developed by a million people over a thousand years ... [and] advanced by minute steps" (6.2.156/451). The innovations allowed architecture first to provide shelter, then added comfort, and finally furnished pleasure as well. The progression affected the configuration and the membrature's walls, roofs, and openings, but he discussed it most amply as it affected the columnar orders and its beginning in the paradigmatic vernacular model, the primitive hut. "In my opinion the column was developed to support the roof." To make its construction noble and permanent "they therefore built columns, beams, even entire floors and roofs out of marble. ... Certainly Nature first supplied us with columns that were round and of wood," and to assure their longevity and strength they strapped them with metal at top and bottom and added bases and capitals that were broader than the shafts, all of which was imitated in their marble descendants (1.10.24–6/69–74).

In close proximity he presents a quite different history of the columnar orders, one that more closely corresponds with his theories rather than with ancient stories. A column is the fragment of a wall left after the first crude construction that provided shelter was opened up. A "row of columns is nothing other than a wall that has been pierced in several places by openings." This satisfied commodity and firmness, but, he continues, men found that "There is nothing to be found in the art of building that deserves more care and expense, or ought to be more graceful (*gratia*), than the column" (1.10.25/71). Tradition now comes even more fully into play. He tells us that there have been many forms of columns resulting from the desire for new discoveries, but none bear comparison with the three kinds that the Greeks tell us about. Much later he identifies their makers as the "Dorons," the Ionians, and the Corinthians who, alluding to Vitruvius' story, "followed at Callimachus' instigation." Alberti, ever the Italian partisan, mischievously questioned whether "the Greeks are to be believed in anything," and then offers a counter tradition when he states that he has "discovered that this [that is, the Doric] was already in use in ancient Etruria" (7.6.201/565).[10] He also prefers above any of the foreign imports a fourth order which he calls the Italian or Italic and we call the Composite (7.6.201/565).[11] We might note that the five orders were not canonized until the next century.

The wall fragment as column comes into its own in Book 6 when Alberti is discussing beauty. "In the whole art of building the column is the principal ornament without any doubt; it may be set in combination, to adorn a portico, wall, or other form of opening, nor is it unbecoming when standing alone" (6.13.183/521). In the next book when he takes up the all-important role of proportioning he twice tells any scribe who might make a copy of the book (his book predated the first printing press in Italy by more than a decade) to write out the numbers to prevent mistakes (7.6.200/565; 7.9.211/589–91). The proportioning of members overlaps with the proportioning of the whole body of the building discussed in our next chapter.

BEAUTY

Here we again encounter the classical triplet of reason, judgment, and nature working together and producing "objects of great beauty and ornament" that give us pleasure (6.4.159/459). Alberti's first definition of beauty, the canonic definition that architects recite whenever pre modern beauty is mentioned, conjoins beauty (rendered in Latin with the root of pulchritude) and ornament and goes quite beyond anything found in Vitruvius.

> *Beauty is that reasoned harmony of all the parts within a body, so that nothing may be added, taken away, or altered, but for the worse. … rarely is it granted, even to Nature herself, to produce anything that is entirely complete and perfect in every respect. … ornament may be defined as a form of auxiliary light and complement to beauty. … beauty is some inherent property, to be found suffused all through the body of that which may be called beautiful; whereas ornament, rather than being inherent, has the character of something attached or additional. (6.2.156/447–9)*[12]

Ornament is definitely not optional (and certainly not a crime). It is the visible presence of the beauty that the lineaments' proportionality implants in the building's material. The lineaments elevate the material that first took shape in the vernacular art of building as the material elements of building, the walls, roofs, and openings, to make them the members with names such as exterior and interior walls, columns, colonnades, porticoes, vaults, embrasures, and so on. They receive the lights and shadows that make visible the lineaments that allow them to serve as ornament.[13] Foremost among them is the columnar order; "In the whole art of building the column is the principal ornament" as we just read. The members are ornaments that provide the ocular presence that can then reach the intellect where beauty's perception will gladden the soul and bring happiness.

Here we are foursquare in the classical tradition where beauty engages reason, harmony, and the coherent unity of members composing a whole body. It encompasses the unity of knowledge that Vitruvius saw in a "well-rounded education" as "a single body ... composed of quite different parts" (1.1.12).[14] Here is Cicero: "the whole content of the liberal and humane sciences is comprised within a single bond of union; since when we grasp the meaning of the theory that explains the causes and issues of things, we discover that a marvelous agreement and harmony underlies all branches of knowledge."[15] It is also the Church that is a single body composed of many members.

The reason that allows all people to perceive beauty is the very quality that they share as a part of their human nature, the faculty that separates them from beasts, that makes justice available to them, and that gives each individual the unique status of being a microcosm of God's cosmic creation where beauty resides (4.1.93/269). Beauty is the binding quality in the universal and the enduring order, harmony and proportionality of nature. The eyes see it and the reasoned intellect perceives it. To those who disagreed Alberti stated that beauty is certainly not to be "judged by relative and variable criteria" or "according to individual taste," as is claimed by those who "deny the existence of anything they do not understand" (6.2.157/449–51). Such people existed then; they are still with us.

Alberti's classical content was steeped with Christian tradition. Here is Saint Augustine on the creation whose parts God had called good but of which when all the parts had been made he said "was very good" (Gen. 1:31).

> *The same can be said for every material thing which has beauty. For a thing which consists of several parts, each beautiful in itself, is far more beautiful than the individual parts which, properly combined and arranged, compose the whole, even though each part taken separately, is itself a thing of beauty.*[16]

Augustine stressed beauty's presence in a unified entity such as the sphere and circle, the equilateral triangle among triangles, the square among rectangles, and so on, and he wrote that proportions allowed beauty to be perceived in things heard and in things seen. Later Boethius, who was identified as one of Alberti's likely unnamed sources, reminded us that proportionality and not likeness is the essential quality in a unity of diverse things, and he gave a detailed treatment of proportionality as proportions.[17]

Later medieval authors, unlike Vitruvius, noted the distinctions between delight and beauty.[18] "Only man," Saint Thomas Aquinas writes, "delights in the beauty of sensuous things as such."[19] What is that beauty? "[L]et that be called *beauty*, the very perception of which pleases."[20] It resides in the object and becomes real to man through the senses in perception and not mere vision, in cognition and not mere ocular sensation.[21] Umberto Eco has pointed out, "Aesthetic perception is not an instantaneous intuition, but a 'dialogue' with its object."[22]

Here as in antiquity beauty is related to the good and now also to the true. Beauty is not truth; it only resembles truth. The beautiful is not a form of knowledge and so it "is not a kind of truth. ... The beautiful ... stirs desire and produces love, whereas truth as such only illuminates."[23] Neither is it goodness, although it resembles goodness, and some of Aquinas' followers asserted that "beauty is a species of goodness."[24] Unlike Vitruvius but in line with classical thought in general Aquinas found a colleagueship between decorum and beauty in the "unity of the moral and aesthetic response to things."[25]

Again Aquinas, on creation: "All things are beautiful because they exist" and have their completeness only in God. Our pleasure in things men make is in proportion to their completeness, and the work of the artist is to make real things that establish the closest possible participation of the individual in that completeness.[26] This presents a variation on imitation and can be reworked to become what can be called the medieval trilogy. "Beauty demands the fulfillment of three conditions. The first is integrity, or perfection, of the thing, for what is defective is, in consequence, ugly; the second is proper proportion, or harmony; and the third is clarity—thus things which have glowing color are said to be beautiful."[27]

With integrity, proportion, and clarity "beauty has its source in God, and the moral truth of art is stressed."[28] We are a long way from symmetry, eurhythmy, and decorum, even farther from commodity, firmness, and delight, and with no interest in ordering, composition, and allocation. But we are on the brink of the Renaissance where Alberti resides.

This beauty is in the whole, complete body of the building that embodies the art of architecture, and it is central to Alberti's treatise. The beauty achieved by reason, harmony, parts, and body are absolute values that the architect knows cannot be achieved in their completeness but that in any work "must be understood *in relation* to the end of the work, which is to make a form [the thing seen] shine on the matter [the material of which it is made]." Because this is so, there exists a numberless number of ways that beauty can shine forth. "Beauty therefore does not consist in conformity to a certain ideal and unchanging type" of a "pseudo-Platonism ... [or] the idealist fancy fair of [neo classicists such as Johann Joachim] Winckelmann and [Jacques Louis] David."[29]

Alberti leaves no doubt that beauty is the end and indispensable content of architecture. In Book 9 in the midst of his final discussion of beauty we find, "The eyes are by their nature greedy for beauty ...," which makes the satisfaction of that greed for beauty to be the ultimate pleasure (9.8.312/845). Here we are far beyond where Vitruvius took us. The pagan offered delight, and so did Alberti as when we find "a certain delight" in "tiny, blinking candles ... arranged in some form or pattern" in churches (7.13.229/631; see also 7.12.223/619). But unlike the pagan Alberti went farther, to beauty, which brings moral content along with it and takes us to God. In the "wondrous works of the heavenly gods" we admire the beauty rather than the utility (6.2.155/445). Nature herself basks in a "daily orgy of beauty—let the hues of her flowers serve as my one example" (6.2.155/445). And as we read in the Prologue, buildings unite "use with pleasure as well as honor," the kind of pleasure that his medieval predecessors had sought in beautiful things and brought them happiness.

IMITATION IN ALBERTI

Alberti, like his medieval predecessors, believed that the beauty of God's creation was the model to imitate to make the beautiful things whose symbolic content was the invisible form of the Divine Mind that is present in His creation. Here the doctrine of creation marks a fundamental division between Christians and pagans who had no declaration such as the one that opens the Hebrew Bible: "In the beginning God created the heaven and the earth." The Christian Bible presents this creation as an ongoing active presence when the Gospel of John begins with the same words as the Hebrew Bible but then identifies the beginning in the Word: "*In principio erat Verbum.*" In John's original Greek the Word (*verbum*) was rendered as *logos*, which encompassed "the Word of the Lord by which the heavens were made ... and ... the Rational Principle which gives unity and significance to all existing things."[30] Another way to put it is this: "In the beginning was the very point of it all."[31]

God could create *ex nihil*, but people are limited to making from creation the things necessary and useful for their lives and for loving God. For that task God endowed them with reason and the unique capacity to imitate.[32] Alberti alluded to these unique endowments in his Prologue when he referred to the architect's "sure and wonderful reason and method," which was surely imitation.[33] He had no more need to name imitation in this role than Vitruvius had had, but he was not as shy as his modern translators who obscure the word under others. We saw it at work when the works of predecessors were imitated to improve the columnar orders from structural props to sources of comfort and pleasure. The precedents in this role were joined by two other sources. One is what nature has made. For example, "The great experts of antiquity ... have instructed us that a building is very like an animal, and that Nature must be imitated when we delineate it" (9.5.301/811). We saw this in our Chapter 1 when entasis was said to resemble a belly and a column a tree. His medieval predecessors had identified things that nature makes as *natura naturata*. Alberti explained the other source when he wrote, "our ancestors learned through observation of Nature herself; ... Nature, as the perfect generator of forms, should provide the models to be imitated. And so, with the utmost industry, they searched out the rules that she employed in producing things, and translated them into methods of building" (9.5.303/817). Those medieval predecessors called this source *natura naturans* by treating nature as the verb *naturare*.[34]

Precedents, nature's products, and the laws operative in nature's production encompass the sources for imitation among the arts of representation, but the last one provides the indispensable basis for the nonrepresentational art of architecture.[35]

We saw that for Vitruvius proportionality was the workman imitation used to satisfy symmetry by transferring proportions from the source to the building. Alberti's imitation is very different. He alerts us to this difference by not cramming a human figure into a circle and square or giving any special authority in the numbers 6, 10, and 16. Numbers necessarily define proportion's ratios, but he found them in a different source, and he treated and applied them with greater complexity and utility than Vitruvius had. He even avoided using the word symmetry, perhaps to signal his departure from Vitruvius' quasi-mechanical method of imitation.

Alberti's imitation rested fundamentally on lineaments. The lines of particular lengths united by particular angles were mental constructs of proportionality that the universal and timeless beauty of the cosmos reveals in God's creation, the whole of nature. He finds proportionality in both passive *natura naturata* and active *natura naturans* while precedents provide models for translating from universal qualities to contingent examples. In these three sources, whether singly or in their twos or threes, the architect's intellect and judgment can discover the proportionality to imitate as the workman's hand is directed to fabricate the members of the walls, roofs, and openings and finally assemble them into the whole body of the building.

Vitruvius had given Augustus the authoritative role in architecture, but Alberti recognized that its better source lay in humankind's natural sociability and the individual's natural aspiration to live nobly and well. In the Christian reading of this central thread of the classical tradition individuals live in an urban setting holding a civil order that they make by imitating God's creation, whether it is the city of Enoch that was the product of the misuse of the will, the city of man that Augustine had defined as a place of concord that hosts the Church, or the Church itself that is the surrogate on earth for the Heavenly Jerusalem to be enjoyed by the redeemed at the end of time. Guiding and improving the governing and building of the good city is tradition and the innovations that make it useful.

> *Many and various arts, which help to make the course of our life more agreeable and cheerful, where handed down to us by our ancestors, who had acquired them by much effort and care. ... The business has grown, I believe, through experience and skill, so that it is now almost without bounds, what with the introduction of the various building types. (1.2.7–8/23)*

These buildings and their members are made by people *acting* in a manner that is natural to them and *using* the natural endowments of reason, memory, and skill. The architect is an agent in God's plan for the world, and his buildings become examples of *natura naturata* and surrogates for *natura naturans*.

In the next chapter we will look more closely at this interaction of the things people make to serve the city's purposes and the proportionality found by imitating nature. Here our attention will be on the individual buildings that are the building blocks of those cities.

ON BUILDINGS

We will begin where an architect begins, with the plan. Alberti defines the *area* or the footprint as one of the six elements and the compartition, that is, the plan within the footprint, as another. The compartition "contributes more to the delight and decorum of a building than to its utility and strength," although, he adds, these three qualities (that is, delight, utility, strength) are so closely related none of them can be "found wanting in anything" (7.1.189/529). (No form follows function here.) Indeed, "the overall division and compartition of lineaments will draw much praise, which is itself the primary and principal form of ornament" (9.1.292/783). Compartition calls on "All the power of invention, all the skill and experience of the art of building." It divides the area into lesser "parts by which it is articulated, and integrates its every part by composing all the lines and angles into a single, harmonious work that respects utility, dignity, and delight" (1.9.23/65). Here he also writes that compartition is composed of rooms made from "close-fitting smaller buildings, joined together like members of the whole body" (1.2.8/23). His method for establishing the compartition is very distant from Vitruvius', which was immersed in convention, and so he simply ignored what Vitruvius had written about building plans. Also uninstructive were the ruins of ancient Rome because they were too ruinous, and so the Florentine paid careful attention to their successors in the many Italian cities that he knew well and that provided precedents for the configurations that would emerge from the compartition. These displayed the role of lineaments in uniting the *area*, compartition, and members into the whole body of buildings, lineaments that the skillful architect could imitate to make a new building.

Alberti explains imitation's role with examples that unsurprisingly begin with the temple, the word he also uses for church. Brief comments about the pagan temple turn to the earliest buildings from "ancient times, in the primitive days of our religion," by which he means the Italic temple that developed from the sepulchers of the Etruscans.[36] Other precedents were the early Christian churches that had been the models for Filippo Brunelleschi's two large basilicas in Florence and other models that he drew on in his own practice, a topic that lies beyond our story. He condemns "the practice of our own times" (7.13.229/629) that demeans the dignity of the sacrifice by stuffing everything with altars, and worse things which he resists mentioning.[37] He then moves on to buildings serving other purposes with an extensive discussion of basilicas that are used for secular justice and are clearly variations on a longitudinal Christian basilica that he includes as a religious building of lesser rank than the principal temple. He brings in imitation's role in serving decorum (7.14–15.230–38/633–49), and he gives the basilica a "lower religious standing" than the principal temple, although the imitation of the latter by the former supports his comment that justice derives its legitimacy from religion (see 7.14.230/633).

This example shows that imitation produces allusion, not rivalry. It supports decorum by abbreviating or diluting formal similarities to place buildings beneath their hieratic superiors. "Since the basilica has the nature of a temple, it should adopt much of the ornament that is appropriate to it; but in so doing, it should give the impression of seeking to imitate rather than rival the temple" (7.14.230/633). "Smaller temples and chapels follow the methods of the larger ones, scaled down according to the importance of the site and the requirements" (5.6.127). And so too for secular buildings where the houses of princes and magistrates "should follow the example of public works; yet they should be handled with such restraint as to appear to seek delight rather than any form of pomp" (9.1.293). Again: the house of a gentleman should imitate the house of a prince (5.17.145). He extends this discussion to the residences of the "humbler folks that ... should follow the example of the rich and emulate their magnificence, so far as their resources allow, though this imitation must be dampened" (5.18.152/435). He also includes remarks, predictably scant, about the buildings for "the common people," a topic that includes farms and urban residences above shops (5.18.152-3/435-7).

The compartition of new buildings would be different in different places because they are to follow the traditions found in the first element of building, locality, a term that addresses the differences found in the various Italian cities. This calls attention to the role of vernacular building practices in traditional building cultures that provide the basis for the arts of building and architecture. New buildings are, after all, made from old buildings or parts of old buildings and are built to express the purposes of the roles they play in the city's political life. Civic council buildings in northern Italy may be as similar to one another as those in Padua, Milan, Bologna, and Cremona where each one is the same but different, or in central Italy as alike as those in Volterra, Siena, Florence, and Montepulciano that again are different from one another. In Alberti's century a building from the first group of cities would be out of place in any of the second group, and so too with private palaces and churches. In Alberti's century regional differences are conspicuous within the newly orderly composition while thereafter the composition's order and its display of the ancient beginnings of its members will be given dominance over regional expression.

To this traditional way of building Alberti made two substantial innovations. One is the greatly expanded list of buildings composing the urban realm that are to receive the attention of architecture and not be left to the art of building. The other is the rigor that Alberti brings to the architect's role in elevating the art of building to the civic art of architecture.

Ancient buildings provided useful but not adequate instruction. They displayed models of decorum's role and taught how to achieve tectonic clarity in the physical material constituting the membrature, but Alberti was not a neo classicist who valued classical form alone or for its associative connection with antiquity. He put architecture in the classical tradition where it was a civic art that required that buildings be beautiful and express their role in serving the civic order, and he used precedents for the volumetric configuration and the material's membrature in the buildings serving modern Italian cities. Although he decried existing buildings as architecturally inept, they nonetheless displayed the locality's way of providing the visible character that expressed their service to the civil order. At their best they were examples of the art of building, but they could still be proper precedents for the configuration's and membrature's matrix of lines and angles that the imitation of nature in its active and passive forms along with the architect's reason, judgment, and knowledge could furnish with lineaments whose proportionality could elevate their successors to architecture whose beauty would shine forth in perception.

NOTES

1. For a brief review of Alberti as architect see Joseph Rykwert, "Theory as Rhetoric: Leon Battista Alberti in Theory and in Practice," in Vaughan Hart and Peter Hicks, eds, *Paper Palaces: The Rise of the Renaissance Architectural Treatise* (New Haven and London: Yale University Press, 1998), 32–50.

2. Jacob Burckhardt, *The Civilization of the Renaissance in Italy*, trans. S.G.C. Middlemore, 2 vols. (New York, et al.: Harper Torchbook, 1958), 1:148ff.

3. Girolamo Mancini, *Vita di Leon Battista Alberti* (2nd edn, 1911; reprint, Rome: Bardi, 1971), 88–90; Anthony Grafton, *Leon Battista Alberti: Master Builder of the Italian Renaissance* (New York: Hill and Wang, 2000), 7, 64, and passim.

4. See inter alia Paul Oscar Kristeller in *Eight Philosophers of the Italian Renaissance* (Stanford: Stanford University Press, 1964) and other studies, and Charles Trinkaus, *In Our Image and Likeness: Humanity and Divinity in Italian Humanist Thought*, 2 vols (London: Constable, 1970). See now also Brad S. Gregory, *The Unintended Reformation: How a Religious Revolution Secularized Society* (Cambridge, Mass., and London: Harvard University Press, 2012), 84–5; 198; and passim.

5. Salvatore Settis, *The Future of the 'Classical,'* trans. Allan Cameron, (Cambridge, U.K., and Malden, Mass.: Polity Press, 2006).

6. See Ingrid Rowland, "From Vitruvian Scholarship to Vitruvian Practice," *Memoirs of the American Academy in Rome*, 50 (2005), 29.

7. Among the modern studies are Françoise Choay, *The Rule and the Model: On the Theory of Architecture and Urbanism*, ed. Denise Bratton (Cambridge, Mass. and London: MIT, 1997), 84–5; Caroline van Eck, "The Structure of *De re aedificatoria* Reconsidered," *Journal of the Society of Architectural Historians*, 57 (1998), 280–97; and, more recent, Caspar Pearson, *Humanism and the Urban World: Leon Battista Alberti and the Renaissance City* (University Park: Pennsylvania State University Press, 2011).

8. Branko Metrović, *Serene Greed of the Eye: Leon Battista Alberti and the Philosophical Foundations of Renaissance Architectural Theory* (Munich and Berlin: Deutscher Kunstverlag, 2005), reviews the extensive literature on lineaments. His ample scholarship always discounts ethical and religious content. Nikolaos-Ion Terzoglou, "The Human Mind and Design Creativity: Leon Battisa Alberti and *lineamenta*," in Soumyen Bandyopadhyay et al., eds, *The Humanities in Architectural Design: A Contemporary and Historical Perspective* (London and New York: Routledge, 2010), 136–46, neglects imitation.

9. Kemp, "From 'Mimesis' to 'Fantasia,'" 288–9.

10. For the Etruscan Doric see Marie Tanner, *Jerusalem on the Hill: Rome and the Vision of St. Peter's in the Renaissance* (Turnhout, Belgium: Harvey Miller, 2010), 155, and Figure 122.

11. "Alberti … anchored the entire history of temple architecture within Italic parameters." Tanner, *Jerusalem on the Hill*, 27.

12. A harbinger is in Pro. 4/11–13; beauty here is pulchritude, not *venustas*.

13. A comment from Roger Scruton was useful here. For ornament see the comment in Alberti, *Ten Books*, trans. Rykwert, et al., 420.

14   McEwen, *Vitruvius*, 60 gives this translation: "For the whole of learning is put together just like a single body, from its members."

15   Cicero, *De oratore*, trans. H. Rackham 2 vols (Cambridge, Mass., and London: Harvard University Press, 1942), III, 21–2.

16   Augustine of Hippo, *Confessions*, trans. R.S. Pine-Coffin (Harmondsworth: Penguin, 1961), Bk XIII, §28, 340–41.

17   V. Zoubov, "Léon Battista Alberti et les Auteurs du Moyen Age," *Medieval and Renaissance Studies* (University of London: The Warburg Institute), 4 (1958), 265–6.

18   Umberto Eco, *Art and Beauty in the Middle Ages*, trans. Hugh Bredin (New Haven and London: Yale University Press, 1986), for Robert Grosseteste and Vincent of Beauvais, the latter of whom referred to Vitruvius' six criteria for architecture, and he defined building as one of the three parts of architecture: *Speculum Doctrinale* (Graz: Akademische Druk- und Verlagsanstalt, 1965), reproduction of *Biblioteca Mundi seu Speculum Maioris* (Douai: Baltazaris Belieri, 1524), II: *Speculum Doctrinale*, XI, 15, E.

19   Tatarkiewicz, *History of Aesthetics*, 2: 259, no. 9, from *Summa Theol.*, I q. 91 a. 3 ad 3; beauty = pulchritudine.

20   Tatarkiewicz, *History of Aesthetics*, 2:258, no. 2, *Summa Theol.*, I-a II-ae, q. 27 a 1 ad 3; beauty = pulchrum (original emphasis). Throughout this chapter beauty translates pulchrum in its various forms.

21   Eco, *Art and Beauty*, 68–73, where Eco explains that the word perception is rendered with *visio*.

22   Eco, *Art and Beauty*, 82. See also Jacques Maritain, *Art and Scholasticism*, revised edn, trans. J.F. Scanlan (New York: Charles Scribner's Sons, 1947), 7–9.

23   G.B. Phelan, "The Concept of Beauty in St. Thomas Aquinas," in *Selected Papers*, ed. Arthur G. Kirn (Toronto: Pontifical Institute of Mediaeval Studies, 1967), 166–71; Maritain, *Art and Scholasticism*, 128–30; 21–22. Eco, *Art and Beauty*, 70–71 stresses the role of form; for its special meaning, see below. Petrarch will disagree.

24   Phelan, "The Concept of Beauty," 155–80; 163, 168–70.

25   Eco, *Art and Beauty*, 15; 70–71; 77–81.

26   Tatarkiewicz, *History of Aesthetics*, 2: 257, no. 1, *Summa Theol.*, I q. 5 a 4 ad 1; beauty = pulchrum; proper proportion = debita proportione; and 2: 260, no. 14, *Summa Theol.*, I q. 12 a 1 ad 4; see also Maritain, *Art and Scholasticism*, 22–3. Here proportionality may be a better term than proportion.

27   Tatarkiewicz, *History of Aesthetics*, 2:261, no. 20, *Summa Theol.*, I q. 39 a. 8; integrity = integritas; perfection = *perfectio*; proper proportion = *debita proporatio*; harmony = consonantia; clarity = claritas. For a recent gloss see Denis R. McNamara, *Catholic Church Architecture and the Spirit of Liturgy* (Chicago and Mundelein: Hillenbrand Books, 2009), 24–7. Phelan, "The Concept of Beauty, 155–80; 177; and Maritain, *Art and Scholasticism*, 23–4.

28   Tatarkiewicz, *History of Aesthetics*, 2: 297.

29   Maritain, *Art and Scholasticism*, 23–4, original emphasis.

30   The interpretation and the quotations are from William Temple, *Readings in St. John's Gospel* (first and second series) (London: Macmillan and Co., 1952), 3–6.

31   I owe this comment to Daniel N. Robinson.

32 Władysław Tatarkiewicz, *A History of Six Ideas: An Essay on Aesthetics* (The Hague, Boston, London: Martinus Nijhoff and Warsaw: PWN—Polish Scientific Publishers, 1980), 247; 254–7.

33 Joan Gadol, *Leon Battista Alberti: Universal Man of the Early Renaissance* (Chicago and London: University of Chicago Press, 1969), part 3, presented a flawed development of imitation's role.

34 Henry A. Lucks, "Natura Naturans—Natura Naturata," *The New Scholasticism* 9 (1935), 23–4, who argues that while Scholastics occasionally used the terminology it is not strictly Scholastic.

35 Alberti had great fun with the folly that pagan gods could display; see his novel *Momus*, trans. Sarah Knight (Cambridge, Mass.: Harvard University Press, 2003).

36 See Tanner, *Jerusalem on the Hill*, Chapter 9.

37 For similar criticism see Antony Black, *Political Thought in Europe, 1250–1450* (Cambridge: Cambridge University Press, 1992), 36.

4

Alberti, Architect and Urbanist

> [L]et it be said that the security, dignity, and honor of the republic depend greatly on the architect: it is he who is responsible for our delight, entertainment, and health while at leisure, and our profit and advantage while at work, and in short, that we live in a dignified manner, free from any danger. In view then of the delight and wonderful grace of his works, and of how indispensable they have proved, and in view of the benefit and convenience of his inventions, and their service to posterity, he should no doubt be accorded praise and respect, and be counted among those most deserving of mankind's honor and recognition.
> (Pro. 2–3/13)

ALBERTI'S REPUBLIC AND ITS ARCHITECT

A building's first obligation is to serve and express the role it is to play in the civil order, to express the source of the authority that builds the city and that its buildings are to serve, and to do so with beauty as its content. These buildings constitute architecture, which is primarily a civic art and is indistinguishable from urbanism. Vitruvius and Alberti used this civic art to serve diametrically opposed authorities. Vitruvius prided himself for being the client of his imperial patron while Alberti presented the architect as no man's client but a citizen who renders his service as a participant in the protection of his city's liberty and assists in the communal task of facilitating each individual's pursuit of the good and the happiness it produces.

Consider the contrasts in three passages. First, as we saw in Chapter 2, Vitruvius gives the emperor credit for the security and prosperity of the empire and "for the construction of suitable public buildings" serving it. (1.Pre.2) Alberti, in a brazen departure from this trope, gives the architect the role of devising and building "whatever can be most beautifully fitted out for the noble needs of man"[1] (Pro.3/7). Second, Alberti asserts that "the skill and ability of the architect have been responsible for more victories than have the command and foresight of any general," which gives to the architect the role that Vitruvius had reserved for the Emperor (Pro. 4/11). And finally, while Vitruvius' emperor enjoyed "divinely inspired intelligence" Alberti gives that intelligence to the architect who, he states, is a person

> *who by sure and wonderful reason and method, knows both how to devise through his own mind and energy, and to realize by construction, whatever can be most beautifully fitted out for the noble needs of man, by the movement of weights and the joining and massing of bodies. (Pro. 3/7)*

Alberti's voice is that of a republican. He was born into a leading family in the Florentine republic, and he valued his attachments to his city and family. In his fictional dialog On the Family the interlocutors are recent forebears who discuss family and civic life. Written to display the qualities of the Italian language, schools in Italy still use it in literature classes. Like all important families, the Albertis had been active participants in Florentine civil affairs. The city was perhaps most alive during the five decades running back from about 1425. In that span's first half the republic was roiled by important families and the lesser people (*popolo minuto*) endlessly jockeying for power while defending the city against aggressive princes.[2] The Albertis, wealthy through heavy involvement in papal finances, supported the lesser people's quest for a greater role, which has earned them the label of the period's "liberals."[3] In the tumult various family members were exiled, then restored, and then banned gain. Battista (he took the name Leon later) was born in exile in Genoa and raised in Venice and the Veneto and began making his career in the employ of curial cardinals. The bans on members of the now weakened Alberti family began to be lifted after Florence had enjoyed more than a decade of relative stability, and in 1428 Leon Battista was allowed to enter Florence.[4]

The Florentine citizens were not political equals. They were arrayed in social-economic-dynastic classes and in patron-client relationships within those classes, but they prized and fiercely defended the liberty that allowed their republic to determine its own affairs and allow individual Florentines to do the same within their niche in the civil order. Elsewhere in Italy and across the Alps princely states in the lands where the Romans had civilized and planted Roman law were being governed by that law's legacy that had developed after Augustus' assumption of authority as "first among equals." It would legitimize government by a single head down into the late eighteenth century. A number of little Italian cities had managed to gain *de facto* independence from negligent princely states, and Florence with Venice, which had been founded outside the empire's temporal and territorial grasp, stood as Italy's great republics under constant and eternal threat from the principalities.

During Alberti's lifetime Florence thrived in an Italy that enjoyed relative security, peace, and liberty where a large body of well trained, well supported, and engaged individuals feverishly absorbed the works left by their ancient forebears. When challenged by princely states the citizens of the republic on the Arno responded with arms and, more enduringly, with the liberal arts of letters, particularly rhetoric and history. For example, Leonardo Bruni (1370–1444), the city's chancellor, argued that Florence's foundation occurred when "those vilest of thieves, the Caesars, the Antonines, the Tiberiuses, the Neros—those plagues and destroyers of the Roman Republic, had not yet deprived the people of their liberty."[5] The princely states countered this rhetoric with histories of their own.[6] On both sides the humanists who waged the battle found that Roman letters had more sting than philosophy and theory.[7]

When Alberti reached Florence he was surely overwhelmed by its new achievements in the arts, especially in Brunelleschi's architecture, Donatello's sculpture, and Masaccio's paintings. In his first treatise on the arts, *On Painting* in 1435–6 (Italian and then in Latin) he proclaimed the superiority for Florence over the ancients.[8] Brunelleschi's huge cathedral dome was "wide enough to cast its shadow over all the Tuscan people," "an enormous structure towering over the skies," and "made as it is without any beam or abundance of wood supports." It is the more remarkable because unlike Brunelleschi, the ancients "had many models to learn from and to imitate."[9] Florentine republicans had built it as a Christian church; no ancient emperor had ever raised its equal for their pagan gods.

His treatise on architecture that followed at midcentury put architecture in the service of the political life that clearly favored republicanism.[10] His political argument drew on the theory that had been developed in the previous century after the papacy had fled to safety in Avignon in 1309 and the little cities in the Papal States in central Italy had fallen into disorder. With their papal overlords gone they had installed new or newly revitalized communal governments not unlike those that had been won from imperial agents in northern Italy more than two centuries earlier. Practice, charters, and power, not theory, justified the authority that these communes wielded until two stellar individuals, Marsilius of Padua (1275/80–c.1342/3) and Bartolus of Sassoferrato (1314–57) took on the task. For Bartolus's troubles Pope Clement VI in 1343 branded him "the worst ever of the heretics," but this did not dethrone the efficacy of their works, which had been developed from the works of Aristotle, Roman jurists and historians, and scholastic tutors and would come to "play a major role in shaping the most radical version of early modern constitutionalism."[11]

Marsilius argued for the separation of sacred and secular affairs just as Christ had done when fingering a Roman coin and Augustine had when finding a home for the Church in the city. Marsilius offered a justification by putting secular justice in the consent of the governed and removed from the hands of priests.[12] For the commune's secular affairs he sought to "secure government by the wise" which was "the human legislator, and ... the human legislator is the people, the whole body of citizens," including priests and laypeople.[13] This wedge would eventually open political equality to all citizens.[14] With Aristotle he believed that sound judgment was a part of human nature and averred that "the less learned citizens can sometimes perceive something which must be corrected in a proposed law even though they could not have discovered it in the law itself."[15] They are also capable of judging things they were incapable of making such as "the quality of a picture, a house, a ship, and other works of art."[16]

Bartolus's contribution was different. He acknowledged that the pope and emperor were the "ultimate legitimizing authority" in their lands.[17] But with support from Aristotle's *Politics*, from Cicero, and from the precedent of ancient Rome he gave greater credence to what men did than to what men had written in more recent centuries. The legal landscape of the period traced papal and imperial authority back to Justinian's *Corpus juris civilis* completed in 534, but Bartolus took a different path. He explained, "if I fail to follow the words of the Gloss" of the *Corpus* it is because "they seem to me to be contrary to the truth, or contrary either to reason or to the law."[18] Communes, he explained, are "governed by 'free peoples' wielding their own *Imperium*." To preserve their liberty, which meant freedom from "servile dominium," whether from external enemies or internal tyrants, they "must be free to choose their own political arrangements, and in particular to maintain their established style of Republican self-government."[19]

In a word, being princes did not make their authority lawful. To the contrary, legitimate authority resided in reason or law that emerged from the reasoned deliberations of the governed. This proto-modern doctrine had had no such clarity and articulation when it appeared in ancient or medieval theory.[20] The cardinal point was that to achieve and maintain their liberty the laws the citizens would obey had to come from their collective reason.[21]

The theory defined ends, which were justice and liberty, but did not specify the number, role, and composition of the various institutions of government or the relationships between them. One size did not fit all: the constitution could be different in every city. The determining factor was the customary civil organization that had developed and changed over time, and it would continue to do so. This custom was the work of history, or tradition, in each city, and this understanding was sanctioned by "most of medieval thought."[22] Here was "a large step towards establishing the distinctively modern concept of a plurality of sovereign political authorities, each separate from one another as well as independent of the Empire."[23]

Marsilius' "whole body of citizens," his "faithful human legislator," was not simply a mass of people in public meetings. A self-governing republic would encompass specialists from among "the weightier part of the citizens."[24] They worked in various councils, one composed of "farmers, artisans, and others of that sort," another being the judiciary that included "advocates or lawyers or notaries." Others were the "'honorable class,'" or the "best men, who are few, and who alone are appropriately elected to the highest governmental offices."[25] An alternative form could have the few or even a single signore exercise governmental authority.[26] This could produce legitimate government by beloved princes such as Federigo da Montefeltro (1422–82), who enjoyed papal investiture as Count and later Duke in the extra mural lands of Urbino and was also annually elected by Urbino's citizens as the signore of their independent commune. His palace straddled the wall between the city and the countryside; its treasured library included a sumptuous copy of Alberti's treatise on architecture.[27] The doctrine also gave cover to an individual or successors in his family who gradually tightened their hold on a city and hastened the atrophy of republican institutions so that princely dominion could take over, and not necessarily without bloodshed.

This political theory also legitimated the Church Council that addressed the Schism and restored the papacy to Rome in 1420. The Council of Constance (1413–18) purged the papacy of its three popes and put a Cardinal from a Roman family on the papal throne as Martin V. Councils as instruments of reform reached back to Constantine's foundation of the Christian empire.[28] Their participants are like the "whole body of citizens," or at least the better part of them.[29] The Council of Constance required that Martin govern with Councils, but he and the next two popes quite predictably dragged their feet, and Conciliarism was defanged by 1449 and authority increasingly migrated to the head and away from the members just as it was doing in the maturing princely nation states throughout Europe. This drift provoked calls for new reforms, and we all know what happened in Germany and Trent in the next century's attempts to find them.

Having different forms of civil order be the protectors of liberty in different political communities rather than putting all of them under a singular form of government describes pluralism, and it flourished in Alberti's century.[30] Protecting that liberty is the very definition of a liberal art's purpose. As Giannozzo Manetti, Alberti's near contemporary, put it following ancient thought, the liberal arts are the arts "worthy of a free man."[31] Alberti considered the art of architecture to be a liberal art, the first person to do so.[32] The architect was free to render services to patrons in different civil orders so long as their purpose was protecting liberty, and he did so during the last quarter century of his life, as a roster of those who drew on his talents as an architect demonstrates.[33]

Alberti made it clear that as a liberal artist the architect's art "gives comfort and the greatest pleasure to mankind, to individual and community alike; nor does she rank last among the most honorable of the arts" (Pro.3/2). He also addressed the architect's patron: when you build well people "realize that you have used your wealth to increase greatly not only your own honor and glory, but also that of your family, your descendants, and the whole city" (Pro.4/13). The period's pluralism appears when he notes, "[T]he greatest and wisest of princes ... consider building one of the principal means of preserving his name for posterity" (Pro.5/13).

THE ARCHITECT AT WORK

We found Alberti's citizen–architect in Chapter 3 whose role Alberti will expand in Book 4 when he turns to the place of buildings in the civil orders of a pluralist culture. Vitruvius could not think in these terms. The civil order and the purposes his buildings were to serve and express were givens, and he could find the required aspect by simply consulting the conventions that tradition transmitted. Alberti was writing when republics and principalities (and the unique civil order of the Church that Machiavelli identified in his *Discourses*) were legitimate civil orders, and this required taking up topics new to theories of architecture.

Because civil orders call buildings into being and not the other way around, Alberti began this topic with a review of the civil orders of states running back to the most remote times. He ignored principalities and, concentrating on the variety and roles of the classes involved in their governing, concluded that these classes differ according to the special talents their members bring to the work of the political community. The best state, he decided, is the one that is organized to make the best use of nature's distribution of talents among individuals. "There is no aspect in which man differs more from man, than that which differentiates him so markedly from the beasts: his power of reason and his knowledge of the noble arts, and also, if you wish, his prosperity and good fortune" (4.1.93/269). Here we find that the state's civil order imitates the order and variety of nature and that that cosmic order's content is reason. He would, therefore, entrust the "care of government" to those "few individuals [who] stand out from the entire community, some of whom are renowned for their wisdom, good counsel, and ingenuity, others well known for the skill and practical experience, and others famous for their wealth and prosperity" (4.1.93/269). "They should administer divine matters according to the principles of religion, set up laws to regulate justice and equity, show us the way to the good and blessed life, and keep watch to protect and eventually increase the authority and dignity of their fellow citizens" (4.1.93–4/267–9). When we recall how he defines the role and special abilities of the architect it becomes clear that he believes that the architect's "knowledge of the noble arts" qualifies him for a role as a magistrate of the city's affairs. It is useful to note that this civil order is found in what people have traditionally done when governing themselves, not in laws inherited from emperors or called down from Heaven as Plato suggested. It is the civil order of a republic.

Alberti then turns to the buildings that a civil order needs. He begins with a prince who governs a city, and opens with a caution to the architect.

> *Above all it is important to establish precisely what kind of person he is: whether he is the sort who governs reverently and piously over willing subjects, motivated, that is, less by his own gain than by the safety and comfort of his citizens, or one who would wish to control the political situation so that he could remain in power even against the will of his subjects. (At 5.1.117/333)[34]*

Alberti calls one a king, whom we can recognize as a person whom the commune elects and reelects to govern willing citizens, while the other is clearly a tyrant whose only authority is power. His residence must be designed to protect him from those he governs, but Alberti adds that even the king's city must be able to defend itself against an enemy attack, and so his palace needs to be linked to a fortress (4.3.117/334, 121–2/345–7). Italy abounds with examples. (He does not mention that Florence's new city hall was the fortified residence for the elected priors during their two-month term with a garrison's barracks on top.[35])

In Chapter 3 we called attention to the role that the first three elements of building, locality, *area*, and compartition, played in drawing on and serving regional traditions. Here we can find them directing the expression of the identity of the local civil orders that citizens can legitimately call on. As an architect Alberti would work in several different localities—Rome, Florence, Rimini, Mantua, and probably Pienza and Urbino. His buildings in these places are easily identifiable as his, but their quite conspicuous differences illustrate the traditions of their locales' building cultures. We can say that he used his reason to excavate them from local traditions of the art of building to serve local civil traditions, a topic we will return to in Chapter 9.

In another comment Alberti recognizes that any new building alters an existing urban condition which it ought to improve. When modifying or extending an extant building the architect must not pervert or incorrectly finish the work of others. "I feel that the original intentions of the author, the product of mature reflection, must be upheld" (9.10.319/865–7). The façade he completed for Santa Maria Novella in Florence illustrates his words. He built a new portal, added a modified pattern above the existing lowest level, surrounded it with columns and their entablature, and added an attic and everything above that except the round window.

4.1 Leon Battista Alberti, façade, Santa Maria Novella, Florence, begun 1458
Source: Photo by author.

ON ARCHITECTURE

In Chapter 3 we encountered Alberti's role for the architect's "sure and wonderful art and method," that is, imitation, in establishing the compartition by using existing buildings as sources for imitation when making new ones, and we saw that this role for imitation was related to the classical tradition's ideas about the natural sociability of people and the Christian's life in the city. In this instance imitation led to new buildings made from old ones in the cities they would serve and enhance.

Now we go a step farther and find that the members, that is, the walls, roofs, and openings that will produce the membrature and the configuration in which they will be arranged will be made to imitate God's creation. The agents for doing so are the lines and angles of the lineaments.

The work will be done by reason, judgment, and nature. In the configuration and the members that make the membrature and, as ornament, make the beauty visible, the lineaments become the actual measured dimensions of the material structure. They size the two-dimensional compartition, its third dimension defining the configuration's volumes, and the members that compose the membrature. We might have expected Alberti to bring the word symmetry into service, but as we noted earlier, the word is missing from his treatise. Instead he adapts Vitruvius' word respond, and he gives it quite a workout.[36] It refers to several general aspects of proportionality.[37] And more specifically, it finds work in proportioning the orders and the other members throughout the body of the building, which makes it the thoroughbred among the horses in his stable.[38] Examples: "the height must be a set proportion of the width" (8.5.258/701). And, the "right and left would have equal dimensions so that they balanced each other out," an anticipation of symmetry's modern meaning (1.12.29/85).[39]

The related word correspond that does the heavier work, the Percheron in his stable, was absent from Vitruvius and from the ancient vocabulary.[40] Note its roles here where it covers the use, application, or quality or ratios and proportions: "These numbers … were not employed by architects randomly or indiscriminately, but according to [alternatively, in correspondence with] a harmonic relationship" (9.6.307/829). "In establishing dimensions, there are certain natural relationships [alternatively, correspondences] that cannot be defined as numbers" but instead are found in roots and powers (9.6.307/829). And, "For us, the outline is a certain correspondence between the lines that define the dimensions" (9.5.305/821).[41] He admonishes architects to compose such that "whole may correspond to whole, and equal to equal;" again, make "all the angles throughout the area balance out and match one another" (1.8.20/57; 1.8.20/57; 7.15.237/645; 8.10.289/773; and 9.4.300/807). Alberti also used respond and correspond to put architecture into defined relationships with things such as music and the scaler relationship between buildings and individuals (1.10.24/69: also 7.10.221/613).

Respond, correspond, and proportionality encompass the third dimension to define volumes rising from the compartition's plan. It also reaches to the configuration's section and to the masses of the membrature's material. Here we find a joint effort that produces a beautiful, proportionate, three-dimensional matrix that the material members as ornament make visible.

We can recognize here Alberti's transfer to architecture of the role that the proportioned lineaments of Brunelleschi's perspective system played. Painters used this invention to produce an ordered facsimile of the world in which people act. Alberti described the method and the benefits it offered the painter in his treatise on painting that he wrote before turning to architecture. This later treatise extends that method to the organization of the spatial void with a three-dimensional matrix of lineaments that become visible not in paint on a two-dimensional surface but in the three dimensions of a building's material membrature.[42] In the treatise on architecture, a three-dimensional art, his translation of lineaments from ordering paint to ordering material takes full flower. It began in his early discussion of beauty in Book 6 where the word respond refers to the task of pulling the other qualities of a building into proportional relationships:

> *In short, all such things will contribute. But whatever they are, they will look worthless unless their composition is precisely governed by order and measure. Each individual element must be arranged according to number, in such a way that even responds to even, right by left, upper by lower; nothing must be introduced that might disturb the arrangement or order; everything must be set to exact angles and proportionate lines. (6.5.164/471)*

Respond is important in this passage, but the Percheron correspond stresses the role of the proportionality of the matrix of compartition and membrature. Examples:

> *[J]ust as the head, the foot, and indeed any member must refer to each other and to all the rest of the body in an animal, so in a building, and especially a temple, the parts of the whole body must be so composed that they all correspond one to another, and any one, taken individually, may provide the dimensions of all the rest. (7.5.199/559)*
>
> *It is the task and aim of concinnity to compose parts that are quite separate from one another by their nature, according to some precise rule, so that they correspond to one another in appearance. (9.5.302/815; more about concinnity later)*
>
> *[E]ven the smallest parts of a building can add charm if they occupy their proper place but if positioned somewhat strange, ignoble, or inappropriate, they will be devalued if elegant, ruined if they are anything else. Look at Nature's own works; for if a puppy had an ass's ear on its forehead ... it would look deformed ... Even cattle are not liked, if they have one eye blue and the other black; so natural is it that the right should correspond to the left exactly.*
>
> *We must therefore take great care to ensure that even the minutest elements are so arranged in their level, alignment, number, shape, and appearance that right matches left, top marches bottom, adjacent matches adjacent, and equal matches equal, and that they are an ornament to the body of which they are to be part. (9.7.310/839)*

Lineaments have now become the dimensioned lines and angles of the membrature's and compartition's proportioned matrix that provide the "infallible way of joining and fitting together those lines and angles which define and enclose the surfaces of the building," as he said when he introduced them in Book 1 (1.1.7/19–21). We have now found several criteria controlling where the material things that compose the six elements of building are to go relative to one another and serve as the ornaments that makes the beauty of the whole body of the building visible and perceptible. Now we can move that beauty in the building to the beauty of architecture whose content imitates beauty's content in nature. Alberti's culminating discussion begins in Chapter 5 of Book 9 where he explains the three steps that carry the names number, outline, and collocation and finally concinnity, all of which he had broached earlier.

Collocation is third, but here we can put it first (9.7.309/387).[43] It puts things in their places according to the dictates of the pattern of the well-proportioned compartition, configuration, and membrature that expresses the purpose of the service it renders to the city's citizens.

Now number, which was first on his list. After a reminder that in dealing with imitation "our ancestors learned through observation of nature herself" he declares that it is "not without reason … that nature, as the perfect generator of forms, should be imitated" (9.5.303/817). Imitation and number are involved with one another in several different ways. He starts by noting that the ancestors' thoughts led them to principles underlying the similarities and differences between the three principal kinds of columns (9.5.303/817). Then, rather banally, he notes that the numbers that are derived from animals tell us that a building's supports need to come in even quantities and its openings in odd ones. Next we learn which numbers the wise agree are the important ones. Among the odd numbers they are three, five, seven, nine, and nine's derivative, forty. He gives instances that tie these to human life and cosmic significance—the seven planets and ages of man, the nine orbs in the sky and nine months for human gestation, and so on. Among the even numbers they are 4, 6, 8, and 10, which embody richer numerical resonances. For example 6 is the product of 1+2+3, and 10^2 is the most perfect of all according to Aristotle because it is the sum of $1^3+2^3+3^3+4^3$ (9.5.303–4/819–21).

Finally, outline (*finitio*) a word whose use by Alberti is difficult to grasp in English and in the modern era.[44] James Leoni's eighteenth-century translation, which he based on Cosimo Bartoli's 1550 Italian translation, called it finishing. "By the Finishing I understand a certain mutual Correspondence of those several Lines, by which the Proportions are measured, whereof one is the Length, the other the Breadth, and the other the Height."[45] We might think of outline as the lines that we see as profiles or silhouettes of solids and as the boundaries we put around solid things when we draw them. Here we can understand that number and outline are inseparable. Outline receives the numbers as dimensions, the bearers of proportions, that govern the membrature's material, which takes us back at proportionality.

The most suitable dimensions as proportions are "taken from those objects in which nature offers herself to our inspection and admiration" and reveal the proportionality (that is, laws; reason) that she uses in her work. (This is the closest Alberti comes to referring explicitly to *natura naturans*.) Alberti sounds like Pythagoras in stating that "Nature is wholly consistent" (9.5.305/821). Augustine endorsed that, and it stands behind his next comment, which is about concinnity. He affirms that "the very same numbers that cause sounds" to be pleasing to the ears "also fill the eyes and mind with wondrous delight." This quality is a harmony that Alberti, who was known to be an excellent singer, defines "as that consonance of sounds which is pleasant to the ears" (5.9.305/823). They occur in ratios that use the numbers one, two, three, four, and eight, which architects employ in pairs for the plans of piazzas and threes for configurations such as "a public sitting room, senate house, hall, and so on" (9.5.305/825).

We are now in the world of numbers that, like lineaments, are denizens of the intellect. Proportions of two numbers follow from the musical analogy. Among the three numbers used for volumes, some are naturally harmonic. Others derive from roots and squares including the cube which is "consecrated to the Godhead" and which generates various other numbers that are irrational but can be produced geometrically. Philosophers have explained yet other methods that are called arithmetic, geometric, and musical means.[46]

These proportions carry the architect only so far. Beyond them lies what Vitruvius called eurhythmy and Alberti left unnamed but entrusted to the judgment of the architect who consulted concinnity. Concinnity? Alberti's Latin word was adequately arcane by 1550 that when Bartoli made the Italian translation he rendered *concinnitas* as *leggiandria* and provided an explanation of it. Concinnity is rarely heard now, but the Oxford English Dictionary shows it had a three-century run that began in the mid-sixteenth century. It meant "Skilful and harmonious adaptation or fitting together of parts; harmony, congruity, consistency," which renders Alberti's meaning very well.[47]

Concinnity is the quality achieved through imitation and correspondence that welds the six elements of building into a beautiful whole building. It polishes the results of numbering, outline, and collocation and is proportionality's quality in a building whose content is the beauty that produces delight. That beauty is peculiar to the building, but it also participates in the pulchritudinous beauty that is a universal quality that different people, different buildings, and different civil orders share, the quality that Augustine had identified as the very good in the many good things in God's creation, the equivalent in the realm of buildings that the *jus naturale* occupies relative to the *jus civile*. It is the universal beauty of nature that, when present in a building, elevates it to architecture and connects it to the beauty of all created things. The eyes enjoy a building's delight, and reason and the soul find pleasure and happiness in the perception of architecture's beauty.

Alberti's medieval predecessors thought of that perception as a cognitive, time-demanding, experience. Alberti agrees, but he also presents it as immediate and forceful. Concinnity, beauty's agent, can be immediately and instantly recognized in a building's "form and figure" a "form, dignity, grace, and other such qualities" that have "some natural excellence and perfection that excites the mind" (9.5.302). The definition of beauty back in Book 6 noted that "as soon as anything is removed or altered, these qualities are themselves weakened and perish." Now he goes in the other direction to emphasize the proportionate unity, that is, the concinnity, uniting all the members, and the building as architecture becomes one with nature and with mankind in nature and mankind as part of nature.

> *Neither in the whole body nor in its parts does concinnity flourish as much as it does in nature herself; thus I might call it the spouse and the soul of reason....*
> *[I]t runs through man's entire life and government, it molds the whole of nature. Everything that nature produces is regulated by the law of concinnity ... Without concinnity ... the critical sympathy of the parts would be lost. (9.5.302–3/815)*

A little earlier Alberti had written that beauty in architecture is found in the unity of the "several elements into a single bundle or body, according to a true and consistent agreement and sympathy ... for otherwise their discord and differences would cause conflict and disunity." To achieve that unity "every rule of beauty" requires "that nature must be imitated" (9.5.301/811). He now moves warily toward rendering his second definition of beauty. He reminds the reader of his first definition by restating that in a beautiful thing nothing may be moved or altered without spoiling the appearance. He now reveals "the three principal components of that whole theory into which we inquire [which] are number, what we might call outline, and collocation. But arising from the composition and connection of the three," he continues, "is a further quality in which beauty shines full face: our term for this is concinnity" (9.5.302/813/15). In this passage the Latin that is rendered as composition and connection in translation are stronger: *compactis* and *nexis*. After a few more preliminaries he has prepared the reader for his second, and final and complete, definition of beauty. The earlier one concerned the necessary condition for this beauty. Then, finally,

> *Beauty is a form of sympathy and consonance of the parts within a body, according to definite number, outline, and collocation, as dictated by concinnity, the absolute and fundamental rule in nature. (9.5.303/817)*

Ornament, an ocular phenomenon, is left out because this beauty is a matter of the perception that addresses a higher unity with the order, harmony, and proportionality of nature than the beauty of an individual member or building. This understanding owes a great deal to what we found in Aquinas and discussed in Chapter 3, and although it invokes integrity and completeness it is not simply the medieval trilogy warmed over.[48] Alberti's identifying concinnity, correspondence's companion, as the "absolute and fundamental rule in nature" tells us that concinnity is what the architect imitates to infuse the whole body of the building with perceptible beauty and elevate it to architecture. David Summers has argued that one aspect of what Alberti identifies as concinnity is bilateral symmetry (not yet bilateral identity). It makes proportionality more intensely visible and reinforces the presence of what Augustine called *convenientia*, or "something like symmetry in the classical sense, that is, proportionality, with a special emphasis upon bilateral symmetry."[49] It "preserves unity and makes the whole beautiful."[50]

Concinnity establishes a relationship between both the things nature makes and the way she makes them, that is, between things God creates and the laws, or principles, or *logos*, or reason revealed in the proportionality and geometry of lines and angles that God uses in creation. These are our old friends *natura naturata* and *natura naturans*. In choosing his sources for imitation Alberti naturally turned to the finest things in the Great Chain of Being, which were the animals, and particularly the human animal. "The most expert Artists among the Ancients," he reports, " … were of Opinion, that an Edifice was like an Animal, so that in the Formation of it we ought to imitate Nature."[51] Consider the human figure, he continues. "One man might desire the tenderness of a slender girl," a character in a comedy might prefer one that is plumper and more buxom, and another might be pleased with a wife who is neither "so slender of figure as to appear sickly nor so stout of limb as to imitate a village bully." They are all beautiful, but they are also different, and in them we can find delight "infused or imprinted" (9.5.301–2/811). His next sentences put delight in an inferior position relative to the beauty that the three women's bodies have in common and which is the quality we ought to imitate. In doing so we must look beyond the differences that lead to different preferences and discover qualities that invest each of them with the beauty that all can perceive as love.

Proportionality, geometry, numbers, physical measurements of material, all of them the operative parts of imitation, are the stuff of the lineaments that the intellect commands.[52] The architect's intellect must be lively, inventive, and conjoined with a God-given talent and indefatigable energy that brings a penetrating analysis to the sources that are imitated, that is, to the things that people had made through imitation within tradition, the things nature creates, and the "rules that she employed in producing things" (9.5.303/817). Here Alberti is planted in the fifteenth century. It is a commonplace in Renaissance studies that to Revelation transmitted in Holy Writ Renaissance artists added the things nature makes, and Renaissance humanists added the great stock of knowledge vouchsafed to unwitting ancient pagans. Earlier, in an anti-Scholastic rant Petrarch had called Plato the "prince of philosophy," a rank given him by truth, "truth which he saw and to which he came nearer than all the others, though he did not comprehend it."[53] Later Erasmus would exclaim: "Saint Socrates, pray for us!"[54]

Jacques Maritain explained that scholastic philosophers had given the artist a "special dignity. He is as it were an associate of God in the making of works of beauty ... artistic creation does not copy God's creation, but continues it."[55] Alberti personalized that medieval position by identifying himself with the works he produced by inventing within imitation on the forward edge of an always innovative tradition. He works with the laws of nature that are evident in the whole realm of things God had created and in nature, that is, the reason, or *ratio*, nature uses in its creation and in its continued operations. In imitating those laws the architect perceives them intellectually, as lineaments and numbers, and from that experience he, and we, may luxuriate in perceiving beauty in architecture and receiving happiness.

ON URBANISM

Alberti's treatise, disarmingly titled *On the Art of Building*, is taken to be a treatise on building buildings, but as we have seen, building is not the same as architecture, and now we will note that the final product of the architect is the urban setting of a civil order. In the classical tradition the city is always the fulfilment of architecture.

The city is the place where people live together in a political community. When Alberti sketched the history of architecture he first presented the organization of civil societies, then the selection and marking out of places to separate private and public things, and then the invention of the art of building and its steady improvement from offering security to comfort and finally to the pleasure that architecture offers to happiness. "Building ... enjoyed her first gush of youth, as it were, in Asia, flowered in Greece, and later reached her glorious maturity in Italy." Seminal in this rise was the work of Asian kings who had the leisure to reflect and the wealth to make buildings that were "impressive as well as graceful" (6.3.157/451). This capsule history makes the works that predated the Romans useless for instructing architects, a bias that prevailed into the eighteenth century.

Alberti's distinction between the delight of mere building and the beauty of architecture was absent from Vitruvius' treatise. It presents beautiful architecture as a complement to the good in the city—a complement, not an attribute, because the beautiful is not interchangeable with the good; the one is a quality of a thing made, the other of an act that is done, but it is natural for men to seek the good and garland it with beauty and to interpret the beautiful city as one that is devoted to the good. Both the good and the beautiful offer pleasure and ultimately happiness, which in architecture and the city it builds was the point of it all in Alberti's history of architecture. Satisfying the Vitruvian trilogy that applies to the art of building is a necessary condition for achieving architecture and building the city. In the classical tradition we can say that the art of building is to architecture as the market is to the city and the goods that the market offers are to the good that fulfills our pursuit of happiness.

During Alberti's lifetime or soon thereafter, and with his involvement in both representational and nonrepresentational arts, his expansion of the art of architecture to embrace the physical and spatial setting of the civil order, that is, as the facilitator and urban integument of the city's purpose, led to depicting the whole urban body composed of members that included the locality, the buildings, and the open areas in spatially convincing relationships to one another.[56]

The city was seen as a unique, particular, earthly place. The image, whether graphic or in actual vision, presents each building as "appropriate in each case" (Pro. 5/15; see also 3.16.91/263). Public buildings stand out from private ones, and the public buildings can be sorted into three categories (*genera*) of ascending importance. One holds lesser, non-institutional public buildings and other urban components (4.3–8.105–16/289–331). A second includes the buildings for the "foremost citizens." In the third and receiving the greatest attention are the public buildings used for the administration of both sacred and secular public affairs and the parts of private buildings used for public purposes.

In the classical tradition the family and the city are similar institutions that differ only in scale. Alberti twice calls a house a miniature city, the second time in a way that recalls Aristotle's explanation of the foundational role of the family in the formation of the city (1.9.13/65; 5.14.140/399). The family that can build an important house and have an important villa will necessarily be occupied in public affairs. Whether a town house or villa house, it ought to have three zones, one private, one semi-private, and one public, and this last zone "should imitate the house of a prince," that is, a person who exercises authority (5.17.145/415–17). The villa is suitable for summers while in the winter an urban residence provides the family with a place to dwell with comfort and civility, and offers the added convenience of having "common retailers and other shops mixed with the houses of the most important citizens" (7.1.192/537).[57]

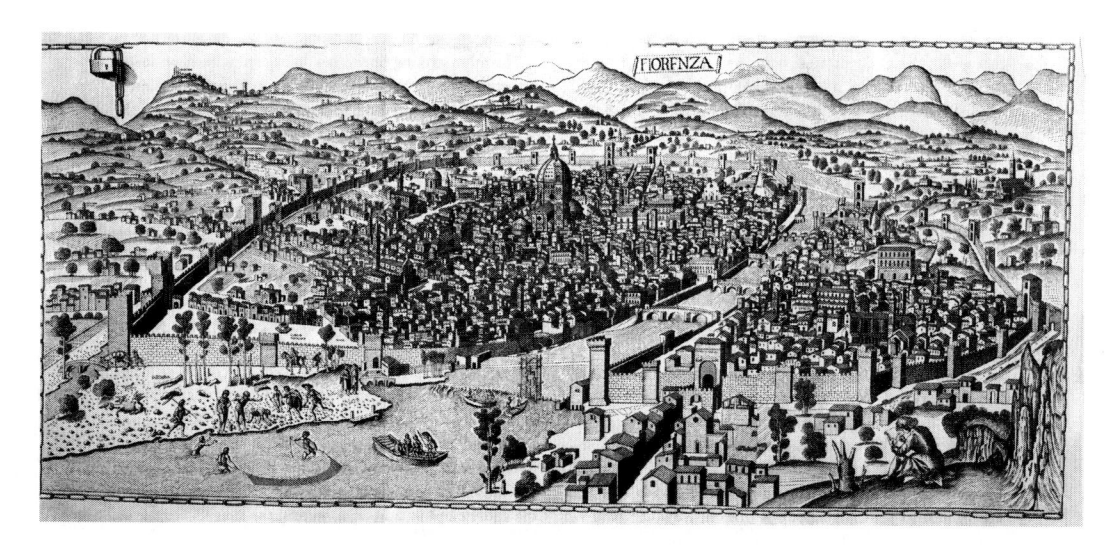

4.2 View of Florence with a Chain, c.1480? c.1510? Woodcut, in the Staatliche Museen Pruessischer Kulturbesitz in Berlin
Source: In the public domain via Wikicommons.

In classical urbanism and architecture decorum must be in command. Decorum calls for honoring the building practices and precedents of the locality and diluting the configuration and membrature of superiors to produce the lesser buildings with a related role. Alberti covers this ground when he pens a rhapsodic paean to the beautiful city right where we would expect it, in his comments about the city's principal church, the one presided over by a great prelate. It is the "greatest and most important ornament of a city" (5.6.126–7/361; 7.3.194/543). He would wish to see it "so beautiful that nothing more complete in appearance could ever be imagined," a place in which a person could not restrain "himself from exclaiming that what he saw was a place undoubtedly worthy of God" (7.3.194/543). It should follow ancient practice and "be executed throughout with such wonderful and exquisite workmanship that those outside are enticed to enter and those within are charmed into remaining longer" (5.6.126–7/361). He endorses the opinion of the ancients that "a people seemed to be truly pious when the temples of the gods were crowded" (7.3.194/543).

"For about the appearance and configuration of a building there is a natural excellence and perfection that stimulates the mind; it is immediately recognized if present, but if absent is even more desired," a statement that applies to "public buildings, in particular sacred ones" (9.8.312/843). Evoking the role that Cicero and Augustine gave to rhetoric he has the church instruct, delight, and move the visitor. The beauty of a church should reach directly into the soul where it will stir the will.[58] Its beauty should draw a person in and have him "start with awe." Then he would gaze upon what he sees, for "There is no doubt that a temple that delights the mind wonderfully, captivates it with grace and admiration, will greatly encourage piety" (7.3.194/543). Within, "I would have nothing on the walls or the floor of the temple that did not have some quality of philosophy" (7.10.220/611). He would reserve the place of greatest dignity for the single sacrificial altar (7.10.220; 229; 240; 228/611; 629; 654; 627 respectively).

Alberti favors a central-plan church because through imitation it will establish the most embracing connection for the worshiper and closest correspondence between the building and God and His creation.

> *It is obvious from all that is fashioned, produced, or created under her influence, that nature delights primarily in the circle. Need I mention the earth, the stars, the trees, the animals, their nests, and so on, all of which she has made circular? We notice that nature also delights in the hexagon. For bees, hornets, and insects of every kind have learned to build the cells of their hives entirely out of hexagons. (7.4.196/549–51)*[59]

Here he expands circularity to include any regular polygon, including the square. These are the lineaments, the bearers of philosophical content, that the mind excited by the vision of beauty uses to perceive beauty and the architect manipulates to induce that perception. The final test of a church's success, we learn, is what we have encountered earlier, which is its capacity to appeal to "whatever learned or unlearned person" who encounters it and so move him that he discovers the presence of God there and uses what he sees as instruction about the nature of God and His love.[60]

The principal church is "the greatest and most important ornament of a city." It should be sited to "lend it the greatest reverence and majesty" (5.6.126/359; see also 7.3.195/549). Here we see decorum at work. We have witnessed Alberti having decorum work with imitation to make the hieratic status of the civil order's institutions visible. It also works with ornament to have the building express the rank and character appropriate to it. Like Vitruvius, Alberti gives it the commanding role in the urban form, but with three differences. First, Vitruvius did so as the client of his imperial patron. Alberti does so as a magistrate in a city. Second, in the fifteenth century the spatial void of the urban realm is being brought under the control of a conceptual homogeneity that will change how cities are depicted. And third, Alberti puts a much wider range of buildings under decorum's command. Alberti realizes that all three roles are central to urbanism, and that when well done, "The principal ornament to any city lies in the siting, layout, fashioning, and arrangement of its roads, squares, and individual works: each must be properly planned and distributed according to use, importance, and convenience" (6.1.191/535).[61] Here architecture and urbanism are indissoluble. The distribution and arrangement of a city's material members are bound by the same principles of architecture as its buildings, and they must be subjected to the equivalents of number, outline, and collocation and have their concinnity embody the criterion of decorum. It is a fundamentally and profoundly civil, material, and spatial understanding of the city, quite unlike any that preceded it.[62] To build this city is the task of the architect Alberti described in the Prologue and instructed throughout the treatise, the architect as citizen and citizen as architect practicing architecture as a liberal art and a civic art.

NOTES

1 Pro. 3/7. This is a precocious assertion of the architect's role; see Carroll William Westfall, "Biblical Typology in the *Vita Nicolai V* by G. Manetti," in J. IJsewijn et al., ed. *Acta Conventus Neo-Latini Lovaniensis* (Leuven: Leuven University Press, 1973), 701–9.

2 For the city studied as most alive when at war see Leo Strauss, *The City and Man* (Chicago: Rand McNally, 1964).

3 Gene Brucker, *The Civic World of Early Renaissance Florence* (Princeton: Princeton University Press, 1977, 39–79 for the story; citing 79. A condensed version of the Ciompi revolt is in Gene Brucker, *Renaissance Florence* (New York et al: John Wiley, 1969), 151–4.

4 Brucker, *Civic World,* 86–7; 90–92; 173; 258; 271; 325–9; 337–40; 488; 500–501.

5 Leonardo Bruni, "Panegyric to the City of Florence," trans. Benjamin G. Kohl, in B.G. Kohl et al., *The Earthly Republic: Italian Humanists on Government and Society* (n.p.: University of Pennsylvania Press, 1978), 135–73, 151.

6 They run through Flavio Biondo, *Italy Illuminated*, ed. and trans. Jeffrey A. White, vol. 1 (Cambridge, Mass., and London: The I Tatti Renaissance Library and Harvard University Press, 2005); see also Philip Jacks, *The Antiquarian and the Myth of Antiquity* (Cambridge and New York: Cambridge University Press, 1993).

7 The literature on these humanists is extensive. The publications of Paul Oskar Kristeller, for example *Renaissance Thought and Its Sources*, ed. Michael Mooney (New York: Columbia University Press, 1979), and his students, for example Trinkaus, *In Our Image and Likeness*, are central. Black, *Political Thought*, 129–35 puts Bruni in the context developed here. Quentin Skinner, "Political Philosophy," in Q. Skinner et al., eds, *The Cambridge History of Renaissance Philosophy* (Cambridge: Cambridge University Press, 1988), 412–30, provides a useful survey.

8 For this date and order see Leon Battista Alberti, *Il Nuovo* de pictura *di Leon Battista Alberti/The New* de pictura *of Leon Battista Alberti*, ed. Rocco Sinisgalli (Rome: Kappa, 2006).

9 Alberti, *Il Nuovo* de pictura, prologue. Smith, "Originality and Cultural Progress," 1992, discusses this passage.

10 Hans Baron, "Leon Battista Alberti as an Heir and Critic of Florentine Civic Humanism," in *In Search of Florentine Humanism*, 2 vols (Princeton: Princeton University Press, 1988), 1: 278–88. Hanno-Walter Kruft, *A History of Architectural Theory from Vitruvius to the Present*, trans. Ronald Taylor, Elsie Callander, and Antony Wood (London and New York: Zwemmer and Princeton Architectural Press, 1994), 44, stated that Alberti "tries to conceal it behind a 'neutral' conception of different political systems."

11 Quentin Skinner, *The Foundations of Modern Political Theory*, 2 vols (Cambridge, London, et al.: Cambridge University Press, 1978), 1: 65 and passim.

12 Alan Ryan, *On Politics: A History of Political Thought from Herodotus to the Present*, 2 vols (New York and London: Liveright Publishing, W.W. Norton, 2012), 273.

13 Leo Strauss, "Marsilius of Padua," in Leo Strauss and Joseph Cropsey, *A History of Political Philosophy*, 3rd edn (Chicago and London: University of Chicago Press, 1987), 275–6.

14 Marsilius of Padua, *The Defender of Peace: The* Defensor pacis, trans. Alan Gewirth, 2 vols (New York: Columbia University Press, 1951–6), reprint of vol. 2 (New York: Harper & Row, 1967), I,xii,4; see Strauss, "Marsilius of Padua," 280ff.

15 For the Aristotle reference see Ryan, *On Politics*, 277; Strauss, "Marsilius of Padua," contrasts Marsilius and Aquinas, 292–4.

16 Marsilius of Padua, *Defender of Peace*, I.xiii.3. I have also consulted Marsilius of Padua, *The Defender of the Peace*, ed. and trans. Annabel Brett (Cambridge: Cambridge University Press, 2005).

17 L.P. Canning, "Law, Sovereignty and Corporation Theory, 1300–1450," in J.H. Burns, ed., *The Cambridge History of Medieval Political Thought c.350–1450* (Cambridge et al.: Cambridge University Press, 1988), 471.

18 Skinner, *Foundations*, 1:53; 9, quoting from Bartolus' Commentary on the Code.

19 Skinner, *Foundations*, 1: 11–12. See also Ryan, *On Politics*; for how "every king within his own kingdom is equivalent in authority to the Emperor;" 283–5.

20 See for example, St Thomas Aquinas, *Treatise on Law*, intro. Stanley Parry (Washington, D.C.: Regnery Gateway, n.d. [1987 printing]), 112–13 for *Sum. Theo.*, Quest. 97, "Of Change in Law," art. 3, "Whether Custom Can Obtain Force of Law," reply obj. 3.

21 Marsilius of Padua, *Defender of Peace*, I,xii,6. Marsilius' Latin that is here translated as "a community of free men" is "communitas liberorum," which accounts for using the word liberty when diction allows it in order to align the political theory with the theme of liberty that was so important to the Florentine republic, as we shall see. "Servile dominium" is the same in English and Latin. For the Latin text see Marsilius of Padua, *The Defensor Pacis*, ed. C.W. Previté-Orton (Cambridge: Cambridge University Press, 1928).

22 Alan Gewirth, "The Basic Themes: Reason, Power, and the People's Will," introduction to Marsilius of Padua, *Defender of Peace*, xxxii–xxxiii.

23 Skinner, *Foundations*, 1:9.

24 Marsilius of Padua, *The Defender of Peace*, I.xii.3.

25 Marsilius of Padua, *The Defender of Peace*, I.xiii.4.

26 Marsilius of Padua, *The Defender of Peace*, I.xvi.

27 For the incipit and information about this and other manuscripts see Alessandro Marchi et al., eds, *La città ideale: l'utopia del rinascimento a urbino tra Piero della Francesca e Raffaello*, (Milan: Electra, 2012), item 7.4.

28 Diarmaid MacCulloch, *Christianity: The First Three Thousand Years* (New York: Viking Penguin, 2010), 211ff.

29 Walter Ullmann, *A History of Political Thought: the Middle Ages* (Harmondsworth: Penguin Books, 1965), 220; see also Antony Black, *Council and Commune: The Conciliar Movement and the Fifteenth-Century Heritage* (London: Burns & Oats, and Shephardstown: Patmos Press, 1979), 10.

30 See inter alia, Black, *Political Thought*, 129. A useful overview is Daniel Waley, *The Italian City-Republics* (New York and Toronto: McGraw-Hill, 1969), with later editions.

31 Giannozzo Manetti, "On Famous Men of Great Age," in *Biographical Writings*, ed. and trans. Stefano U. Baldassarri et al. (Cambridge, Mass., and London: Harvard University Press, 2003), §11, 115. See also Leon Battista Alberti, "Fate and Fortune," trans. Arturo B. Fallico et al. *Renaissance Philosophy: The Italian Philosophers* (New York: The Modern Library, 1967), 33–40.

32 See Carroll William Westfall, "Painting and the Liberal Arts: Alberti's View," *Journal of the History of Ideas*, 30 (1969), 487–506; reprinted in William J. Connell, ed., *Renaissance*

Essays II (Rochester: University of Rochester Press, 1993), 130–49; and "Society, Beauty, and the Humanist Architect in Alberti's *De re aedificatoria*," *Studies in the Renaissance*, 16 (1969), 61–79.

33 See Robert Travernor, *On Alberti and the Art of Building* (New Haven and London: Yale University Press, 1998), 79–124. For different views of Alberti's service to the papacy see Carroll William Westfall, *In This Most Perfect Paradise: Alberti, Nicholas V, and the Invention of Conscious Urban Planning in Rome, 1447–44* (University Park and London: Pennsylvania State University Press, 1974), 63–77, and Manfredo Tafuri, *Interpreting the Renaissance: Princes, Cities, Architects*, trans. Daniel Sherer (New Haven and London: Yale University Press, 2006), Chapter II, "Civic esse non licere: Nicholas V and Leon Battista Alberti," reviewed extensively in Grafton, *Leon Battista* Alberti, 295–315.

34 For more about the distinction see for example the Conciliar apologist John of Segovia, quoted in Antony Black, *Monarchy and Community: Political Ideas in the Later Conciliar Controversy 1430–50* (Cambridge: Cambridge University Press, 1970), 45.

35 For it see Jürgen Paul, *Il Palazzo Vecchio in Florenz* (Florence: Leo S. Olschki, 1969); and Marvin Trachtenberg, "What Brunelleschi Saw: Monument and Site at the Palazzo Vecchio in Florence," *Journal of the Society of Architectural Historians*, 47 (1988), 14–44.

36 See Hon and Goldstein, *From* Summetria *to* Symmetry, 113. Their use of the word proportion here is misleading. *Respondere* has more to do with the composition of elements within a body, as Alberti will use the term, than with the proportional relationships. Also misleading is their rendering of *respondere* as correspond, as modern translations commonly do. The same fault appears on 116 and 117.

37 Among the places they can be found are the following: 1.9.23/65; 7.9.212/593; 3.2.63/177; 3.11.78/225; 3.6.111–2/319; 6.7.168/483; 6.12.182/519; 7.4.197/553; 7.8.207/581; 7.9.212/593; 8.7.276/745.

38 Diverse examples are at 8.3.251/687; 8.6.262/713; 9.5.305–9/821–39; 1.13.31/89; 7.10.219/607; 7.10.219/607: 8.6.264/717; 8.8.281/757; 2.1.33/97, 9.2.295/793, and 10.5.330/903.

39 Other examples are at 8.10.289/773; 9.7.310/839; and 9.7.310/839.

40 Neither correspond, respond, nor symmetry carry the purely formal and mechanical meaning that the word symmetry currently has within architecture. Hon and Goldstein, *From* Summetria *to* Symmetry, 116, opine that Alberti "introduced a new principle into architectural aesthetics ... [and implicitly] forged a new technical term."

41 Here are additional uses of correspondence: 9.6.308/831; 9.3.297/797; 9.6.306/827; 9.6.308/831; 9.6.308/833; 9.9.314/853; and 9.6.308/831.

42 Important comments on this relationship are in Giulio Carlo Argan and Nesca A. Robb, "The Architecture of Brunelleschi and the Origins of Perspective Theory in the Fifteenth Century," *Journal of the Warburg and Courtauld Institutes* 9 (1946), 96–121; Rudolf Wittkower, "Brunelleschi and 'Proportion in Perspective,'" *Journal of the Warburg and Courtauld Institutes* 16 (1953), 275–91; Westfall, "Society, Beauty, and the Humanist Architect"; Norris Kelly Smith, *Here I Stand: Perspective from Another Point of View* (New York: Columbia University Press, 1994).

43 Rykwert et al. translate it as arrangement. Using collocation rather than composition signals the difference between a representational art such as painting and architecture, which is not.

44 It refers to the boundary between what is a material object and the void it inhabits. Outline, which suggests a visual property, fails to convey the sense that the outline is an intellectual property of a material thing. Metrović, *Serene Greed*, appendix; and

Tavernor, *On Alberti*, 43 give the usages of others that include Metrović's "shape-defining properties" (32), measured outline, delimitation, boundary, measure, and proportionality.

45 Leone Battista Alberti, *Ten Books on Architecture*, trans. James Leoni, 3 vols in 1, (London: Thomas Edlin, 1726), Italian-English en face; II: 9.5.196; in the London, Edward Owen, for Robert Alfray, 1755 edn, ed. by Joseph Rykwert (London: Alec Tiranti, 1955), 9.5.196; in Rykwert et al., 9.5.305; Orlandi, 821. The word has the advantage of suggesting that the outline is the result of the hands of the workman having produced the results of the lineaments of the architect, but it is now archaic. See also Leon Battista Alberti, *L'architettura*, trans. Cosimo Bartoli (Florence: Lorenzo Torrentino, 1550), 9.5.340.

46 The standard explication of the arithmetic, geometric, and musical proportions is Rudolf Wittkower, *Architectural Principles in the Age of Humanism*, 3rd edn (London: Tiranti, 1962), part 4, §3.

47 The OED's citations occur in reference to the frame of the world, to dance, to music, and most extensively and lastingly in language, which supports the observations of various authors concerning his source for the word and the concept. Hartmut Wulfram, *Literische Vitruvrezeption in Leon Battista Albertis* De re aedificatoria (Munich and Leipzig: K.G. Saur, 2001), 298–301, with earlier sources cited at 299, n. 7, argues that Alberti drew the word from its extensive use in rhetoric where it was allied with decorum. More comprehensively, Christine Smith, "Alberti's Description of Florence Cathedral as Architectural Criticism," *Architecture in the Culture of Early Humanism* (New York and Oxford: Oxford University Press, 1992), 87, calls attention to its analogy to the *mediocritas* of Aristotle's *Nichomachean Ethics* and at 89 to its meaning in rhetoric not as "a quality, but as a relation, connecting opposites in such a way that perfection is the result;" Cicero used it in this way. At 95–6 it also carried theological content when the mean and the connecting of opposites was an attribute of the nature of God, a concept that Alberti's contemporary Nicholas of Cusa developed.

48 Vasilij Pavlovič Zubov, "La théorie architecturale d'Alberti," trans. Rénata Feldman, in *Albertiana*, 3 (2000), 11–62; 36–7 and passim, stresses the differences between the "metaphoric" symbolism of Durandus and Aquinas's "organic" connection to the universe of God's creation which is also Alberti's position about how a building bears meaning.

49 David Summers, *Michelangelo and the Language of Art* (Princeton: Princeton University Press, 1981), 441, calls Augustine's passage on a building "one of the most careful discussions of bilateral symmetry in all aesthetic literature."

50 Summers, *Michelangelo*, 441.

51 Alberti, *Ten Books*, 1726, 9.5.194. Contrast Rykwert et al., 9.5.301; Latin in Orlandi, 811.

52 Zubov, "La théorie," 33–41 and passim.

53 Francesco Petrarch, "On his own Ignorance and that of many Others," trans. Hans Nachod, in Ernest Cassirer et al., eds, *The Renaissance Philosophy of Man* (Chicago and London: University of Chicago Press, 1948), 107–8.

54 In *The Godly Feast* of 1522; see Lynda Gregorian Christian, "The Figure of Socrates in Erasmus' Works," *The Sixteenth Century Journal*, 3:2 (October 1972), 1–10.

55 Maritain, *Art and Scholasticism*, 49.

56 For earlier comments on this topic, which lies beyond the scope of this book, see Westfall, *Paradise*, Chapter 5, and now David Friedman, "'Fiorenza': Geography and Representation in a Fifteenth Century City View," *Zeitschrift für Kunstgeschichte*, 64

(2001), 56–77, who challenges the traditional c.1480 dating of the Florence image to c.1510; also Juergen Schulz, "Jacopo de'Barbari's View of Venice: Map Making, City Views, and Moralized Geography before the Year 1500," *The Art Bulletin*, 60 (1978), 425–74.

57 For farming villas see 5.14–18 and 9.9.1–4. See also Leon Battista Alberti, "Villa," in *Opere Volgari*, ed. Cecil Grayson, (Bari: Gius. Laterza & Figli: Scrittori d'Italia, no. 218, 1960). Alberti argued that it is better to raise a family in a city than in a villa; *I Libri della famiglia*, ed. Cecil Grayson, vol. 1 (Bari: Gius. Laterza & Figli: Scrittori d'Italia, no. 218, 1960), 200–202; Leon Battista Alberti, *The Family in Renaissance Florence*, trans. Renée Watkins (Columbia: University of South Carolina Press, 1969), 194.

58 Renaissance belief reversed the relative importance of the intellect and will. Petrarch, *On His Ignorance*, 105, wrote, "It is better to will the good than to know the truth." Commentary in Trinkaus, *Image and Likeness*, 48; see also Kristeller, *Eight Philosophers*, 17.

59 Supplying the trees from Orlandi.

60 See similar comments about paintings in Alberti, *Il Nuovo de picture*, §28; §40; §62.

61 Discussed above. Here Alberti expands on the medieval role of the locations of buildings relative to one another that can allow a city to resemble Jerusalem or Rome; see Wolfgang Braunfels, *Mittelalterliche Stadtbaukunst in der Toskana,* 3rd edn (Berlin: Mann, 1966), and Marvin Trachtenberg, "Scénographie urbaine et identité civique: réflexion sur la Florence du Trecento," *Revue de l'Art*, 102 (1993), 11–31.

62 See Carroll William Westfall, "Making Man's Dignity Visible in Buildings: The Foundations in Leon Battista Alberti's *de re aedificatoria*," in Daniel N. Robinson et al., ed., *Human Nature in its Wholeness: A Roman Catholic Perspective* (Washington, D.C.: Catholic University of America Press: 2006), 144–59.

5

Vitruvianism and Palladio

AFTER ALBERTI

Leon Battista Alberti's treatise on architecture was published in 1485, the first treatise on architecture to be printed.[1] It was followed the next year by Vitruvius' treatise, which quickly put Alberti's in the shade. Alberti's dense, Latin, humanist content and its republicanism did not appeal to a Europe that was becoming increasingly princely. Vitruvius' was also shorter, his theory was simpler, and it came with antiquity's sanction. In 1511 Fra Giovanni Giocondo's seminal small folio Latin edition with 136 woodcut illustrations, readable text, a glossary, and dedicated to Pope Julius II "would turn out to be one of the most influential books of the sixteenth century. It served as a fundamental basis for the practice of architecture in early modern Europe, and through its circulation among European merchants, colonists, and missionaries, for the rest of the world."[2] Before Alberti's saw print again in Italy in 1546 another half dozen editions or translations of Vitruvius appeared including the extensively illustrated folio translation and commentary of Cesare Cesariano in 1521.[3] The new century belonged to Vitruvius.

A pair of treaties that remained unpublished until the twentieth century reveal the slight role of Alberti's revisions to Vitruvius. Although written by Tuscans, Vitruvius provided their authors with the model for the architect, perhaps because their patrons were princes and as the century moved on Florentine republicanisms was increasingly becoming a hollow shell. The treatise of the Florentine sculptor-turned-architect named Antonio Averlino, who came to be called Filarete (c.1400–c.1469), or lover of virtue, is a meandering, picaresque dialogue with his patron, Francesco Sforza, perhaps for fireside chats during Milan's long winter evenings.[4] The important benefit the more talented Sienese painter, sculptor, engineer, and architect Francesco di Giorgio Martini (1438–1502), who produced three versions of his musings and drawings, came from Alberti's instruction about lineaments, but for imitation and proportionality he stuck with Vitruvius. He made some fine drawings of the standing rather than supine Vitruvian man, and was clearly in tune with his generation's increased interest in man as a microcosm by applying human proportions directly to the configurations of buildings.[5]

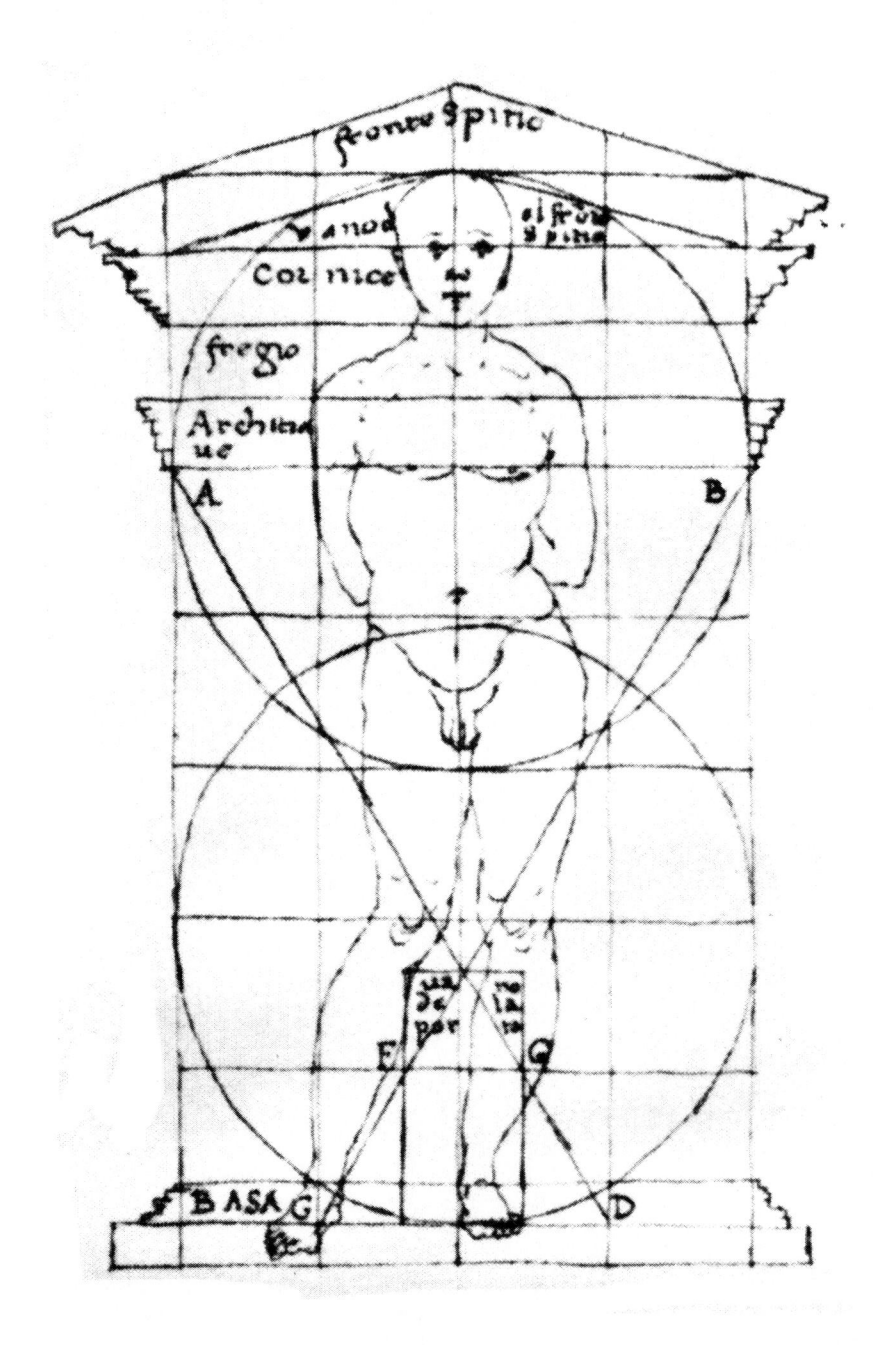

5.1 Francesco di Giorgio Martini, "Man, Church, and Proportions"
Source: Codice Magliabechiano II.I.141, fol. 38ᵛ, Biblioteca Nazionale di Firenze. Image in public domain.

The important newly-published book was the well-illustrated quarto in Italian by another Sienese, Sebastiano Serlio (1475–1554). As a young architect he was swept into the imperial undertaking that Pope Julius II commanded in rebuilding and augmenting Rome's buildings and urbanism with Saint Peter's Basilica as its centerpiece. A whole generation of Italian architects was trained in the building yard where Bramante presided with the sobriquet Vitruvius. In 1540 Serlio's book and experience would earn him a call to the court of Francis I in France where he flourished.

Serlio's fame comes from his book, not his few buildings. Narrow in scope but appealing to both architect and patron, its several chapters, that is, books began appearing in 1537.[6] Most of Alberti's topics are absent from the completed corpus: the difference between building and architecture and their respective criteria; imitation's sources in nature; the primacy of proportions; beauty as more than *venustas*; and architecture as urbanism. His focus is on the art of building with his only reach toward architecture in his comment that the square is the "most perfect" of rectangular forms and is closer to "the mind of God, which is perfection itself … The further man moves away from God, taking pleasure in earthly things, the more he loses that initial goodness which was granted him in the beginning."[7] He stressed appearance in Vitruvius' sense of *aspectus* with a corpus of canonic buildings providing the governing conventions. But he did make two important contributions to theory.

One of these is his adaptation of painter's perspective to lineaments in building. Featured in Books 1 and 2, he calls them *linea occulte* or hidden lines within the perspective constructions that Alberti had taught to painters but which Alberti had given a very different role in his treatise on architecture. Serlio knew Alberti's treatise on architecture but he drew more from how Francesco di Giorgio had used lineaments in delineating plans, sections, and elevations than from Alberti while pushing lineaments farther into the process of design. Perspective constructions present the outlines of various members of a building and guide their collocation into whole bodies that resemble the patterns of canonic membratures and whole buildings. That is, they serve representation based on precedents, and do not serve in imitating nature. Serlio's mentor Baldassare Peruzzi was a master in using perspective for paintings and for drawings made to assist on the building site.[8] Serlio learned from him, and he wed Alberti's perspective for painters with Vitruvius' comment about composition (*dispositione*), which involves depicting the plan, elevation, and scenography (that is, perspective) of a building, but lacking is any role for concinnity. Perspective, he explained, enables "the architect, when he wishes, to reveal his concept in a visible design."[9] He acknowledges Vitruvius' connection of perspective to stage sets in the last images in Book 2 with illustrations of the comic, tragic, and satiric stage sets.[10]

Serlio's second important contribution was the cataloguing and illustrating of models for architects to consult. Architects had collected models in their sketchbooks clear back into the middle ages, but Serlio's book democratized models by putting them in a treatise anyone could buy. They and brief comments about them are the content of Book 3, *On Antiquities*. The Pantheon came first followed by other ancient buildings and then by several "modern ones" (his term), first a longitudinal and a centralized plan for Saint Peter's, Bramante's dome for the still-unfinished building, and other buildings or projects including Bramante's Tempietto di San Pietro and Cortile del Belvedere in the Vatican, Raphael's Villa Madama, and Giuliano da Maiano's Poggio Reale near Naples along with his alterations to make it suitable for France. No random assemblage, the book presented a carefully considered catalogue of canonic buildings with plans, sections, interior and exterior elevations, and details constituting the best models for making new ones using the method he soon presented in Books 1 and 2.

Images sell books, which is why Book 4, "On the Five Styles (*manieri*) of Building," came first (1537) followed by Book 3, "On Antiquities," in 1540. Books 1 and 2 with theory followed five years later. Book 4's first image is a clear and attractive woodcut that illustrates and names the five orders with their proportions presented in brief, inconspicuous notations. These establish the canon of the five orders, and the name he used, orders, replaced the earlier name, genus. Placing them on a common base and using a common scale facilitated comparison between them: the similarities are obvious but so are the differences because they are all different in the same way, in Alexander Tzonis's felicitous phrase. The material in this book, Serlio wrote, "is more relevant and more important than the others for understanding the different styles (*manieri*) of building and their ornaments."[11]

Serlio's images initiated the ascent of the image to dominance over the word. Vitruvius' images had been lost and Alberti's treatise lacked them, but the 1511 Vitruvius used them to illustrate the text and the pairing of text and image made them codependents. They formed a self-contained loop that the architect did not need to leave and initiated imitation's course to desuetude. Books would provide models to use as precedents to adapt and modify and explain a method for doing so. Alberti's inquisitive and inventive method of imitation will recede and emulation will become the dominant method with the columnar orders serving as the emblem of the building's identity with classical architecture. A number of books will expand the range of models for the orders and vouch for their authenticity, the first one being Giacomo Barozzi da Vignola's *Regola delli cinque ordini*, a picture book with only the briefest text. First published in Rome in 1562, it has been followed by others and by dozens of editions right up to 1999.[12]

Theory remained the provenance of Italian authors until the seventeenth century with one notable exception: Philibert de l'Orme (c.1514–70). A member of an old French family of builders, de l'Orme was in Rome in the late 1540s. When Serlio was in France adapting Italian ideas to French traditions de l'Orme was working French traditions into Italian models. With his buildings and treatise (*Le premier Tome de l'Architecture*, 1567) he tried to elevate the architect to a higher status than that of a mere craftsman only to find to his discomfort how great a sway monarchs hold over their subjects. We will encounter his treatise in Chapter 8.

Serlio, the rise of Vitruvianism in the service of princes who were enjoying increasing power, and the Roman Church's reaction to the Reformation would soon inhibit the continued exploration of Alberti's role for architecture's service to the political order. Instead, the several arts in Italy would commit themselves to expressing the basis of the authority of princes and kings and the doctrines of the Church. Machiavelli's sneer at the sacred basis of Church governments—they "are upheld by superior causes, to which the human mind does not reach"—became reality and was extended to princes who joined prelates in finding important roles for Vitruvian architects.[13]

DELLE ANTICHITA

Questo tempio è a Tiuoli sopra il fiume Aniene. alcuni lo dicono il tempio di Vesta, gran parte rouinato, & è di opera Corinthia ben lauorato, & eleuato dal piano di terra dalla parte dauanti quant'è il basamento: ma dalla parte di dietro è eleuato piu di sette braccia disotto del basamento.

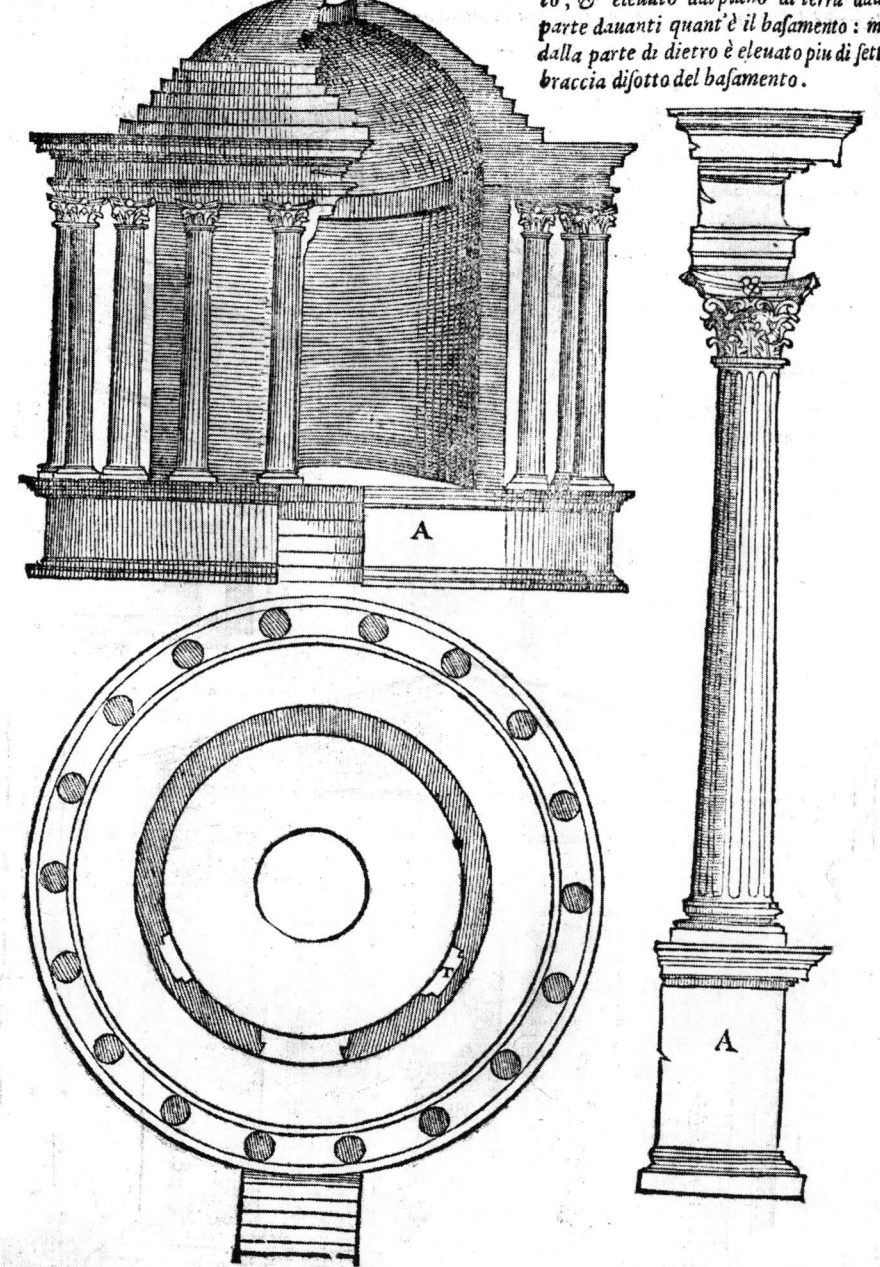

5.2 Sebastiano Serlio, Temple of Vesta, Tivoli
Source: Tutte l'opere d'architettura, Venice, Francesco de' Franceschi Senese, 1584, Book 3, *On Antiquities*, xxvii (60ᵛ). Image provided by the University of Notre Dame's Architecture Library.

DELLE ANTICHITA

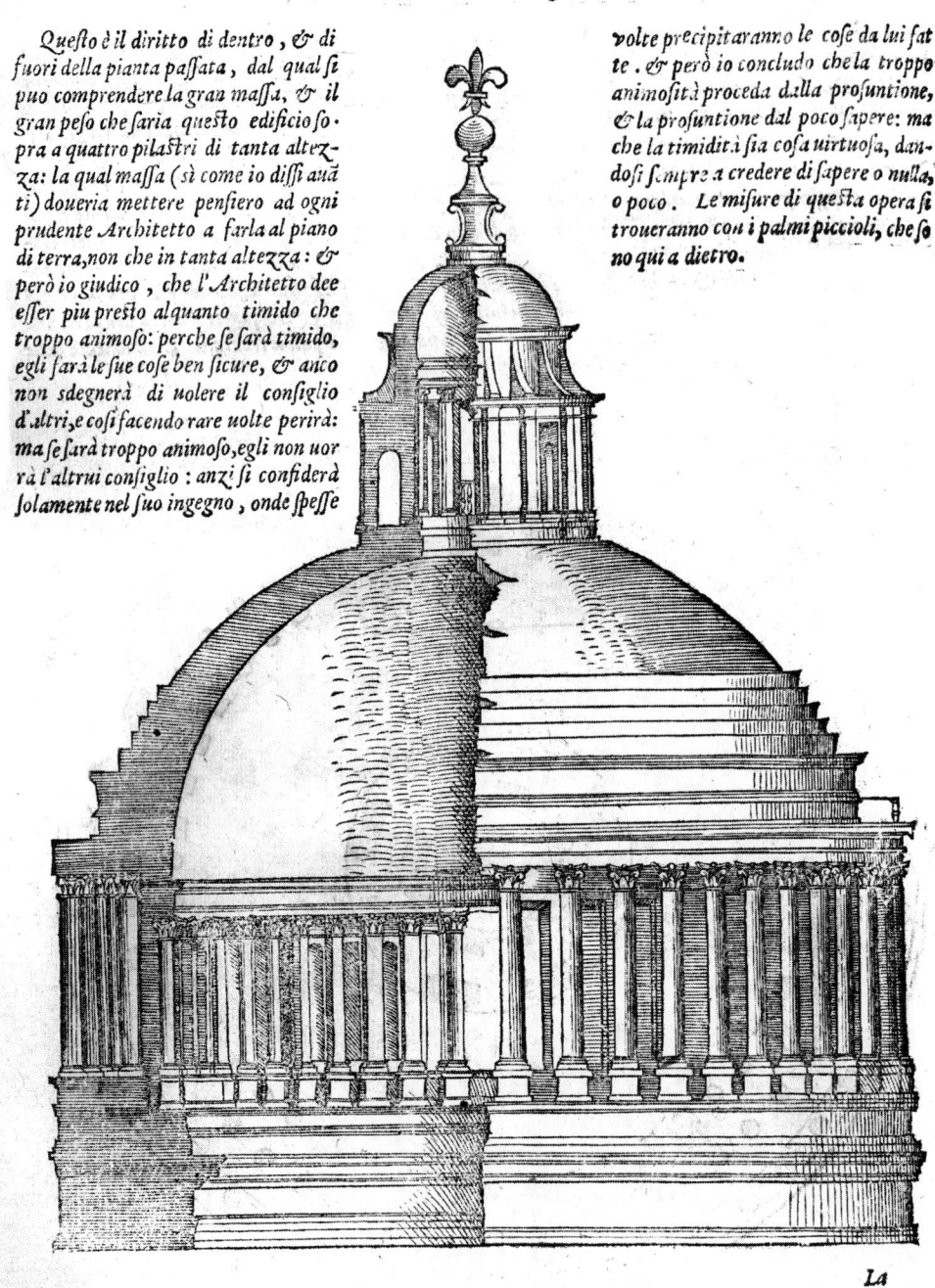

Questo è il diritto di dentro, & di fuori della pianta passata, dal qual si può comprendere la gran massa, & il gran peso che saria questo edificio sopra a quattro pilastri di tanta altezza: la qual massa (sì come io dissi auāti) doueria mettere pensiero ad ogni prudente Architetto a farla al piano di terra, non che in tanta altezza: & però io giudico, che l'Architetto dee esser più presto alquanto timido che troppo animoso: perche se sarà timido, egli farà le sue cose ben sicure, & anco non sdegnerà di uolere il consiglio d'altri, e così facendo rare uolte perirà: ma se sarà troppo animoso, egli non uorrà l'altrui consiglio: anzi si considerà solamente nel suo ingegno, onde spesse volte precipitaranno le cose da lui fatte. & però io concludo che la troppo animosità proceda dalla prosuntione, & la prosuntione dal poco sapere: ma che la timidità sia cosa uirtuosa, dandosi sempre a credere di sapere o nulla, o poco. Le misure di questa opera si troueranno con i palmi piccioli, che sono qui a dietro.

La

5.3 Sebastiano Serlio, Bramante's Dome, Basilica of Saint Peter
Source: Tutte l'opere d'architettura, Venice, Francesco de' Franceschi Senese, 1584, Book 3, *On Antiquities*, xl (66ᵛ). Image provided by the University of Notre Dame's Architecture Library.

5.4 Sebastiano Serlio, The Five Orders
Source: Tutte l'opere d'architettura, Venice, Francesco de' Franceschi Senese, 1584, Book 4, *On the Five Styles of Buildings,* iiii^r (127^r). Image provided by the University of Notre Dame's Architecture Library.

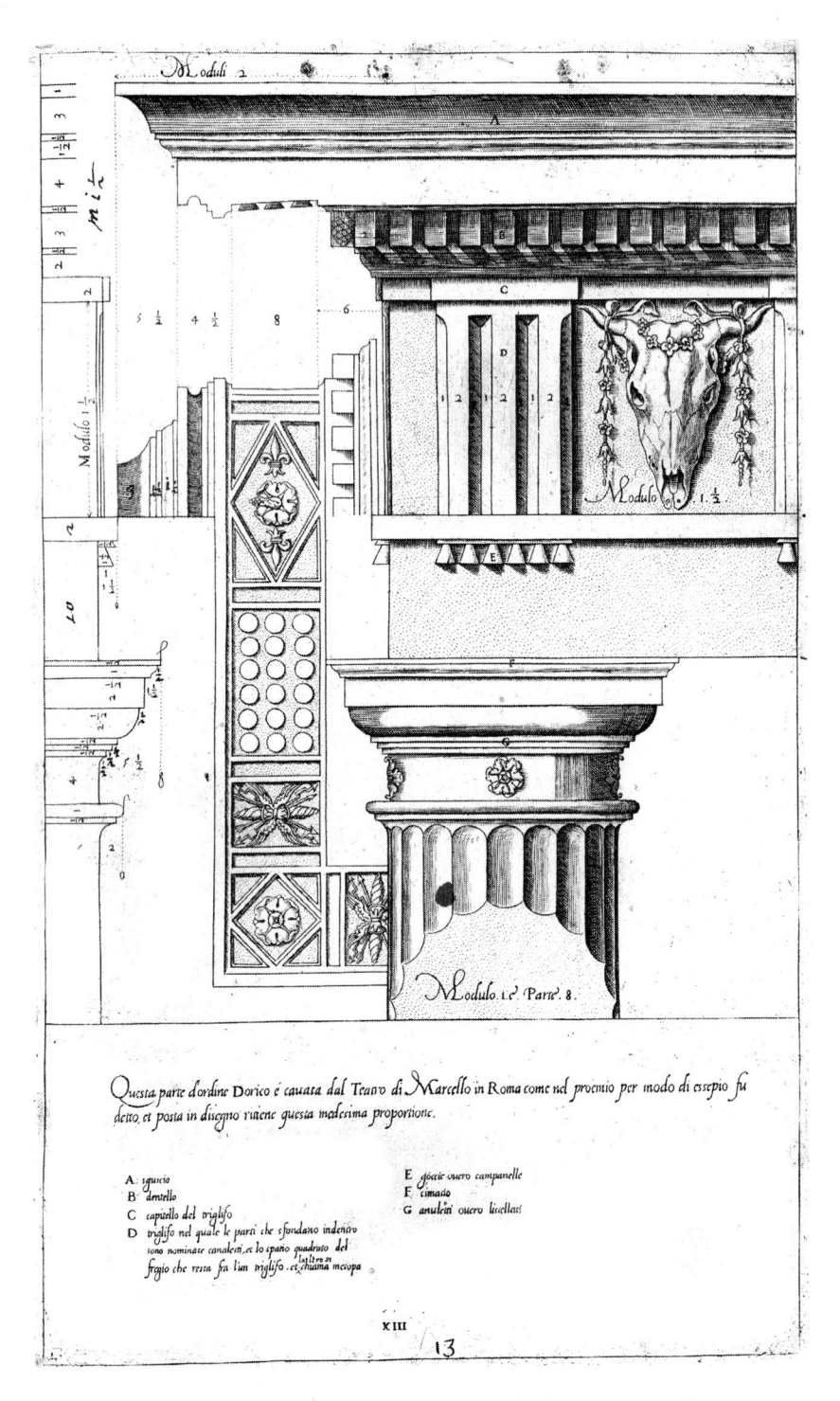

5.5 Giacomo Barozzi da Vignola, Doric at the Theater of Marcello
Source: Regola delli cinque ordini d'architettura, Rome: Francesco de Pauli, [after 1602], Plate 13. Image provided by the University of Notre Dame's Architecture Library.

PALLADIO

The exception was in Venice, Italy's last republic left standing. A city better known for printing books than for writing them, in 1615 Vincenzo Scamozzi would compile the massive and choppy book that is more a recapitulation than an original contribution, and it would enjoy a minor reputation.[14] He was the executor of the works that Andrea Palladio (1508–80) left unfinished at his death and served as a Palladian expositor for English visitors. Palladio's *Four Books on Architecture*, an Italian octavo from 1570, has been acknowledged as the only book whose influence can rival that of Vitruvius'. It is short, it uses exquisite woodcuts to illustrate the text and clear texts to explain the images, it presents beautiful images of canonic models both ancient and modern, it includes details of the five orders and their collocations, and it offers images and brief descriptions of his own buildings, a practice architects have followed ever after as advertisements to potential clients. Published in many editions and translations it, along with his many villas, palaces, and churches accessible in Venice and the Veneto, make him perhaps the best known early architect among architects and probably laypeople today.[15]

Palladio's importance, especially in Britain and America, can hardly be overemphasized. He wrote that he intended his *I quattro libri dell' architettura* to allow people "to understand many passages in Vitruvius reputed to be extremely difficult."[16] But Alberti's ideas are more important for his own work in a world in which "Vitruvianization" was smothering Alberti's ideas and Venice was a thorn in the side of princely states.[17] He declared that he had "elected as his master and guide Vitruvius," but he also stated that his authority for the measures of the orders had been "not so much in line with what Vitruvius teaches but according to what I have observed in ancient buildings" (1.12.17). He also credits "other brilliant men who have written on so noble an art," including Alberti whose name follows Vitruvius' and who emerges from a close reading of the text as the more important mentor.[18] His abbreviation of Alberti's treatise transmitted the Florentine's arguments concerning the distinction between building and architecture, proportionality and the unity of diverse parts, beauty, and the roles of imitation, nature, reason, tradition, and lineaments to those in successive generations who were equipped to grasp its content. Absent is attention to perspective, which Alberti had absorbed into lineaments, and pluralism, which was a dead issue in the Veneto.

Several patricians in the Veneto provided the tutelage and Roman education that raised this Padua stonemason to being an architect. Settling in Vicenza he built palaces and villas for them and their friends. Among the most important were the Barbaro brothers, near contemporary Venetian patricians and authors of learned treaties. Marcantonio had him build their incomparable Villa at Maser, and Danielle's Vitruvius translation and commentary included Palladio's plates in both its handsome 1556 folio and the 1567 quarto revision. It also covers Alberti's syllabus except for urbanism but with the notable addition of the century's attention to man as microcosm: "The force of numbers brought together among themselves in just proportions is divine. [They constitute] the fabric of this universe that we call the world and also the little world" that is the human person. "All the secrets of the arts consist of proportionality."[19] Proportionality will "satisfy the delight of the eyes with beauty and a gracious manner" with a form based on lineaments. This is accomplished with human intelligence which is imperfect "and a great distance inferior to the divine intellect." The design (*disegno*) must imitate nature.[20] Barbaro understood Vitruvius much as Alberti did, and so Palladio must have as well.

Barbaro, Alberti, and Palladio put lineaments before *structura* and thereby stress reason and intellect as guides for the architect. In not putting the five orders together on a single page they were less likely to be read as mere emblems of proportionality. They are, as Alberti had written, "by far the most important [ornaments] that can be applied to a building," and like Alberti, Palladio introduced them immediately after his discussion of walls (1.11.17).

Palladio took imitation seriously. He gave the word two meanings. In its light meaning it means follow as when he referred to Vitruvius' use of the module to dimension the proportions of the orders rather than some particular measurement such as the *braccio*, which differs from city to city (1.13.19). It also simplifies the construction process and assures an internally coherent proportionality between the members and the whole body.

More consequential is his statement, "architecture imitates nature (as do all the other arts)" (1.20.55). Imitation and tradition establish the link between what people did, what nature and the Creator do, and what the architect ought to do. The ancient architects first built with wood. "[T]aking as their model trees" they made them more slender at the top while bases, triglyphs, modillions, dentils, and the other parts of buildings introduced additional refinements.[21] Nature provides the model.

> [O]ne cannot but curse that way of building which, departing from what the natural order of things teaches and from that simplicity which appears in the things created by her, generates, as it were, another version of nature and deviates from the true, good, and beautiful method of building. ... And though variety and novelty must please everybody, one should not, however, do anything that is contrary to the laws of this art and contrary to what reason makes obvious. ... (1.20.55)

While this sounds like Marc-Antoine Laugier's reductionism two centuries later it is a condemnation of willfulness unbridled by reason, devoid of sound judgment, and ungoverned by nature. In the chapter titled "On Abuses" he catalogues recently produced examples of intemperate novelty at the expense of proportionality and congruence that lead to a "bruttissimo aspetto." The examples he identifies on new buildings are scrolled forms on supports that suggest that something soft is supporting something hard; split pediments that suggest that the roofs are incapable of protecting inhabitants from rain, snow, and hail; cornices with too great a projection into a room that "will make it narrow and displeasing" and always "look as though they are about to collapse" and will frighten those standing underneath; "large cornices on small columns;" and garlands and rings around columns that make them appear less, not more, secure and stable.

Serlio illustrated many of these without calling them abuses. More recently they had become fashionable, especially among court architects such as those who, in *Lives of the Artists* in 1564, Giorgio Vasari had called the "academicians," among them Vasari himself. They were more interested in following the latest fashions; Palladio was more interested in the best models such as those of "Bramante, a supremely talented man and observer of ancient structures, [who] built marvelous buildings in Rome." He was "the first to put into light that good and beautiful architecture which had been hidden from the time of the ancients till now" (4.17.276).[22] Others followed, and he names nine of them, beginning with Michelangelo, without noting their abuses (4.17.276).[23] Like Serlio, he presented images of ancient buildings and only one modern one other than his own, Bramante's Tempietto, that was surely abuse free and therefore worthy to join the authoritative ancient buildings. These provided models for imitating their sources in nature in the three guises that Alberti had identified, precedents, things nature made, and nature's laws.

Palladio is as artful as Alberti had been in weaving Vitruvius' ideas into his text and modernizing them. After quickly dispatching commodity, firmness, and *venustas* he covers Vitruvius' symmetria, eurhythmy, and decorum with compartition largely submerged under various Alberti-isms in which respond and correspond do the work without lapsing into bilateral symmetry. For example, he observes that "all well-designed houses have places in the middle and in the most beautiful parts to which all the others respond and can be reached from."[24] Similarly, the plans, elevations, and vaults of rooms are configured with proportions that the woodcuts render as numbers and as geometric figures that lock the three dimensions together to produce a whole body from the members, a topic that scholarship on Palladio's use of proportions has made easily available (1.22–4.57–60).[25]

Palladio's compartitions and membratures follow the well-known Venetian precedents in the way doors and windows interrupt the walls and the columnar units such as porticoes and loggias depart from predetermined proportionality. Here is an experienced architect fitting members onto the *area* with a proportionality that unifies them into a whole body that will "match the size of the building, the character of patron, and the things that must be brought in and out" (1.25.60–61). "The windows at the right must correspond to those on the left and those in the upper story must be vertically above those below ... and be placed enfilade "so that someone standing in one part of the house is able to see across to the other, which brings in beauty and fresh air in the summer and other advantages" (1.25.55; 60–61).

Palladio's discussion of decorum reveals the profundity of his understanding of architecture as urbanism. In the first chapter of Book 2 he couples the Italian word *decoro* with *convenienza* and *commodità*, or suitability and commodity. Decorum involves two qualities. First, decorum must see to it that the members of the building are commensurate with the whole so that large buildings have large members, medium ones medium, and small ones small. And second, it requires that the building must be "appropriate to the character of the person who will have to live in it, and of which the parts will correspond to the whole and to each other." Equating the building's and the inhabitant's character recalls Vitruvius' prescriptions but translates it to describe the "grand gentlemen, mostly in a republic," who were the magistrates in Alberti's treatise, the magistrates in the Veneto, and Palladio's patrons. They need large halls where their clients come to await and salute them and seek their assistance and favor, as do judges, lawyers, and merchants. "[S]maller buildings of lesser expense and ornament will be appropriate for men of lower status."[26] Alberti's echo appears in the advice that "the architect pay particular attention to those who want to build, not so much for what they can afford as for the character of building that would suit them," and then see that the parts match the whole and that "the appropriate decoration is applied."[27]

In sacred structures decorum, "one of the most beautiful aspects of architecture," is even more important. The most perfect shape for a temple is circular. "[I]t alone amongst all the plans is simple, uniform, equal, strong, and capacious. ... it is perfectly adapted to demonstrate the unity, the infinite existence, the consistency, and the justice of God. Besides which, no one can deny that greater strength and durability are needed more in temples," and this shape provides it (4.2.216). Palladio's churches are absent from the treatise; it was published before they were built.

Palladio's anthropomorphic analogy follows Alberti in not imprisoning the human figure in a square, circle, or column but using it as a model for the configuration. "[O]ur blessed God has arranged" the human figure such that "noble and beautiful parts" are easily visible and the "less pleasant and agreeable" are in obscure places. So too should a house be: the "loggias, halls, courtyards, magnificent rooms, and large staircases" should be placed with "the most important and prestigious parts in full view and the less beautiful concealed as far from our eyes as possible thereby "making the whole beautiful and graceful" (2.2.77–8).[28] He notes, as Alberti had, that this is more easily done on rural sites than on the often constricted and irregular urban ones.[29]

Finally, Palladio's lineaments constitute the geometric matrix of proportions that generate the configuration's hollow rooms and position the solid membrature. The proportions in the book's plates are often not present in the buildings, whether from workmen's errors or knowledgeable adjustments to circumstances, but that makes no difference to those who consult his transportable text with its seductive images that always present the buildings at their best and most complete. We might think of them as resembling the penultimate phases of the method Alberti said he used when designing, the one before actually beginning construction (9.10.317/861–3). Jorge Hernandez suggested that Palladio's use of Alberti's lineaments can account for the distortion in the treatise's half elevation of the Villa Rotunda that shows the bottom of the dome running as a straight line rather than as a circle segment that an intersection of a circle segment would actually make with the roof's slanted plane.[30] The text's image is the guide to the perception of the building's beauty and not a factual image that geometric perspective or not-yet-invented photography would make. Lineaments produce the true depiction, not the factual one, the one we perceive and not merely the one we see.

Palladio's text exemplifies the continued reinterpretation of Vitruvius' treatise, the foundation of the theory of architecture in the classical tradition, an epitome and a revision of theory and not a departure from or challenge to it. It is also an Alberti handbook. Both architects amplified and modernized theory and did not reduce or nullify its argument. Like Alberti's, it presents the parts of that tradition that a knowledgeable person can expand into the full curriculum.

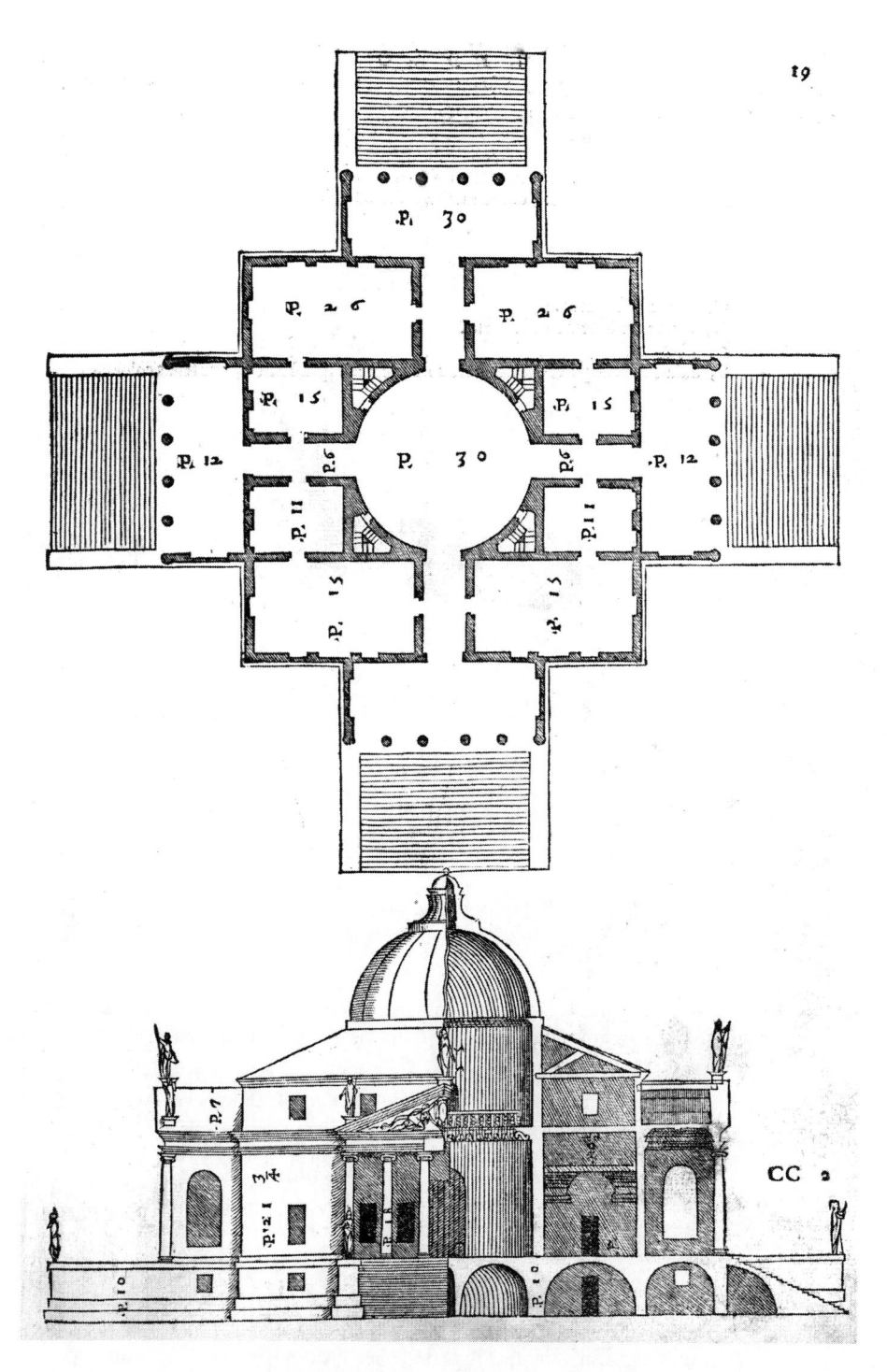

5.6 Andrea Palladio, Villa Capra, la Rotonda
Source: I qvattro libri dell'architettvra, Venice: D. de' Franceschi, 1570, II, 19.
Image provided by the University of Notre Dame's Architecture Library.

His brief comments about what lies at the core of Alberti's treatise and the classical tradition identify Palladio as more indebted to Alberti that to Vitruvius, although that ancient architect is among the household gods. Both of Vitruvius' most important modernizers cast the architect in the mold of a liberal artist who uses his civic art to make buildings that make cities and serve and express the purposes of the institutions that build them, but they work as citizen–magistrates of the city and not as clients of patrons. Their role is to make beauty perceptible by embodying the order, harmony, and proportionality of nature as a counterpart to the city's devotion to the good. Palladio, more explicitly than Alberti, teaches that the architect "generates, as it were, another version of nature" that does not deviate "from the true, good, and beautiful method of building …" (1.20.55–6).

NOTES

1. An Alberti edition in Paris in 1512 was the first to divide the books into chapters with Jean Martin's French translation coming in 1553. An Italian translation appeared in Venice in 1546 and another, the well-regarded Cosimo Bartoli translation, the first with illustrations, in 1550 in Florence with reprintings in 1565 and 1568.

2. Ingrid Rowland, "The Fra Giocondo Vitruvius at 500 (1511–2011)," *Journal of the Society of Architectural Historians*, 70 (2011), 285.

3. Vitruvius, *De architectura*, trans. and comm. Caesare Cesariano (Como: Gotardo da Ponte, 1521).

4. See Kruft, *A History*, 51–5; and Filarete, *Treatise on Architecture, Being the Treatise by Antonio di Piero Averlino, Known as Filarete*, facsimile and trans. with notes by John R. Spencer, 2 vols (New Haven and London: Yale University Press, 1965). The first critical edition is Anna Maria Finoli and Liliana Grassi, ed., *Trattato di architettura*, 2 vols (Milan: Polifilo, 1972).

5. Francesco di Giorgio Martini, *Trattati di architettura ingegneria e art militare*, ed. Corrado Maltese (Milan: Il Polifilo, 1967); Lawrence Lowic "The Meaning and Significance of the Human Analogy in Francesco di Giorgio's Trattato," *Journal of the Society of Architectural Historians*, 42 (1983), 360–70. For microcosmic man in the fifteenth century Ernst Cassirer, *The Individual and the Cosmos in Renaissance Philosophy*, trans. Mario Domandi (New York: Harper and Row, 1964), remains the standard treatment.

6. Sebastiano Serlio, *Sebastiano Serlio on Architecture*, trans. and comments Vaughan Hart and Peter Hicks, 2 vols (New Haven and London: Yale University Press, 1996–2001). The first five books were first published "as a set" in Venice in 1551 (xxxiii). They make the first English translation, which was from the Dutch by Robert Peake; London, 1611, also New York: Dover, 1982. The first one to be published, Book 4, concerned the columnar orders: *Regole generali di architetvra sopra le cinqve maniere de gliedifici … per la magior parte concordano con la dottrina di Vitruvio* (Venice: F Marcolini, 1537). Later came Book 3, *Antichità di Roma* (Venice, 1540); Books 1 and 2 on geometry and perspective (Paris, 1545); Book 5, *Diverse forme de' tempij sacri* (Paris, 1547); and *Libro extraordinario* with various portals published in Lyons, 1551. The posthumous publications are Book 6, habitations, and Book 8, Roman camps, both remaining in manuscript until well after 1900, and Book 7, various residences, threats to buildings, and the modernization of older buildings (Frankfurt, 1575). All are in Hart and Hicks.

7. Serlio, *Architecture*, Book 1, 19.

8   See Ann C. Huppert, "Envisioning New St. Peter's: Perspective Drawings and the Process of Design," *Journal of the Society of Architectural Historians*, 68 (2009), 158–77.

9   Serlio, *Architecture*, Book 4, 253, when referring to the content of Book 2.

10 See Vaughan Hart, "Serlio and the Representation of Architecture," in Hart and Peter Hicks, eds, *Paper Palaces: The Rise of the Renaissance Architectural Treatise* (New Haven and London: Yale University Press, 1998), 170–85. We need not pursue the connections between these and urbanism.

11 Serlio, *Architecture*, Book 4, 253.

12 Giacomo Barrozzi da Vignola, *Canon of the Five Orders of Architecture*, trans. with intro. by Branko Mitrović (New York: Acanthus Press, 1999).

13 Niccolò Machiavelli, *The Prince*, trans. Harvey C. Mansfield, Jr. (Chicago and London: University of Chicago Press, 1985), Chapter 9.

14 Vincenzo Scamozzi, *L'Idea della architecttura universale* (Venice: self-published, 1615).

15 Three circumstances enhance Palladio's reputation today. First, Modernists accept his buildings' roles in plans and elevations of Le Corbusier's buildings. Second, that role is legitimated in Colin Rowe's essay, "The Mathematics of the Ideal Villa," first published in the *Architectural Review* in 1949 and subsequently in a collection of essays, *The Mathematics of the Ideal Villa and Other Essays* (Cambridge, Mass., and London: MIT: 1976; 1982 paperback). The mathematics are in proportions that Rowe, a student of Rudolf Wittkower, found by applying his tutor's study of proportions that would appear in the 1949 scholarly version of *Architectural Principles*, 1st edn (London: Alec Tiranti, 1952). Third is the appealing monograph by James S. Ackerman, *Palladio* (Harmondsworth: Penguin, 1966).

16 Andrea Palladio, *I Quattro libri dell'architettura* (Venice: Domenico de'Franceschi, 1570); *The Four Books on Architecture*, trans. Robert Tavernor and Richard Schofield (Cambridge, Mass., and London: MIT, 1997), Book 4, 213 in the translation whose pagination is used here and below with book, chapter, and page in the notes and in parentheses in the text; the translation supplies the original pagination in brackets in the margin.

17 The apercu and the term "Vitruvianization" are from Choay, *The Rule and the Model*, 182 and passim.

18 1.For.5; 4.For.4. Here are a few instances; others will appear in what follows. He presents *venustas* as *bellezza* and as a union making a "ben finite corpo" (1.1.6). In the chapter on abuses (1.20) he presents the five orders as "gli ornamenti dell'Architettura." He then moves quickly to "Natura" as the standard to seek through imitation, which rings more of Alberti than Vitruvius (1.20.55). Finally, he refers to the ancient "bellezza, & venustà" of architecture's "belle proportioni, & della ornate maniera di fabricare" that was lost and then brought back to light by Bramante (4.17.276).

19 Vitruvius, *I Dieci libri dell'architettura*, trans. and commen. Danielle Barbaro (Venice: Francesco de'Franceschi Senese, 1567), 3.1.108; republished (Milan: Polifilo, 1987), ed. Manfredo Tafuri.

20 Vitruvius, *I Dieci libri*, 1567, 1.3.37. The intertwining of Alberti, Palladio, and Barbaro is a theme that runs through Margaret Muther D'Evelyn, *Venice and Vitruvius: Reading Venice with Daniele Barbaro and Andrea Palladio* (New Haven and London: Yale University Press, 2012).

21 Compare Alberti, 1.10, discussed above in Chapter 4.

22 The translation's "to make known" for metter *in luce* (put into light) obscures the allusion to the long-standing trope that Renaissance artists and architects restored to light an art that had been buried for many centuries, for example in the life of Cimabue, Giorgio Vasari, *The Lives of the Most Excellent Painters, Sculptors, and Architects*, trans. Gaston du C. de Vere, ed., Philip Jacks (New York: Modern Library, 2006), 23 and passim.

23 Other abusers whom he found praiseworthy were Sansovino, Peruzzi, Antonio da Sangallo, Sanmichele, Serlio, Vasari, Vignola, and Leoni Leone.

24 I.22.57; and 1.21.56–7 (with *respondino* translated as correspond) are examples. Hon and Goldstein, *From* Summetria *to* Symmetry, for Alberti, p. 113; for Palladio, p. 119.

25 Provocative is George Hersey and Richard Freedman, *Possible Palladian Villa (Plus a Few Instructively Impossible Ones)* (Cambridge, Mass.: MIT, 1992).

26 2.1.77. Serlio in Book 6 also covered the whole range of buildings from "hut" to "the most sumptuous palace for a prince."

27 Palladio: 2.1.77; following Alberti, at 9.11.

28 The backs of his villas are often blank.

29 Alberti, 9.2; it is worth comparing Palladio and Alberti at 9.1 on the compartition of residences.

30 Jorge Hernandez, "Palladio in Contemporary Academy and Practice" (paper presented at symposium, *From Vernacular to Classical: The Perpetual Modernity of Palladio*, School of Architecture, University of Notre Dame, June 10–12, 2011).

6

Events in the Classical Tradition on the Continent

Politics is the art of living well together. That art exhibits the good that the community seeks through the governance of a civil order that binds its members. In the classical tradition the good that the civil order seeks is justice. To achieve that good it builds the city whose beauty is to be the counterpart to the good. The civil order controls what is built, which means that in the lives of citizens, politics is more important than architecture.

Alberti and Palladio put architecture and urbanism in service to the political life of free cities. From their rise in ancient Greece and in Florence and Venice, they sought justice through the collective reasoning of the community. The enemies of those cities were legion, and often stronger. They had taken Cicero's life and had made Augustus the patron for Vitruvius to serve. Augustus' model was Alexander the Great and among their successors were Julius II and kings with names like Louis, James, and George. These princes exercised authority by analogy to the role of the head over the members of the body, of the sun that gives light to the universe, of God's activities in His creation, as successors to the Jewish kings arrayed on the façades of French cathedrals, as executors of the imperial law the ancient Romans had planted, and so on. In this chapter we will return to the story of the Vitruvianism that we saw take root in the first part of the previous chapter. In the next chapter we will return to Alberti's and Palladio's modernization of the classical tradition.

FROM IMITATION TO EMULATION

Vitruvianism sank deep roots in Rome when the papacy initiated a rebuilding project that the princes of Europe would soon emulate. The papal program began, as Marie Tanner has demonstrated, with the same interplay between local traditions and connections with antiquity that Alberti advocated and that he probably assisted Nicholas V in initiating in the Vatican in 1447.[1] A new Basilica of Saint Peter would replace Constantine's decrepit Basilica. It would exhibit imperial grandeur with distinctly Italic origins. A half century later Julius II and Bramante, with greater resources, ambitions, and knowledge gained by archaeological investigations and experience in building in the *modo antico*, revived, expanded, and revised the project that would eventually become the Vatican complex that exists today. Modeled on ancient imperial Rome, for more than four centuries it provided the benchmark for architectural achievement in Rome and throughout princely Europe. It led the way to making local traditions in architecture mere garnishments in buildings whose principal expressive content was the imperial authority of their princely builders.

This emphasis on the authority of a single head found its counterpart in the arts. The Platonizing doctrine that nature, or God, endows a few artists with a genius that elevates them to god-like status began to challenge the longstanding relationship between God as creator and man as maker in Florence when Alberti was alive. In the generation younger than him was heard the suggestion that "art may be more perfect than the object of its imitation, i.e., nature. [Marsilio] Ficino called art 'wiser than nature.'"[2] No heresy here yet: Leonardo da Vinci referred to the artist as creator whose activities were broadly analogous to nature's work in the microcosmic order.[3] But the genie was out of the bottle.[4] Consider Pietro Bembo's epitaph for Raphael's tomb in the Pantheon: "Here lies Raphael; by whom nature feared to be outdone when he lived, and when he died, feared that she herself would die." The final step to god-like status for genius artists, the one that Romanticism would secularize, is found in the second edition of the *Lives of the Artists* in 1568 where Giorgio Vasari divinizes Michelangelo, a status long attributed to him.[5] Here we find the "greatest change in the history of the concept of imitation. It made the classical theory of art into the academic."[6]

Artists driven by the demiurge of genius chafe under the obligations of the liberal artists who are citizens defending the liberty of their city. The model art among these liberal arts was oratory, which Cicero had placed first among them because it provided evidence of "our greatest advantage over the brute creation [which] is that we hold converse with one another, and can reproduce our thoughts in word."[7] But divinely inspired artists set themselves higher, which makes them poor citizens, and with the expansion of princely states the arenas for citizen–architects were quickly shrinking. These genius–artists are also poor clients of princely patrons, as the relationship between Julius II and Michelangelo and the lives of Romantic artists attest. The princes' solution was to flatter them and let their genius illuminate the virtue of the princes who let them shine. This strategy was not always successful, as Louis XIV's attempt to harness Bernini demonstrated; all the king could show for his troubles was a wonderful bust of himself.

The most reliable option for training the few artists who might be geniuses and the many who are not involved giving aspiring artists a shot at fame and glory where they might glow in light radiating from their patron-sun as the moon does from its superior orb. To train and corral them, princes established academies that made artists into academicians. This replaced their status as liberal artists while still elevating them above mere craftsmen. Academies also assured that the artists would be loyal clients by controlling patronage and the choice of the models that were used in their instruction. The first academy was founded in Florence where the beleaguered republic had finally succumbed to princely authority in 1534. Vasari outlined its organization and purposes in 1563 with Cosimo I, Grand Duke of Tuscany along with, quite cleverly, the aged Michelangelo as its titular *Capi*.[8] The Accademia del Disegno moved the training of artists out of masters' workshops where, as guildsmen, they had been involved in the governing order of the Florentine republic. In 1571 they were relieved of guild membership and made into courtiers dependent on the good will of the prince. Cosimo's academy soon ran out of steam, but the Accademia di San Luca in Rome in 1577 instituted its own flourishing program, and in the next century princes all across Europe harnessed architects into academic programs.

The word *disegno* or design in the academy's title refers to basing paintings, sculpture, and architecture on drawn lines. Vasari, like Serlio, ignored Alberti's distinction between lines in architecture and those in the arts of representation. Vasari's lines are not what Alberti had named lineaments, although he came close when he said that their "chief use indeed is in architecture, because its designs (*disegni*) are composed only of lines (*linee*), which … are nothing else than the beginning and the end of his art." This overlooks their role in configurations and membratures that govern Vitruvius' *fabrica* and Alberti's *structura* that are of no concern to painters and sculptors. Vasari states that these lines make the drawings that the architect passes on to craftsmen for execution. Here we find Vasari and not Vitruvius or Alberti as the inventor of the clean-handed academic architect who is uninvolved in construction.[9]

Vasari's academic program taught artists in the three arts of design to begin their work with lines that imitate nature by emulating the best models of the ancients and the moderns.[10] Lines and emulation of models remain at the heart of the academic method. The models in Italy both within and outside academies were principally works by Michelangelo, Leonardo, and Raphael while elsewhere and at other times the canon differed according to taste and the patrons' interests.

Beginners started by using line "in copying (alternatively: portraying; *ritrarre*) figures in relief" and moving on to copying "from nature. … Hold it moreover for certain, that the practice that is acquired by many years of study in drawing (*disegnando*) … is the true light of design (*disegno*) and that which makes men really proficient." Earlier here he had written that ultimately, design is "not other than a visible expression and declaration of our inner conception and of that which others have imagined and given form to in their idea." The artist learns how to "express in drawing the conceptions of the mind and anything else that pleases him," and it begins in what is seen.[11] Vasari's emphasis on what is seen takes us back to his source, which is in Alberti's treatise on painting where he explained how to people with figures what he in his *Lives* (for example, of Masaccio and Ucello) calls the *casamento* or little house that the perspective construction makes. These figures Alberti "took from nature" by first tracing the linear silhouette or circumscription of things seen, then composing those circumscriptions into bodies engaged in a narrative, and completing the facsimile by reproducing their reception of light in the colors, shades, and shadows on the figures and things filling the scene. Vasari recapitulated the method when he wrote, "we are indebted above all to Masaccio, seeing that he, as one desirous of acquiring fame, perceived that painting is nothing but the counterfeiting (*contrafare*) of all the things of nature, vividly and simply, with drawing and with colors (*col disegno e co'colori*)."[12] This emphasis on design with color in second place defines Florentine art while Venice reversed the order.

In his only elaboration on his method Vasari presents five parts of the arts of design in a way that makes architecture a red-headed stepchild. It can lay claim to only two parts as its own. They are rule (*regola*), which is "the process of taking measurements from antiquities and studying the ground-plans of ancient edifices for the construction of modern buildings," and order (*ordine*), or the rules for correctly assembling the pieces of the Doric, Ionic, Corinthian, and Tuscan orders. It seems that nothing had been added to the art of architecture since Vasari explained in his "Life" of Brunelleschi that when he and Donatello were exploring Rome they found "nothing of the good that they did not measure" and where they recovered the "good ancient Orders." In continuing his elaboration on his method he has architecture join the other arts in using the third part, proportion (*misura*), which is common (*universale*) to all three visual arts and involves having "all bodies ... made correct and true, with the members in proper harmony." But correct and true relative to what, we might ask? Architecture must begin to feel like a wallflower when we find proportion overlapping with the fourth part, design (*disegno*), which involves "imitating the most beautiful things of nature in all the figures both sculpted and painted, that reproduce everything that the eye sees ... with absolute accuracy and precision." Architecture might as well leave the dance before it reaches the fifth and final part, manner (*maniera*), where "the greatest possible beauty" is achieved by "constantly copying (*ritrarre*) the most beautiful objects, and joining together these most beautiful things, hands, heads, bodies, and legs."[13]

Vasari falls into the all too common fault of treating architecture as an art of representation. Alberti did write, "Of the arts the ones that are useful, even vital, to the architect are painting and mathematics" (9.10.317/861). He put mathematics to work all through the treatise, but he said nothing explicitly to move his theory of painting into his theory of architecture. Instead, he was leery of paintings because they can draw attention away from the architecture.[14] Inside churches, where even reliefs are less welcome than maxims, he calls for a pavement with "musical and geometric lines and shapes so that the mind may receive stimuli from every side" (7.10.220/609–11). The architect elevates buildings to architecture by imitating nature's concinnity. In Vasari's emulation precedents presented as models teach the artist how to extract the ideal from nature without consulting nature to make paintings and sculptures that can reveal concinnity only at second hand, as proportions, or Vasari's *misura*.

Emulation is invaluable in training artists who can practice all three arts at a high level. It dominated education in the span running from Vasari's academy through the Ecole des Beaux Arts and its American surrogates in the first third of the twentieth century. In a stable tradition the emulation of canonic precedents plays a more prominent role than the imitation of nature in the ongoing tasks of designing buildings and in architecture's counterparts in the civil order which include framing laws and administering them justly. Those canonic precedents set the parameters for acceptable invention. But eventually canonic precedents become overly familiar and shop worn and new precedents, or even the refreshment that only imitation can provide, is necessary. Too great a dependence on emulation and its precedents inhibits finding the inventive innovations to new contingencies and seeking precedents that will give buildings and laws new life. If these inventions are unanchored by the governing that the imitation of nature imposes we get what Palladio called abuses. Examples in architecture are the relatively short-lived fashions that carry the stylistic labels of Mannerism, which was a licentious excursion from the stolid, storied antique manner of the sixteenth century, and Rococo, which is an exhibition of license within an already licentious Baroque. These are examples of the mimetic rivalry that emulation within a rigid tradition encourages. In Modernist practice the cycles are shorter and the extremes more excessive but emulation still finds a valued if unacknowledged home.

In emulation, he who chooses the canonic precedents controls the education and artistic production. Academicians select precedents to curry the favor of their sponsors while the patrons dictate the precedents that carry the expressive content they want. Alberti's advocacy of an architecture that imitates to serve civil orders seeking the good through their imitating nature is an open-ended method. Emulation works in a closed loop. Alberti's method requires pluralism of the kind that permeated the authoritative institutions of Church and State. In the sixteenth century when Thomas More was martyred and Erasmus was hounded into isolation comity fell victim to bellicosity. The Church reasserted its claim to its imperial foundations to solidify its position while the states that had not absorbed ancient Roman imperial law into their lands successfully rejected the authority of the Church in Rome. In imperial Rome's new descendants Vitruvius' relation to his patron provided an excellent model for the role of the artist and architect whose chosen models were artists such as Raphael, Michelangelo, and Bramante whom Julius II had used to legitimate the claims of the Holy See. In the next century came their ingenious emulators, geniuses such as Gianlorenzo Bernini and Francesco Borromini whose works only aroused both admiration and incomprehension in the lands of the Protestants that rejected the doctrines that their works expressed.

Today even agnostics and republicans can enjoy the artistic achievement in works from the period whose arts express doctrines of the Church and claims of the princely states that they cannot accept. The dissociation of admirable form from unacceptable content began to take hold in the later seventeenth century when skepticism began to assault the content. Before long the arts of design slipped the doctrine's harness and sought out content that offered simpler pleasures and delights. Music and poetry embarked on a similar path, and they combined to become the indisputable five members of the Fine Arts or Beaux Arts club, eventually even ceasing being arts of design and becoming arts of creation.[15] We will encounter them again later in this chapter.

PERRAULT'S RADICAL REVISIONS

A trunk road turned off from the Italian academies and ran over the Alps where Louis XIV found that academies fitted his program of personal and consolidated rule like his bejeweled gloves fitted his hands. Richelieu, his father's Prime Minster, in 1635 had established the Académie Française, the first academy in France. Its purpose was to protect and promote the nation's vehicle for expressing its unique culture, the French language. The Sun King endorsed establishing academies to promote the *gloire* he sought for France which was himself. In 1671 came the Royal Academy of Architecture "to regulate French architectural production."[16] This was a forum for discussion by a select group of established architects. The academy was to assure that the learned practice of architecture was truly and visibly elevated above the craft of building done by guildsmen and to assure that the architecture that served the king was a conspicuously French architecture that achieved the highest standards exemplified by the architecture serving the ancient emperors.

Its sister academy for painting and sculpture taught drawing, and the architecture academy's director Françoise Blondel offered lectures to selected apprentices. His many publications included a three-volume *Cours d'architecture* (1675; 1683; new edition 1698) that remained important in the education of architects in France for more than a century. This erudite compilation of authoritative theories and commentaries from Vitruvius to his present day was intended to promote the role of the new science of mathematics in serving the proportions that had traditionally been the source of beauty in buildings. Blondel's interests were shared by the Academy whose sessions involved extended discussions of the treatises its members most valued: Vitruvius, who provided the "'true' tradition of Antiquity," and Palladio, Scamozzi, Vignola, Serlio, and Alberti, followed later by de l'Orme, Jean Bullant, Jacques Androuet du Cerceau, and even Henry Wotton.[17]

The academician and medical doctor Claude Perrault whose credentials in architecture included his role in designing the east front of Louis' Louvre brought to the discussions a very different focus from Blondel's.[18] Claude's brother Charles, who "invented" the genre of the fairytale, conducted the Quarrel of the Ancients and Moderns that concluded that modern French achievements in the arts had surpassed those of antiquity. Claude agreed and supported France's claim to uniqueness in the notes of a handsome folio translation of Vitruvius published in 1673. He claimed that symmetry and eurhythmy were identical and, declaring that proportion was the same thing, threw it into the lot.[19] This emptied symmetry of its role in imitation and removed the role of ratiocination. He replaced that bundle with formal mirror-image bilateral likeness across an axis. He named the bundle symmetry and made it into a completely internal, formal property, although it did carry with it the "reasoned relationship (*rapport*) between proportionate parts" whose model is the human body where "there is relationship (*rapport*) between the elbow, the palm, the hand, the finger and other parts."[20]

A decade later Perrault published *Ordonnance for the Five Kinds of Columns after the Method of the Ancients*, which has been called the translation's "necessary complement."[21] Here Perrault expanded his assault on the classical tradition's fundamental principles of beauty that his translation had broached. Beauty is not present in an object. When he was done the only thing left of beauty as the classical tradition had always understood it was its name.

Perrault's demolition was complete. What was taken to be beauty in an object did not participate in universal, enduring, eternal beauty. Beauty was not a property that is accessible to perception; the visual properties of what we see are all that is required for its enjoyment. The beauty we see in a thing has no relationship to the beauty we find in other expressions, such as music. And finally, beauty has no connection with the order or the harmony or the proportionality of the cosmos.

Note how the diction of the 1708 English translation put it. There are "two sorts of Beauties in Architecture, namely, those that are founded on solid convincing Reasons, and those that depend only on" something else. The beauty that depends on those "reasons," is "the Richness of materials, the Grandeur and Magnificence of the Structure, the Exactness and Neatness and Performance … ." The second basis of beauty depends only on "Preposession [sic.] and Prejudice," and it is in "the Symmetry, which denotes that kind of Proportion, which produces an evident and remarkable Beauty." By prejudice he means nothing more than what we are accustomed to. Universal beauty, then, is one thing, and beauty identified with the words customary, subjective, arbitrary, or relative is quite another.

And universal beauty is not what it used to be. It arises from qualities that are in buildings and in which all people find pleasure simply by virtue of humankind's *sensus communis*, or sense that they all possess as a part of their human nature. This is where proportions survive in Perrault's scheme, because he finds that one aspect of this universal beauty is in "the Correspondence of the Parts of a Column with its Whole" as in "the entire Body of Man, and all its Parts, or upon the Resemblance that a Fabric may have to the first Buildings, that Nature taught Man," that is, the primitive hut. Another way to put it is that beauty is in materials and in pleasure but not in perception or the happiness that exceeds mere pleasure.

Perrault then deflates imitation into mere copying and deprives it of being the source of universal beauty classically understood. If "Imitations and Resemblances" produced "Grace and Beauty" then

> the greatest Beauty would consist in the most exact imitation. Neither the imitation of Nature, nor Reason, nor good Sense, are then the Foundation of those Beauties, which we fancy we see in Proportion, Order, and Disposition of the Parts of a Column; and it is impossible to assign any other cause of the Agreeableness, than Custom.[22]

In a passage that in our next chapter we will find will not pass muster across the Channel, Perrault tells us that no *sensus communis* can inform us

> to be displeas'd or pleas'd with the Proportions of Architecture. … [for this] we must be instructed by a long Observation of the Rules, which Use alone has established, and of which, good Sense could never have given us the least Knowledge: as in the Civil Laws, there are some which depend on the Will of the Legislators, and the Consent of the People, which the natural light of Equity does not discover in us.[23]

Universal beauty is a crude beauty accessible to everyone while the superior beauty, customary beauty, can be discerned and produced by those who have a cultivated taste. It is also a possession "which distinguishes true architects from those that are not so."[24] It is no surprise to find that Perrault has followed Vitruvius to delight and never reached the beauty that his successors had found. His beauty is in the eye of the beholder, and it is not open to reason's assessment or disputation.

6.1 Claude Perrault, The Five Orders
Source: A Treatise of the Five Orders of Columns in Architecture, trans. John James
(London: Benj. Motte, 1708), Plate I. Image provided by the University of Notre Dame's Architecture Library.

Perrault founded his argument on the undisputable facts brought forth by the methods of the empirical sciences that treated numbers as integers within the logic of mathematics and vanquished any challenge coming from received opinion. He noted that the measurements of buildings whose proportions were considered the canonic examples of beauty and good taste failed to yield proportions that the treatises said would make them beautiful. Even optical adjustments, the adjustments that eurhythmy controlled, failed to rescue the old doctrines. QED "The partisans of optical adjustment presupposed that the eye can be deceived. This," Perrault counters, "is not so; if deception occurs, it is not due to the eye, which never fails, but to our judgment, which interprets the optical sensation wrongly." "[C]hanging architectural proportions in order to correct visual shortcomings is a bad practice."[25]

Perrault's argument fitted the king's program, as the word *ordonnance* in its title made clear. That word identified "rational political decrees that led to the regimentation of life under the reign of Louis XIV."[26] After Perrault had dismantled the authority of the classical orders he offered a rational and easy-to-remember series of proportions for the columnar orders that assured that French architects could build tasteful buildings.

The book's premise is that the orders alone assured good taste and that architecture was an art that made stand-alone buildings that were unconnected to urban issues.

Vasari, Blondel, and Perrault agreed that knowledge of proportions is essential to gain command of the orders, but beyond that their agreement ended. Blondel argued vigorously against Perrault's position, and although Perrault's easy method never took hold he ultimately carried the day. His claim that the classical columnar orders are difficult to design has been proven by inept examples that have proliferated in direct proportion to their being excised from the education of architects. Even those who learn to emulate the examples in Vignolesque books of the orders stop short of understanding that they are not mere pasties that attest to a building's status or claim to a place in tradition. When nothing more than taste justifies their use they are easily disposed of when taste changes and they fall out of fashion.

ARCHITECTURE'S NEW ALLIANCES

Perrault's assault on tradition would eventually achieve victory on the Continent, but while slow in coming, it was complete.[27] He had begun the removal of traditional content from architecture. Others would take their turn and suggest new content, with the rest of this chapter reviewing some of what they found.

Although the old reasons for finding pleasure in a thing were made passé, just to say, "I just like it," was unfulfilling, so around mid-century the new field of philosophy called aesthetics was invented to provide reasons. It claimed no role in the practice of art. "Aesthetic theory is a branch of philosophy, and exists for the sake of knowledge and not as a guide to practice."[28]

But one might ask, knowledge of what? To find an answer a person might conduct empirical inquiries into his sensations and impressions, as Edmund Burke did.[29] Beauty, he concluded, is "that quality or those qualities in bodies by which they cause love, or some passion similar to it," such as "the sense of affection and tenderness."[30] But he found beauty paltry compared to a quite different, newly identified sensation. In 1712 James Addison had found it pleasurable, in 1726 Francis Hutcheson noted it, and finally in 1759 the young Burke named it the sublime and gave it currency.[31]

> Whatever is fitted in any sort to excite the ideas of pain and danger, that is to say, whatever is in any sort terrible, or is conversant about terrible objects, or operates in a manner analogous to terror, is a source of the sublime; that is, it is productive of the strongest emotion which the mind is capable of feeling.[32]

Deformity such as the abuses that Palladio lamented are regrettable, not sublime. "[M]ost of those Objects which excite Horror at first, when Experience or Reason has remov'd the Fear, may become the occasions of Pleasure; as ravenous Beasts, a tempestuous Sea, a craggy Precipice, a dark shady Valley."[33] Four years later Emmanuel Kant put the difference in an aphorism: "The sublime *moves*, the beautiful *charms*."[34] In buildings Kant found the sublime in a hugely large or hugely tall building, and Burke in one that is "dark and gloomy."[35]

The master of the sublime in architecture was Giovanni Battista Piranesi (1720–78) whose etchings are intended to make the beautiful perceptible rather than to stir the feelings and move the emotions. Their dramatic contrasts of light and dark, exaggerated relationships in scale, uninhabitable points of view, and other devices intensify the emotional impact of their representations of ancient and modern Rome, especially for spectators to whom the sublime was a newly discovered pleasure. Even more intensely sublime are his *Carceri d'invenzioni* that served the appetite for the fantastical, provocative, irrational, and threatening. They have become lodestones of taste among Modernists.

The sublime got a mate in the picturesque, which grew up with it in England. The term was applied to a visual treatment given to rural land considered not for its productivity but for the pleasure it offered to sight. In earlier ages the garden hemmed in, governed with geometry, and trimmed the view of nature. Now it was to be seen as raw or, actually, "natural," as it appeared in the paintings of light-drenched Italian landscapes like those by Claude Lorraine that the English Milordi were bringing back from their Grand Tour. The sublime and the picturesque would increase their demands on the viewers' emotions and become the tutors of Romanticism found in the more emotionally demanding experiences of ferocious Alpine thunderstorms, solitary figures on lonely beaches, and buildings that evoked days of yore, ruins that revealed the assaults of time, and massive piles that conquered the assaults of nature. With this we find that the associations formed with the subject matter offered more pleasure than the work's formal properties.[36]

As people increasingly wanted what they saw to offer them easily accessible pleasures the appeal of the difficult content of the higher genres waned. As Samuel

6.2 Gianbattista Piranesi, *Carcere di inventione* 14, c.1749/50– c.1761
Source: Cooper–Hewitt, Smithsonian Design Museum, in public domain via Wikicommons.

Johnson (1709–84) said, "I would rather see the portrait of a dog I know, than all the allegorical paintings they can shew me in the world."[37] But contentless form was unacceptable, and people came up with new content for buildings.

One was called character, which had been there all along but was now isolated, named, and given a great deal of freight to carry. Here is Marc-Antoine Laugier (1713–69) in 1753:

> *What makes up the character of a building is the genre chosen and the destination it is intended for. Churches, palaces, private houses, corps-de-logis, pavilions, domes, towers—these are the various main genre. Different destinations give rise to more or less lofty ideas and call for a simple, elegant, noble, august, majestic, extraordinary or prodigious manner.*[38]

Here it is in current diction: particular functional types call for particular expressive characters. A church ought to look like a church, a courthouse like an important place, and a house like a home.

Character soon gathered a large, fresh series of adjectives to give refined meanings. Jacques-François Blondel (1705–74), the dominant educator in architecture in France in the decades before the Revolution, enumerated "over sixty architectural qualities that include the noble, sublime, and terrible; masculine, solid, and virile; feminine, light, and elegant; as well as the servile, licentious, dissimilar, ambiguous, frivolous, barbarous, cold, sterile, poor, and the flat."[39] In 1780 Nicolas Le Camus de Mézière elevated character's importance when he aligned it with *convenance*, or propriety, decorum.[40]

Architecture considered as a silent language that conveyed character arose as a topic in the last decades of the century. Called *architecture parlante*, the original poster children are the 50 relatively small tax-collecting stations called *Barrières* that Claude-Nicolas Ledoux (1736–1806) built along the tax wall of Paris between 1785 and 1788.

6.3 Claude-Nicolas Ledoux, Barrière de la Villette, Paris, 1788, by an unknown artist in 1810
Source: Bibliothéque de France, in the public domain via Wikicommons.

In its strict sense if expression is language and not mere noise, utterance, or Babel it must be embedded in reason and make statements, but *architecture parlante* aims directly as the emotions. Ledoux's *Barrièries* express the state's power to impose taxes but are not connected to a reasoned basis for doing so. Similarly, the images he and Étienne-Louis Boullée (1728–1799) produced of vast, unbuildable, bloviated buildings with sharp contrasts of light and dark, countless repetitions of similar architectural elements such as the orders, and vast stretches of unrelieved surfaces are unbuildable and unusable but they are sublimely unbound by reason. They evoke sensations, and their only identity comes from the labels on the renderings: a national library (1778), a *Métropole* (a religious structure for an unknown religion, 1781), a Cenotaph for Newton (1784).[41] An English doctor recognized this role for a reason-less linguistic analogy when he gave his reaction to a hospital or asylum for the insane by George Dance, Jr. He had found no "beauty in it … It always excited gloomy reflections in his mind, and gave him no other idea but that of an hospital for the reception of mad persons."[42]

The linguistic analogy has become a long-standing staple in discourse about architecture. Toward the end of the eighteenth century Antoine Chrysostôme Quatremère de Quincy gave it serious theoretical treatment; we will meet him in Chapter 9.[43] It made a cameo appearance in one of the many editions of the important engineering textbook that Claude-Nicolas-Louis Durand wrote for Napoleon's engineering school: "The elements [of architecture] are to architecture what words are to speech, what notes are to music."[44] And it remains a common trope today.[45] It is the featured content of a popular little book written to accompany a series of talks on the BBC in 1963 and still in print, *The Classical Language of Architecture* by Sir John Summerson (1904–92). A language of architecture, it tells us, is like a "'uniform' worn by a certain category of buildings." The classical language uses traditional formal elements that developed from the columns and their combinations that were first used in the "classical" world of ancient Greece and Rome.[46] The examples of Blenheim Palace, the Louvre of Louis XIV, and Saint Peter's Basilica use "force and drama in order to overcome our resistance and persuade us into the truth of what they have to tell us—whether it is about the invincible glory of British arms, the paramount magnificence of Louis XIV, or the universal embrace of the Roman Church." Note that there is nothing in this "uniform" or expressive content that goes beyond the emotional response to "invincible glory," "paramount magnificence," or "universal embrace." When those buildings were new, he tells us, their significant and symbolic content was conveyed with a rhetorical language that is a dead language for us moderns. He treats their speech as emotional utterance: "You cannot use the orders lovingly unless you love them; and you cannot love them without persuading yourself that they embody some absolute principle of truth or beauty." In his final chapter, "Classical into Modern," he decides that the content of architecture is in its forms that are disciplined by principles of grammar based on rationality, a characteristic common to classical and Modernist architecture. The classical "uniform" used to display those principles; now Modernist forms do, which makes Le Corbusier "the most inventive mind in the architecture of our time …, one of the most classical minds."

Le Corbusier and other Modernists did believe that their architecture and the revolutionary political program it would serve were based on principles and reason, and they believed that the works of modern engineers and technicians were the best models for architecture. They rejected the classical tradition and emulated machines for their new architecture that would hurry the future into existence. But content derived from emulation can never be richer than that of its models, and the speech of buildings based on emulating concrete colossi and machines such as steam ships and automobiles cannot be richer than that of a technical manual. Buildings based on the machine analogy remain mere buildings and cannot become architecture even if they offer the delight of forms molded by light or the visual counterpart to the sound of a well-tuned straight-eight internal combustion engine or a bicycle equipped with a Campagnolo derailer. Impressive as they might be as Fine Arts self-expressions, of their technological means, or their functional roles, these buildings are mere utterance that lack the content of the speech that separates mankind from the brutes and offers to expand our humanity and fulfill our human nature with happiness.

FROM ARCHITECTURE TO HISTORY

Character and the linguistic analogy joined league with associationism to become the Romanticism that dresses buildings like ventriloquist dummies that would say whatever architects wanted them to say. Pugin, Ruskin, Viollet-le-Duc, and others did so. Their heirs are architects who use buildings to present the content of idiosyncratic interpretations of architecture and of the world, esoteric theories of their own devising, or theories imported into architecture from other fields.

The most common ventriloquist dummies today are the buildings that proclaim that they occupy a precise place in a chronological narrative that history preordained for them. Time moves, buildings document the movement, and the buildings in each era speak the language of architecture with a distinctive style. In this sequence old styles are forgotten, new ones become old, and the newest ones point to the future. The style of a building belongs only to its time, and what we build now must be "of our time."

This interpretation of history gives to chronological sequence the authority that used to be enjoyed by three other, quiet different, categories of judging a building's success: its achievement in the art of architecture, its service to an institution of the civil order, and its contribution to the urban order. These three categories are very much in evidence in Serlio's and Palladio's collections of buildings where even the distinction between ancient from modern models can melt.

These three categories belong to a narrative that valued continuity and relished innovation within tradition. In the eighteenth century continuity began to be parsed as a chronological sequence in which the past was understood as prelude to the present and progress would improve the future, and the Fine Arts were given a prominent place in identifying the best ages. Voltaire (1694–1778) identified these as the age of Philip, Alexander, and Pericles in Greece, of Caesar and Augustus in Rome, then of the Medici in Florence, and finally of Louis XIV. Meanwhile, Johann Joachim Winckelmann (1717–68) shifted the focus from what men did to the formal qualities of the art objects they had made. The quality of a civilization was determined by the quality of its art, and its art became more important than its history's instruction about how to live in the world. Winckelmann gave Greek art a new prestige that launched a revival of all things that recalled ancient Greece.[47] Before long people were finding high artistic value in the art objects of other times and places, and these were assembled into a narrative that stressed the separateness of civilizations from one another and equipped them with distinctive names: ancient, Gothic, Renaissance, and so on. Further explorations into distant times and places enlarged the corpus, refined the divisions, and brought previously unknown or unregarded things in Greece, Pompeii, China, and elsewhere into the narrative. Organizing the past as a series of ruptures displaced the earlier interest in a tradition's continuities and innovations, a scheme that Sir Banister Fletcher illustrated in the "Tree of Architecture" that we saw in Figure 1.1.

This new kind of history depended on treating a building or other product of artisanship as an art object. As early as 1300 English was using the word "art" to stand for skill with the content of the thing offering evidence of the artisan's skill and making it valuable in itself without reference to anything outside itself and offering pleasure simply in seeing it. When this art object that was valuable merely as an art object was inserted into the historical narrative we find a new conception of art that Louis Dupré identified as one of the Enlightenment's "major achievements."[48] Art now became interpreted as an autonomous enterprise with Kant writing that no consideration of an art object's use was needed. Because architecture must necessarily serve a use it ended up last among the arts but not removed from disinterested aesthetic consideration or deprived of moral content.[49]

As a famous dictum puts it, the art object presents "the perfect appearance of the good."[50] But note that the morality that a building symbolizes here is unconnected to the civil order it serves and expresses, and, more urgently, to the urban realm to which the building necessarily contributes. Architecture here is dissociated from the political life it serves.[51] Kant went father in offering a new aesthetics of beauty. He accepts a person as a rational creature and therefore a participant in universally valid reason, but beauty is still in the eye of the beholder. If an individual judges beauty to be present it is indisputably present, but for those who do not find it present its presence remains beyond disputation. The result, paradoxically, is that while its presence or lack thereof is beyond disputation the beauty may participate in the universal and general, and so the concept of beauty remains a much disputed topic today.[52]

Kant's position left a gap between form and content, and others rushed to fill it, with two deserving attention here. One gap filler was the role found for form and content by a succession of French (and other) governments seeking legitimacy after the Revolution. They modernized their regimes and absorbed the rapidly changing social, economic, commercial, and industrial demands of the modernizing world, all the while using associationism to express their national identity and continuity with their past. The issue was especially pressing in France where their dramatic Revolution had broken the connection to its long history. To display a restored continuity it sponsored the Ecole des Beaux Arts whose program of instruction taught architects how to serve new functions while emulating ancient and especially French precedents. Its graduates would serve the state's demands by expressing Frenchness in the buildings serving the institutions of the French nation.

The other gap filler was Hegelianism. It absorbed the sequential historical narrative displayed in Fletcher's "Tree" as a replacement for the classical tradition's qualitative assessments, and it supplied it with the motive power that made disruptive changes from era to era that the sequence of styles chronicled. The classical tradition's explanation that architects imitated nature by using reason, judgment, and nature dissolved. Replacing it was the irresistible force of Hegelianism's world historical spirit operating on builders, architects, and everyone else who made the cultural products of an age. This spirit (*Geist*) that made progress inevitable influenced the actions of individuals in each successive era (*Zeit*). The architect, knowingly or unknowingly, simply obeyed the influences of the *Zeitgeist*, and the appearance, the formal qualities, the image, of what he made told the whole story and served as a symptom of the age. Imitation was now obsolete.

> Art as imitation seems to possess what truth it does, not necessarily in virtue of anything in itself as image, but in virtue of something external to it. Hence its value does not reside in the image as such, but depends on an external relation binding image and original. This dependency of imitation seems to make art derivative and of secondary importance compared to the original it imitates.[53]

Now it would make visible the *Zeitgeist*, the spirit of that moment or era, rather than the enduring, unchanging, and unattainable beauty of the cosmic order or even models it emulated.

Hegel's plot featuring the irresistible influences of the spirit and the chronicle of progress in the historical narrative that divided the past into a sequence of eras progressing to a blissful future on earth gave architecture new and very important content. History and its buildings no longer contributed to an understanding of men's actions as a civil being and his fate in a natural world that included his human nature. Now it addressed man's destiny, and his destiny lay in the future. Projections into the future rather than the reasoned judgment that had accumulated within useful traditions now controlled the culture of architecture. This about-face made tradition obsolete and licensed the avant-garde to invent forward-looking theories that explained practice from the limited viewpoint of the present, and it obliged the architect to fulfill those projections. The Modernist architect plays the role that Vitruvius had defined for him except now he worked under the tyrannous *Zeitgeist* rather than in the service to a divine emperor.

We have now reached the present, orthodox, and nearly hegemonic understanding of the history of architecture and the theories that accompany it. Imitation, beauty, and tradition, the identity of architecture with urbanism, and the relationship between a building and the authority that licenses it have been fenced out along with the rest of the classical tradition. This is the story that unrolled on the Continent. Across the Channel a different story unfolded, and it would eventually include America. It will occupy us for the rest of this book.

NOTES

1. Tanner, *Jerusalem on the Hill*.
2. Władysław Tatarkiewicz, *Six Ideas*, 247; 272–3, where he quotes from Ficino's *Theologica Platonica*. See also Rudolf and Margot Wittkower, *Born Under Saturn: The Character and Conduct of Artists: A Documentary History from Antiquity to the French Revolution* (London: Weidenfeld and Nicolson, 1963), 34–8; 98; Rudolf Wittkower, "Individualism in Art and Artists: A Renaissance Problem," *Journal of the History of Ideas*, 22 (1961), 291–302.
3. Martin Kemp, "From 'Mimesis' to 'Fantasia,'" 382.
4. Erwin Panofsky, "Artist, Scientist, Genius: Notes on the 'Renaissance-Dämmerung,'" in *The Renaissance: Six Essays* (New York and Evanston: Harper Torchbooks, 1962), sect. vi; Panofsky, *Idea*; Paul Oskar Kristeller, "The Modern System of the Arts," in *Renaissance Thought II: Papers on Humanism and the Arts* (New York, Evanston, and London: Harper Torchbooks, 1965), 179; Tatarkiewicz, *Six Ideas*, 247.
5. The topic is treated extensively in Summers, *Michelangelo*.
6. Tatarkiewicz, *Six Ideas*, 273.
7. Cicero, *De Oratore*, I.viii.33.25.
8. I have drawn principally on Vasari's *Lives* and on Nikolaus Pevsner, *Academies of Art Past and Present* (Cambridge: Cambridge University Press, 1940), 33–49; 54–66; Wittkower, *Born Under Saturn*, 11, 232–4; and Karen-edis Barzman, *The Florentine Academy and the Early Modern State* (Cambridge: Cambridge University Press, 2000), for a history; 59 for the guilds, and Chapter 6 for their guild-like activities. See also Mark W. Roskill, *Dolce's "Aretino" and Venetian Art Theory in the Cinqecento* (New York: New York University Press, 1968).

9   For example, Vitruvius, 1.2.15.

10 For a recent and useful study of emulation see David Mayernik, *The Challenge of Emulation in Art and Architecture* (Burlington, Vt.: Ashgate, 2013); at 28 he follows the not uncommon misattribution of Platonic content to Alberti's ideas.

11 Giorgio Vasari, *Vasari on Technique*, trans. Louisa S. Maclehose (New York: J.M. Dent, 1907; reprinted New York: Dover, 1960), §74–5, 205–8.

12 Vasari, *Lives*, "Masaccio," 96–8.

13 Vasari, *Lives*, Preface to the Third Part, 221–6.

14 Here Vasari is in accord with Peruzzi, Serlio's mentor, and like Vasari noted for his large perspectival paintings as well as his buildings.

15 Authoritative is Kristeller, "The Modern System of the Arts," who conjectures that the name *arti del disegno* is the origin of the term Beaux Arts. However, Tatarkiewicz, *Six Ideas*, 20, and 60, traces the term to the sixteenth-century Portuguese *boas artes* of Francesco da Hollanda, Michelangelo's biographer, but notes that it "did not take root" until the latter part of the eighteenth century. In Paul Oskar Kristeller, "Afterword: 'Creativity' and 'Tradition,'" in Michael Mooney, ed., *Renaissance Thought and the Arts* (Princeton: Princeton University Press, 1990), 250; we read, "In the nineteenth century, this attitude became pervasive, and we might note with surprise that an age that found it difficult to believe God created the world out of nothing apparently had no difficulty in believing that the human artist would create his work out of nothing."

16 See now Anthony Gerbino, *Françoise Blondel: Architecture, Erudition, and the Scientific Revolution* (London and New York: Routledge, 2010), who is largely followed here. Consult also the quite useful study by Indra Kagis McEwen, "On Claude Perrault: Modernizing Vitruvius," in Vaughan Hart and Peter Hicks, *Paper Palaces: The Rise of the Renaissance Architectural Treatise* (New Haven and London: Yale University Press, 1998), 321. For Louis XIV's academy, see Nikolaus Pevsner, *Academies of Art*, 16–17.

17 Choay, *The Rule and the Model*, 184–5; and 380, nn. 69–72; Gerbino, *Françoise Blondel*, 59.

18 See Robert W. Berger, *The Palace of the Sun King: The Louvre of Louis XIV* (University Park Pennsylvania State University Press, 1993).

19 *Dix livres d'architecture de Vitruve*, corrigex et tradvits nouvellement en françois, avec des notes & des figures (Paris: J.B. Coignard, 1673). The next year he made the content of his commentaries available in an abridgement; *Abregé des dix livres d'architecture de Vitruve* (Paris: J.B. Coignard, 1674), with an anonymous English translation appearing in 1692. The edition quoted here is the revised and enlarged second edition of 1684; 9, and 11, n.8. Hon and Goldstein, *From* Summetria *to* Symmetry, 127–34 is useful. See also Kruft, *A History*, 133–6.

20 Perrault, *Dix livres*, 1684, 11, n. 9; for the translations I thank Samir Younès. Although it is only likeness and not yet the absolute equality that will come a century later. Kant in 1794 and the French mathematician Adrien-Marie Legendre (1752–1833) would articulate symmetry as mirror image likeness across an axis. Extremely productive in mathematics and the physical sciences, in architecture it led to reductionism that obscures the basic kinds of symmetry used in the Renaissance, bilateral, reflective, translator or glide, and rotational, illustrated in Hersey and Freedman, *Possible Palladian Villas*, 17. For all this see also Hon and Goldstein, *From* Summetria *to* Symmetry, esp. 52–65; 112–19; 127–34.

21 Claude Perrault, *Ordonnance des cinq especes des colonnes selon la methode des anciens* (Paris: J.B. Coignard, 1683). The quoted words are those of Alberto Péres-Gómez,

"Introduction," Claude Perrault, *Ordonnance for the Five Kinds of Columns after the Method of the Ancients*, trans. Indra Kagis McEwen (Santa Monica: Getty Center, 1993), 1. For background see Wolfgang Herrmann, *The Theory of Claude Perrault* (London: A. Zwemmer, 1973), 31–9. For the discussion in the Academy, which began with the manuscript in 1681, see Kruft, *A History*, 136.

22 Claude Perrault, *A Treatise on the Five Orders of Architecture*, trans. John James (London: Benj. Motte, 1708), vi–ix. In Perrault, *Ordonnance*, 176. In note 6 we find a misleading interpretation. It treats imitation as copying and comments on "subsequent generations," which are not Perrault's concern, and makes no comment on imitation as previous generations had understood it. The authorship of the translation's notes is not noted.

23 Perrault, *A Treatise*, x–xi; and Perrault, *Ordonnance*, xiii, emphasis added. Here is a modern translation: To be pleased by proportions "requires the discipline of long familiarity with rules that are established by usage alone, and of which good sense can intimate no knowledge, just as in civil law there are rules dependent on the will of legislators and on the consent of nations that a natural understanding of fairness will never reveal." Perrault, *Ordonnance*, 1993, 54. How jarring this statement would be to Englishmen will become clear in Chapter 8.

24 Perrault, *A Treatise*, ix–xi; and Perrault, *Ordonnance*, 1683, xiii and xii, a right Tast [sic.] = bon goust; true architects = vrais Architectes.

25 Herrmann, *Claude Perrault*, 74–5; 77.

26 Pérez-Gómez, "Introduction," 36.

27 Péres-Gómez, "Introduction," 27, refers to this as the "'crisis of representation' of our own day. ... For the first time in history, the inherent connection between a visible form and an invisible content becomes an issue." See also 36–7.

28 Bernard Bosanquet, *A History of Aesthetic*, 2nd edn (London: George Allen & Unwin, 1904), ix.

29 Edmund Burke, *A Philosophical Enquiry into the Origin of our Ideas of the Sublime and Beautiful*, 2nd edn, 1759, ed. Adam Phillips (Oxford: Oxford University Press, 1990), Part III, citing Sections I–V, "Proportion Further Considered," and quoting Section I, 83.

30 Burke, *A Philosophical Enquiry*, I.vii.36; I.xviii.47. For Burke's extension of Perrault's ideas see Wolfgang Herrmann, *Claude Perrault*, 138–9.

31 The word is ancient. Burke argued that taste has principles and is a universal human possession composed of "sensibility and judgment" whose qualities "vary exceedingly in various people," running from defective to acute. *A Philosophical Enquiry*, Introduction, 13, 22. More about this will be presented in Chapter 8.

32 Burke, *A Philosophical Enquiry*, I.vii.36; also I.xviii.47.

33 Francis Hutcheson, *An Inquiry into the Original of Our Ideas of Beauty and Virtue in Two Treatises*, revised edn, ed. Wolfgang Leidhold (Indianapolis, Liberty Fund, 2008), I.VI.11.62. More will be said about Hutcheson in Chapter 8.

34 Immanuel Kant, *Observations on the Feeling of the Beautiful and Sublime*, trans. John T. Goldthwait (Berkeley, Los Angeles, and London: University of California Press, 1960), Sect. 1, 47, original emphasis. For observations on Kant's later work in aesthetics see Scruton, *The Aesthetics of Architecture*.

35 Kant, *Observations*, Sect. 1, 49; Burke, *A Philosophical Enquiry*, II, xv.

36 There is a large literature on nature and Romanticism. I mention here only the classic essay by Arthur Lovejoy, "'Nature' as Aesthetic Norm," *Modern Language Notes*, 42

(1927), republished in *Essays in the History of Ideas* (New York: Capricorn Books, G.P. Putnam's Sons, 1960), 69–77.

37 In George B.N. Hill, *Johnson Miscellanies*, 2 vols (Oxford: Oxford University Press, 1897), 2: 15.

38 Marc-Antoine Laugier, *An Essay on Architecture*, 2nd edn, trans. Wolfgang and Anni Herrmann (Los Angeles: Hennessey & Ingalls, 1977), 62–3. The translation renders genre as style.

39 Samir Younés, "Type, Character, and Style," in Alireza Sagharchi and Lucien Steil, eds, *New Palladians: Modernity and Sustainability for 21st Century Architecture* (London: Artmedia, 2010), 37, referring to Jacques-François Blondel, *Cours d'architecture, ou traité de la décoration, distribution & construction des bâtiments; Contenant les leçons données en 1750, & les années suivantes*, 8 vols. (Paris, 1771–77); (the last two volumes were written by Pierre Patte), 2: 229–32. See also the useful discussion by George L. Hersey, *High Victorian Gothic: A Study in Associationism* (Baltimore and London: Johns Hopkins University Press, 1972), Chapter 1. In 1905 Julien Guadet reissued Jacques-François Blondel as, *L'architecture français* (Paris: Librairie centrale des beaux-arts, É. Lévy, 1904).

40 Samir Younés, *The Imperfect City: On Architectural Judgment* (Farnham, Surrey, and Burlington, Vermont: Ashgate, 2012), 169. Its title is *Le Génie de l'Architecture, ou l'Analogie de cet art avec nos sensations*. See Rémy G. Saisselin, "Architecture and Language: The Sensationalism of Le Camus de Mézière," *The British Journal of Aesthetics*, 15 (1975), 239–54.

41 Étienne-Louis Boullée, *Treatise on Architecture, A Complete Presentation of the Architecture, Essai sur l'art*, ed. Helen Rosenau (London: Alec Tiranti, 1953); also, *Architecture, Essai sur l'art*, ed. Jean-Marie Pérouse de Montclos (Paris: Hermann, 1968). They were soon forgotten but then were discovered by Modernist historians; see the chapter devoted to Emil Kaufmann in Anthony Vidler, *Histories of the Immediate Present: Inventing Architectural Modernism*, (Cambridge, Mass., and London: MIT Press, 2008). Kaufmann's magnum opus, *Architecture in the Age of Reason: Baroque and Post-Baroque in England, Italy, and France* (Cambridge, Mass.: Harvard University Press, 1955), published posthumously, has a laudatory "Foreword" by Joseph Hudnut, the Harvard Dean who hired Walter Gropius.

42 John Soane, *Memoirs of the Professional Life of an Architect between the Years 1768 and 1835* (London, 1835), 21, quoted in Jeffrey A. Cohen and Charles E. Brownell, *The Architectural Drawings of Benjamin Henry Latrobe*, Part 1, (New Haven and London: Yale University Press, 1994), 9.

43 A longer version of the material on the linguistic analogy is in Carroll William Westfall, "Classicism and Language in Architecture," *American Arts Quarterly*, 27: 1 (2010), 17–27. The essential introduction, written as a contribution to the genealogy of modernism, is Sylvia Lavin, *Quatremère de Quincy and the Invention of a Modern Language of Architecture* (Cambridge, Mass., and London: MIT Press, 1992). For its later development see Samir Younés, *The True, the Fictive, and the Real: The Historical Dictionary of Architecture of Quatremère de Quincy* (London: Andreas Papadakis, 1999), Chapter II, "Architecture and Language."

44 *Précis des Leçons d'Architecture*, 2 vols (Paris: Didot, 1819; republished Nördlingen: Uhl, 1981), 1: 29; discussed without citation in the informative Chapter 17 on the linguistic analogy in Peter Collins, *Changing Ideals in Modern Architecture 1750–1950*, 2nd edn (Montreal & Kingston, etc.: McGill-Queen's University Press, 1998), 179. This passage is not found in the first edition, 1802–5, translated by David Britt as *Précis of the Lectures of Architecture* (Los Angeles: Getty Research Institute, 2000), or in the 1840 edition

(Brussels: Meline, Cans), although this one does have two references to language, at 33 and 35. Durand did not acknowledge that Perrault had rejected the analogy between music and architecture.

45 The linguistic analogy should not be confused with linguistics, which can provide a useful analytical tool. See for example Gianfranco Caniggia and Gian Luigi Maffei, *Interpreting Basic Building: Architectural Composition and Building Typology*, trans. Susan Jane Faser (Florence: Alinea, 2001), which Gibson and Richard Worsham brought to my attention.

46 John Summerson, *The Classical Language of Architecture* (London: Methuen, 1964), 7; the word classical, and the inverted commas are his; further page citations are unnecessary for this short book. Alan Powers, "John Summerson and Modernism," *Twentieth-Century Architecture and its Histories*, ed. Louise Campbell, (n.p.: Society of Architectural Historians of Great Britain, 2000), 153–75, writes that ever since Summerson encountered Le Corbusier's writings in the mid-1920s he had looked at the future prospects of architecture, for good or ill, through the lens Le Corbusier had supplied, although as his involvement in history deepened his engagement in current movements lessened.

47 For the broadcast of the discoveries in ancient Greek architecture see Dora Wiebenson, *Sources of Greek Revival Architecture* (London: A. Zwimmer, 1969). The first notable publication of Paestum is Thomas Major, *Ruins of Paestum* (London: T. Major, 1768), with a concurrent French edition and a German edition in 1781. For Greece, James Stuart and Nicholas Revett, *The Antiquities of Athens*, 5 vols (London: J. Haberkorn, 1762–1830), preceded by Julien-David LeRoy, *Les ruines des plus beaux monuments de la Grèce* (Paris:Guerin & Delatour, 1758).

48 *The Enlightenment*, 78; Chapter 4.

49 Immanuel Kant, *Critique of Judgment*, trans. James Creed Meredith (Oxford: Clarendon Press, 1928), Book I, 1,§4;II,1,§51,54. Poetry ranked first.

50 *Critique of Judgment*, II,1,§32;2, App. §60. For this rephrasing see Anthony Savile, "The Sirens' Serenade," in Anthony O'Hear, ed., *Philosophy, the Good, the True and the Beautiful, Royal Institute of Philosophy Supplement: 47* (Cambridge: Cambridge University Press, 2000), 250.

51 Kant exemplifies a position that Frederick Turner, *Beauty: The Value of Values* (Charlottesville, and London: University of Virginia Press, 1991), esp. Chapter 3, excoriates for its emphasis on the concept of the disinterest in beauty, if not its uninterest in the beauty of things.

52 Scruton, *The Aesthetics of Architecture*, uses this putative indisputability to prove its disputability.

53 William Desmond, *Art and the Absolute: A Study of Hegel's Aesthetics* (Albany: State University of New York Press, 1986), 6, quoted in Daniel N. Robinson, "Aesthetics, Phantasia and the Theistic," in Charles Taliaferro and Jil Evans, eds, *Turning Images in Philosophy, Science, and Religion: A New Book of Nature* (Oxford and New York: Oxford University Press, 2011), 151.

7

The Classical Tradition's Fate West of the Channel

MEANWHILE IN BRITAIN

The French Revolution and its immediate aftermath in other states on the Continent ended the tradition of law that based authority on the body of law that descended from ancient imperial Rome with the Church grafted on.[1] When people as a mass rejected that authority they became atheistic regicidal mobs. The government they cobbled together stabled horses in Notre Dame Cathedral in Paris, and Versailles, royalty's most conspicuous expression, was saved from destruction only by the heat of the day that wearied a Parisian mob bent on wrecking it.

ENGLAND'S LAW

Across the Channel Britons watched with apprehension. The ancient Romans had only a brief and light presence in England, and its legal structure easily withered in the face of the island's indigenous source of authority. At the center of that authority was English common law, "the only great system of temporal law to come out of the Christian centuries."[2] One of English law's landmarks, Magna Charta from 1215, states, "[T]he English Church shall be free and shall have all her rights and liberties, whole and inviolable."[3] Henry VIII broke with Rome and made the monarch the head of the Church in England while the Elizabethan Religious Settlement of 1559 that was fulfilled in the Act of Toleration in 1689 made openness to disagreement the (imperfect) heart of the Church of England and largely stilled the suspicion of anything sniffing of popery. Meanwhile, the division of civil authority between commoners, peers, and royalty survived by being constantly adjusted to address changing circumstances.

The Church cares for the soul and cures human frailty "through her sacraments and the grace of God" while the state looks after this mundane life, doing so with a generosity of spirit embedded in the legal tradition in which "Everyman is presumed to be a good man until the contrary is proved by lawful evidence." In the years when the Roman Church was being racked by ever greater dissent Erasmus and Sir Thomas More, two great men of words, articulated a common law position when they agreed men are more "knit together by friendship and benevolence than by covenants and leagues, by hearty affection of mind than by words."[4]

English jurists knew the words that Aristotle, Augustine, Aquinas, and others had written, but their training and experience with common law cases were authoritative in ways that political theory, philosophy, and bodies of written law were not. The common law resided in a body of precedents that originated in local and customary laws that often remained valid as customary law in those villages or districts. This was the bottom-up experience that became common law when it encountered the adjudication based on reason and tradition in royal courts and was written in law books and treatises that were revised when new cases revealed the necessity for innovations. The whole system was based on the ongoing interaction between bottom-up cases and top-down judgments.

The dynamics of the common law tradition occurred within a framework of natural law that played a very different role from natural law's presence in the legal structure that had descended from imperial Rome. On the Continent the law set the standard for what a person was to be and how he was to behave; its intent ran back to the Romans' imposition of that standard on the diverse peoples it had brought into its orbit. Over time it had been adapted to support monarchic regimes and to define Catholicism, Frenchness, and so on as it gradually drifted away from its foundation on natural law. Meanwhile, natural law remained foundational in English common law whose central tenet held that every individual is, by nature, a free and lawful man (*liber et legalis homo*) and has been endowed by nature with the capacity to know right from wrong and truth from falsehood. Called synderesis and working as the conscience, it provided each individual with the freedom to perfect his unique human nature in his pursuit of happiness. While the purpose of positive law based on the legacy of ancient Roman law was to make a person a Roman or a Catholic or a Frenchman, the purpose of common law is to allow each individual to respond for himself to the ancient admonition, "Know thyself."

The common law operated without a statute or law handed down by the man in the saddle telling him what is right and what is wrong. Corollaries are that everything is allowed until it is forbidden; that a person is presumed to be innocent until he is found guilty; that a person has the right to confront an accuser and defend himself against the charges made in the presence of a judge who is qualified to interpret the laws and precedents and conduct the hearing; that a jury composed of the defendant's peers (not of the realm but of the litigants) or, if the accused chooses, a judge, assesses the facts of the case and pronounces a verdict; and, eventually, that a person cannot be a fair judge of his own actions.

But men are imperfect. They are endowed with a conscience but also with a will that can cloud their judgment and lead them astray. When that occurs, who is to set the right path before them? In his last letter Thomas Jefferson reminded us who is not to do so: "the mass of mankind has not been born with saddles on their backs, nor a favored few booted and spurred, ready to ride them legitimately, by the

Grace of God."[5] Instead, it must be discovered, uncovered, or found in experience and judgment governed by reason, the endowment of all men, and validated by "reason and nature," a pair we have encountered earlier and will again. Experience, reason, and nature guide the community in formulating laws and using them with fairness. These ordinances instruct and the judgments correct wrongdoers in a community that is "knit together by friendship and benevolence ..., by hearty affection of mind," that formulates them and accepts them as precedents for future adjudication.[6] This nature-based law fills the voids when positive law is lacking. It is notable that there were no positive (statutory) law enactments in place to justify bringing Nazi leaders to the bar in Nuremburg in 1946.[7] And in England in that same year "no English statute has defined or forbidden murder or manslaughter or rape or attempted suicide or assault or false imprisonment. The judges of the Common Law, recognizing and enforcing the principles of natural law and ethics, defined these crimes and punished the criminals."[8] The natural law basis of common law tells us that if we transgress what is right, we can be held accountable because "we should have known better," although we are free to argue otherwise.

This system of law articulates "the necessary principles and rules of moral actions. These principles and rules of natural law have their origin in the order of the world and in a view of man as a part of that order; and in a study too of the inner constitution of man, of psychology and of ethics, and the metaphysical foundations of our being." Richard O'Sullivan continues, reasoning from those principles puts man at the acme of the Great Chain of Being as it exists in the terrestrial realm. It is in the "aspiration and appetite and perfection. The appetite of the mind is for the True and the appetite of the will is for the Good." He reminds us that the true and the good that are vouchsafed to man to seek in this world are only the truth and the good that are accessible in this world, and that is the truth and the good whose acquisition is the end of the public good of men bound together in friendship in society. Their place in the final end of man lies beyond that society, and on that basis the state's reach into an individual's personality is limited. Put shortly, a man may be tried for what he writes, speaks, or does but not for what he thinks or believes.[9]

This system of law is founded on necessary truths, that is, truths that are not derived from Holy Writ, Revelation, or theology but are congruent with our human nature and the nature of things that we extract by using moral reasoning. The sacred has no place here. They concern the secular. They are indifferent to religious beliefs, based as they are on self-evident truths that we share with all sane men of good will and to which we give a particular form in our community.[10] They are known before illustrations of them are offered. Otherwise it would be impossible to make moral judgments about new acts that are either contemplated or accomplished. These judgments are akin to other things we know are true through the reason and nature of the thing. For example, a whole cannot be less than the sum of its parts even without doing the math, and every effect must have a cause whether or not we know the cause, the effect, or their connection. These are propositions that came into being when nature did, and stand outside time. They are propositions of reason, not of empiricism, such as learning that a hot stove hurts when we touch it. We will come across these propositions again a little later.

This interaction between natural law, moral reasoning, and the experience of a community gives common law pliability, flexibility, and adaptability to the ever-changing circumstances of our life in nature. In the two centuries that began in the fifteenth century these qualities were sorely tested in England and in the Continent's positive law regimes. People had to cope with increased access to the storehouse of ancient writings and new ideas that printed books quickly put in the hands of an ever increasing number of literate people. They were given reports of strange lands, people, beliefs, and customs and of unheard of flora, fauna, and natural wonders in distant, newly discovered lands. And they were given new tools in ever more precise apparatus for measuring and looking and more powerful mathematics for digesting the data. We have reviewed some of the responses on the Continent. To them can be added what happened in the civil order. When its traditions were challenged the remnants of natural law claims and the elaborate structure of positive law that supported the increasingly centralized and consolidated monarchic nation states were met with increasingly rigid inflexibility. When violence and revolution ensued, the British were not surprised.[11] In the series of regimes that were born from revolution the old habit of seeking to prescribe how people ought to live remained in place. Meanwhile, in England, common law traditions provided ballast that let its ship ride out the storms.

NATURE AND HUMAN NATURE

The French *philosophes* were in the thick of things, and Francis Bacon, Isaac Newton, and René Descartes were their idols as the workshops of their busy minds absorbed what flowed in from aboard and was observed at home. Empiricism in the hands of the British led to very different outcomes. Unlike the French, the British were less willing to separate humankind from nature in their inquiries, which led them to seek reasonable revisions to the received, traditional knowledge about the laws of nature and the nature of man. As Daniel Robinson has explained, for the physical scientists those laws existed in a nature that is a perceptual affair. For them,

> *The laws of science must describe nature as it is experienced, not the way it "ought" to be. To the extent that Aristotle had preconceived notions about how nature "ought" to be and to the extent that succeeding generations of rationalists were guided by his preconceptions, then, to these extents, the modern era begins with the rejection of the authority of Aristotle. Bacon, the empiricist, led the British movement away from Aristotle and his Scholastic following. On the Continent, the leading spokesman for the new era was René Descartes.*[12]

Descartes was a pathfinder on the Continent but not in Britain where the paths with the beginning in Newton, Bacon, and John Locke were very different with some of them leading deep into the classical tradition and to the American colonies.

Central to the received knowledge was the primacy of the role of God's government of man and the cosmos. In France Christianity would be debased and even eventually if only temporarily banned. In Britain men had been tutored by the common law and the nature law, and they used the natural endowments of reason, memory, and skill to extract from the nature God had created the laws of nature that were operating in the physical order and the natural law that guides the moral order without bringing God into their conclusions.

In 1611 John Donne, the Dean of Saint Paul's Cathedral in London, voiced the unsettled prospect that "A new Philosophy calls all in doubt … / 'Tis all in peeces, all cohaerence gone." Donne's anxiety was overly hasty as a rapid survey will demonstrate.[13] Professor Rudolf Wittkower used Donne's conclusion to argue that in England "the whole structure of classical aesthetics was overthrown from the bottom." The last redoubt of that structure, he proclaimed, is found exactly a century later in Anthony Ashley Cooper, Third Earl of Shaftsbury (1671–1713).[14] We would be well served to review Wittkower's review.

The English were well aware of developments in France but followed their own path. Christopher Wren, Newton's great friend and collaborator and who had spent eight months in Paris in 1665–66, articulated the traditional classical position in the mid-1670s, the one that Claude Perrault would challenge in 1673 and assault in 1684. Wren explained,

> *There are two Causes of Beauty, natural and customary. … Natural is from Geometry, consisting in Uniformity (that is Equality) and Proportion. … Geometrical Figures are naturally more beautiful than other irregular; in this all consent as to a Law of Nature. Of geometrical Figures, the Square and the Circle are most beautiful, … Customary beauty arises through Familiarity or particular Inclination [that] breeds a Love to Things not in themselves lovely. Here lies the great Occasion of Errors … .*[15]

A generation later in a collection of papers Shaftesbury would expatiate on the familiar classical position. In his "Advice to the Author" he brought together nature, music, art, architecture, and morality. When a man declares to "the Students and Lovers of the Art" of music, he writes,

> *"That the Measure or Rule of HARMONY was Caprice or Will, Humour or Fashion;" 'tis not very likely he shou'd be heard with great Attention, or treated with real Gravity. For HARMONY is Harmony by Nature, let Men judg ever so ridiculously of Musick. So is Symmetry and Proportion founded still in Nature, let Mens Fancy prove ever so barbarous, or their Fashions ever so Gothick in their Architecture, Sculpture, or whatever other designing Art. 'Tis the same case, where Life and MANNERS are concerned. Virtue has the same fix'd Standard. The same Numbers, Harmony, and Proportion will have place in MORALS; and are discoverable in the Characters and Affections of Mankind; in which are laid the just Foundations of an Art and Science, superior to every other of human Practice and Comprehension.*[16]

He then quickly presents the traditional classical differentiation between universal or absolute beauty and customary or arbitrary beauty when he tells us,

> *whether the Writer be Poet, Philosopher, or of whatever kind, he is in truth no other than a copist after NATURE. His Style may be differently suted to the*

different Times he lives in, or to the different Humour of his Age or Nation: His Manner, his Dress, his Colouring may vary. But if his Drawing be uncorrect, or his Design contrary to Nature; his Piece will be found ridiculous, when it comes thorowly to be examin'd. For Nature will not be Mock'd.[17]

The imitation of nature lies behind these remarks, and beauty retains its traditional role of establishing reciprocity between object and subject. But something has changed, and it will be developed in later British authors. Louis Dupré has observed here a new emphasis on the subject at the expense of the object in that "The harmonious proportions of nature become truly beautiful only when viewed as symbolic of the mind's own harmony," a position not unlike Kant's a century later but poles apart from Claude Perrault's.[18]

Nevertheless, from 1711 through reprints and new editions down to 1790 Shaftsbury's *Characteristicks* made available the argument that harmony in the mind united an individual with a people and with the good and the beautiful, and that things such as buildings are comprehended within a unity of knowledge that embraces nature and theory and practice in aesthetics, politics, and architecture. Shaftsbury brought into the argument the ideas about an individual's common sense, a sense that is shared in common among people, as well as the role of natural knowledge and the fundamental role of reason. The argument also reaches into the equation of beauty and truth that is especially evident in architecture and the necessity of using simple forms to make these connections perceptible to the mind.[19] Here we can see the uniquely British reciprocity of bottom-up (the subject) and top-down (the object) in full swing.

Several authors who followed John Locke and who were identified with the Scottish Enlightenment wanted to know how individuals would perceive the beauty in beautiful things.

Francis Hutcheson (1694–1746), Locke's student and the protégé of Shaftsbury whose grandfather had supported and nurtured Locke, understood that to support conclusions he needed evidence, which "for him seems to be a proof from experience, which cannot be supported by other sufficient reasons."[20] "Let it be observ'd," Hutcheson wrote in 1726,

> *that in the following Papers, the Word Beauty is taken for the Idea rais'd in us, and a Sense of Beauty for our Power of receiving this Idea. ... In the following Sections, an Attempt is made to discover "what is the immediate Occasion of these pleasant Ideas, or what real Quality in the Objects ordinarily excites them."*[21]

That "real Quality" turns out to be "Uniformity amidst Variety," which produces the pleasure that beauty provides. This formula retains the reciprocity between object and subject found in classical aesthetics, but it shifts the burden from beauty in the object to beauty as the content of the subject's pleasure. It offers agreement with Locke's empiricism by arguing that while men are not endowed with innate ideas they nonetheless possess an inner sense that allows them to receive "Ideas of Beauty from all Objects in which there is Uniformity amidst Variety."[22] This capacity reveals a design or intention of the designer who is the cause of the universe and is a wise and good deity. The uniformity is exhibited in a variety that reveals itself in different genre of art objects and in different nations. An example is in the parts and proportions of buildings in different nations and among different Europeans, found in

> the ornaments in each of our five Orders, ... yet there is even among them a Proportion retain'd, a Uniformity, and Resemblance of corresponding Figures; and every Deviation in one part from that Proportion which is observ'd in the rest of the Building, is displeasing to every Eye, and destroys or diminishes at least the Beauty of the Whole.[23]

Relative beauty is a subordinate companion apprehended in the "Conformity, or a kind of Unity between the Original and the Copy," with his word copy being better read as imitation (I.IV.I.42). In poetry it appears as metaphor and in painting in resemblances. In architecture, a nonrepresentational art, "A Rude Heap of Stones" reveals an absence of absolute beauty (I.VI.I.61–2). Elsewhere we read,

> although a Cylinder, or Prism, or regular Solid, may have more original [that is, absolute] Beauty than a very acute Pyramid or Obelisk, yet the latter please more, by answering better the suppos'd Intentions of Stability, ... This may be the reason too, why Columns or Pillars look best when made a little taper from the middle, or a third from the bottom, that they may not seem top-heavy and in danger of falling. (I.IV.v)

Further on he states that the "accurate Observation" of one or two parts of a regular object, as opposed to an irregular one, "often leads to the Knowledge of the Whole: Thus we can from a Pillar or two, with an intermediate Arch, and Cornice, form a distinct Idea of a whole regular Building, if we know of what Species it is, and have its Length and Breadth" (I.VIII.ii.78–9). Perceiving the pleasures of relative beauty, then, depends upon the building's imitation of its "species" that presents the appearance of a building serving a particular purpose. It is no stretch to see that Hutcheson draws a parallel between the order of the universe and the order of a beautiful building, and the connection of that order with the end or purpose of the universe and of the building.

Hutcheson explains that different people bring different "Tempers, and past Circumstances" to perception which provokes different "Associations of Ideas" in different people. These differences must not be confused with "Conceptions ... of Beauty or Deformity." For example, we join "the faint Light in Gothick Buildings" to "Ideas of something Divine" (I.V.xi–xii.67–9). As a consequence he gives a very important role to custom, education, and example, the topic of Section VII. Education may "make an unattentive Goth imagine that his Countrymen have attain'd the Perfection of Architecture; and an Aversion to their Enemys the Romans, may have join'd some disagreeable Ideas to their very Buildings, and excited them to their Demolition." But more importantly, education and custom may allow us to "grow conscious of a Pleasure far superior to what common Performances excite" (I.VII.iii.73).

Hutcheson twined this inquiry with one that concerned "our Ideas of Virtue or Moral Good." In the former he argued against Descartes; here he takes on Hobbes. People do not do the good solely out of self-interest but because we attain happiness by perceiving that which is good. We do so independently of our will through our "moral Sense, which makes rational Actions appear Beautiful" (II.I.1.89–91). This sense may be sharpened by "Custom, Education, Example, or Study ... but they never could have made us apprehend Actions as amiable or odious" (II.I.vii.99). The "universal Foundation of this moral Sense" is love or benevolence with no anticipation of personal advantage but which is repaid with esteem, gratitude, honor, and so on (II.IV.1.136–7; II.V.1ff).

While beauty gives us an immediate pleasure the good operates a little differently. It provides us with happiness in our reflection on benevolent actions. We do not hold innate ideas about beauty and harmony or in the benevolent and good. Instead, the "Author of Nature," equipped us with the

> Sense of Beauty ... [and] has given us a Moral Sense, to direct our Actions, and to give us still nobler Pleasures; so that while we are only intending the Good of others, we undesignedly promote our own greatest private Good. (II.I.viii.99–100)

This good of others is the common good or the public good, which we can see as the highest good. Shaftsbury held this understanding of the aesthetic and the moral, and it held through Hume, but things change with Kant who emphasizes disinterest, which moves it out of the public arena.[24] It runs the full gamut in the response from pure and disinterested to pricks of conscience at the opposite extreme. "Chastity is itself a powerful Charm in the Eyes of the Dissolute, even when they are attempting to destroy it." In like manner, benevolence disposes a person to "a Love of Poetry, Musick, the Beauty of Nature in rural Scenes, a Contempt of other selfish Pleasures of the external Senses ... . a Delight in and Emulation of every thing which is gallant, generous and friendly" (II.VI.v.171).

In 1757 David Hume (1711–76) made the most persuasive argument about how bottom-up (individual judgments) and top-down (consensus among the best disinterested judges) guide taste, a word he uses to refer to aesthetic judgments, in assessing the relationship between customary beauty and the indubitable presence of universal beauty. In a brief essay "Of the Standard of Taste" he had posited that the basis of inquiries into judgments of taste "is the same with that of all the practical sciences, experience; nor are they any thing but general observations, concerning what has been universally found to please in all countries and in all ages" (210). "It appears then, that amidst all the variety and caprices of taste, there are certain general principles of approbation or blame, whose influence a careful eye may trace in all operations of the mind. Some particular forms or qualities, from the original structure of the internal fabric, are calculated to please, and others to displease" (214).

There is, however, that "species of philosophy, which ... represents the impossibility of ever attaining any standard of taste. The difference, it is said, is very wide between [rational] judgment and sentiment [which deals with taste]."[25]

The sentiments alone provide no reliable, reasoned judgments. Neither do "geometric truth and exactness." These can only provide guidance that is then superseded in actual beauty (211f). Beauty offers pleasure, and pleasure resides in the sentiment that may be sound or defective.

> *If in the sound state in the organs, there be an entire or a considerable uniformity of sentiment among men, we may thence derive an idea of the perfect and universal beauty. ... Though some objects, by the structure of the mind, be naturally calculated to give pleasure, it is not to be expected, that in every individual the pleasure will be equally felt. (215)*

Furthermore, "it must be allowed, that there are certain qualities in objects, which are fitted by nature to produce those particular feelings" (217). "Thus, though the principles of taste be universal, and nearly, if not entirely the same in all men; yet few are qualified to give judgment on any work of art, or establish their own sentiment as the standard of beauty" (228). The "true standard of taste and beauty" is found in the "joint verdict" of critics with a "Strong sense, united to delicate sentiment, improved by practice, perfected by comparison, and cleared of all prejudice" (229).

Hutcheson had called attention to architecture's necessity of serving utility, which he identified as offering relative beauty while leaving intrinsic beauty to the Fine Arts. Utility received an additional dimension when Henry Home, Lord Kames (1696–1782) worked decorum into that equation. Dwelling houses include palaces, he wrote, and both must exhibit "congruity," which means the identification of its status. A palace is a dwelling of an aristocrat who occupies a position of authority, and it has the duty to be exemplary of the good and the beautiful, a model for people enjoying the liberty that we saw Shaftsbury praise. It must therefore please the eye, which requires the "Regularity and proportion" that are intrinsic to beauty.[26]

Kames also takes up imitation in architecture. It is "original" rather than imitative as poetry and painting are. In them variety may abound, but in "original" works "the timid hand is guided by rule and compass; and accordingly in architecture strict regularity and uniformity are studied, as far as consistent with utility"[27] (702). ("Original" here does not mean without precedent.) Regularity, uniformity, proportion, and congruity "are all equally essential" (706). But he dissents from other aspects of imitation, as when he states that proportions that are agreeable to the eye have nothing to do with the proportions that music uses to charm the ear. Nor do the "reasoning and philosophy" of Vitruvius and his successors (whom he does not name) validate them. But he explicitly rejects Perrault's position that in the columnar orders

> *the beauty of these proportions is entirely the effect of custom. This betrays ignorance of human nature, which evidently delights in proportion, as well as in regularity, order, and propriety. ... [I]f these proportions had not originally been agreeable, they could not have been established by custom.*[28]

The beauty may not be an analogue of nature's beauty (although he does not deny this), but it is squarely in the nature of man to take pleasure in the perception of intrinsic, universal, absolute, enduring beauty.

Rather quickly the ground supporting this position ran out and the source of pleasure moved from perception to sensation. The Lockean perceptions that Hutcheson had mentioned and that he and others had built on were displaced by extrinsic qualities that provided associations for the pleasure of the mind. Sir Joshua Reynolds said so in the 15 *Discourses on Art* delivered to the Members of the Royal Academy and printed separately from 1769 onward. Even though he gave only a few brief comment about architecture, its presence here solidified its identity with painting and sculpture as a Fine Art. He acknowledged that architecture is not a representational art (his term was "imitative art") but was, like music and poetry, one that "applies itself ... directly to the imagination, without the intervention of any kind of imitation." It does so "by means of association of ideas." Ancient buildings call to mind our natural "veneration for antiquity," and the "ancient customs and manners [conjured by] ... the castles of the barons of ancient chivalry" are "sure to give us delight." Now Sir John Vanbrugh, whose works had fallen out of favor across the century, is rehabilitated in a telling comment. "Vanbrugh appears to have had recourse to some principles of the Gothick architecture; which, though not so ancient as the Grecian, is more so to our imagination, with which the artist is more concerned than with absolute truth."[29] Now comes Romanticism and Richard Payne Knight who tells us that our encounters with nature, principally in viewing landscape, and in particular a manufactured picturesque landscape, provide the pleasant sensations we cherish. In differentiating this beauty from the sublime he glosses the term beauty in its "customary idiom." "[N]ot only in English, but in all the other polished languages of Europe, both ancient and modern; kalos in the Greek, *pulcher* in the Latin, *bello* in the Italian, and *beau* in the French, being constantly applied to moral and intellectual, as well as to physical or material qualities."[30] But the gloss carries a hollow sentiment. That language, written in the first decade of the new century, had behind it the momentum of a century in which the British had avoided the dismemberment that had been achieved on the Continent.

Behind the thoughts that carried the words to Knight we find that while custom trumps theory, custom must be digested with reason and experience and be in concord with our very nature. We might note that here custom is another word for tradition and that this position is held in the land of the common law that is congruent with the natural law within the classical tradition.

BRITAIN'S COLONIAL STUDENTS BECOME AMERICANS

The British colonies in the North American were peopled primarily by emigrants from Britain. They were governed from England, and England was their home country. The colonists who would cut their ties with their mother country and carve out a new nation had been schooled in British traditions in law and architecture. Like their home-country countrymen they had little truck with the new developments in the intellectual realm in France. The problems the colonists had were with their distant and increasingly overweening overseers across the sea, and when it came time for them to "dissolve the political bonds" with those who had proven themselves tyrants, they did something never before done. They founded a new nation on a proposition, one that was discovered through reasoning about the nature of man, one that had to be proven and that they, imperfect men that they were, set out to validate. It was the proposition that men govern best when they govern themselves and imitate the best possible model of government, which is perceptible in the order, harmony, and proportion of nature's moral order. The tutor in this enterprise was the fund of actual experiences of men across the centuries and in their unique experiences in governing themselves in their own religious and civil orders. Thomas Jefferson put it quite succinctly: "Every species of government has its specific principles. Ours perhaps are more peculiar than these of any other in the universe. It is a composition of the freest principles of the English constitution, with others derived from natural right and natural reason."[31] The words are from his recently printed *Notes on the State of Virginia* that he sent to James Madison from Paris on September 17, 1787, which coincidently was the date the Constitution's drafting was completed in Philadelphia.[32]

Historians of architecture, in their zeal to find a leading place for the United States in their narrative, identified it in the buildings in the later years of the nineteenth century that served the uses of the industrial, commercial revolution. The top-most building in Fletcher's "Tree" is a commercial office building, the Flatiron in New York by Daniel H. Burnham completed in 1902. It is emblematic of the newest era in his sequence of styles, and used the new technologies introduced in the dynamic modern era. Only the building's refusal to eschew traditional forms prevents its being admitted among the first icons of Modernism.

This narrative fails to account for the originality of the architecture that served the new federal republic with buildings that it labels as inferior if precocious examples of the neo classicism that Europeans would produce. The narrative misses why they appear as they do and what their content is.

They were built to serve and express the purposes of the role their users and residents played in the civil order. They are, in other words, squarely within the classical tradition, and their builders were that tradition's heirs and stewards. The Founders looked to that tradition for guidance and to their experience, reason, and judgment to amend it to produce the best possible regime. They knew this was not the same as the best regime or the best buildings but the best possible regime and buildings within traditions of governing and building that were always capable of improvement by absorbing suitable innovations. And they understood that they were to be based on the imitation of nature, which provided the common foundation for both. This is the nature as understood in the classical tradition, the nature that is omnipresent in the Founder's thought and rhetoric, that held the events and the accumulations that run back to ancient Greece, that the Renaissance had given new content, life, importance, and currency to, that the British civil order had reinforced with its millennium of experience with two complementary sources of authority in governing, top down and bottom up. The Founders charged their former overlord with losing the balance between head and members and moving into tyranny. Their antidote to tyranny was to spread the authoritative institutions in a ramified, descending network with the family, whose individual members were educated, informed, and involved citizens, as the foundation of the whole structure.

The nature that they imitated, the nature that runs through the western, classical tradition, did not depend upon any particular divinity for its content of the good, the true, and the beautiful that collectively constitute justice. Nature endures unchanged and unknowable in its completeness in its order, harmony, and proportionality, unchanged across time and in so far as the affairs of humankind are concerned. It includes humankind, and is governed by "the Laws of Nature and of Nature's God" with indifference to god's identity or even his presence, just as he is in the lines: "for the support of this Declaration, with a firm reliance on the protection of divine Providence, we mutually pledge to each other our Lives, our Fortunes and our sacred Honor." Individuals may seek that divine protection according to their lights, which is quite different from invoking it to justify the nation's actions or the arrangement of its institutions. The work of the Founders was the work of like-minded men who lived their lives within the classical–Christian tradition, who shared broad beliefs about the nature of God, of the world, and of mankind and who were willing to overlook minor differences of opinion and even fundamental differences of religious belief in the interest of the greater good that came from a common, human devotion to a public good. They sought to assure the perpetuation of that same good will by excluding religious authority from the making and executing of laws and judgments. The God who inhabited the recent span of the nearly two millennia of that tradition was congruent with those laws of nature, but those laws are not dependent on that God or extensions of him or of any other divinity. Nature is imitated to provide the authority to order and govern a free people who enjoy the liberty to live their civil lives within a community with no unbidden meddling by God in its or their affairs. Those are the laws that "entitle" their civil order to enjoy "the separate and equal station" with other civil orders.

Thomas Jefferson found the roots of the American Revolution in the British government's unjustified intrusions into the colonies' affairs. These interfered in the exercise of the rights that "nature has given to all men ... of establishing new societies, under such laws and regulations as to them shall seem most likely to promote public happiness." The colonists had carried those rights to North America just as their "Saxon ancestors had, under this universal law," carried them to Britain.[33] In Britain they established "that system of laws which has so long been the glory and protection of that country."[34] The government in England has proven incapable of protecting those natural rights. As Jefferson put it in the Declaration dated July 4, these rights are founded on "self-evident" truths, the first of which is that "all men are created equal, that they are endowed by their Creator with certain unalienable Rights, that among these are Life, Liberty and the pursuit of Happiness. ..."

The Founders contrived institutions that recognized its citizens as the common law had, as individuals, each one a free and lawful person (*liber et legalis homo*) and now explicitly a member of a whole body of citizens that would govern itself by majority rule while honoring minority rights. The Founders benefited from the experience and tradition of their British predecessors and avoided the traps that would soon be springing across the Channel. They necessarily worked within existing contingent circumstances, which left the deep fault of excluding many people. Many of the faults have been remedied, but conspicuous exclusions remain.

We know this because the ideals were articulated in timeless rhetoric that set the standard of justice and leads us to recognize the facts that fall short of the truths while that same rhetoric persuades men of good will to identify the facts that are incongruent with those truths and empowers them to work to banish the shortcomings.

The new nation's first civil order proved barely adequate to win independence, and in 1787 the Founders set about drafting a new Constitution that, amended, endures. To become the law of the land the whole body of citizens, directly or indirectly, was called on to ratify it. To rally New Yorkers to that end three Founders penned 87 essays collected as the *Federalist Papers* that provide a penetrating understanding of classical political theory and practice. Here we find a still instructive argument based on the congruity between the enduring, unchangeable *jus naturale* present in a reasonable nature and its imitation in the best available articulation of the *jus civile*, which was their immediate concern. Consider a few passages. In *Federalist # 51* James Madison reminds us, "what is government itself but the greatest of all reflections on human nature? If men were angels, no government would be necessary." "Justice," after all, "is the end of government. It is the end of civil society." Later, in *Federalist # 78*, Alexander Hamilton tests the positive (statutory) law of the *jus civile* against a higher standard, which is "the nature and the reason of the thing," or *jus naturale*.

In the beginning of *Federalist # 31* we find Hamilton writing, "In disquisitions of every kind there are certain primary truths, or first principles, upon which all subsequent reasonings must depend." He offers four examples from geometry, including "all right angles are equal." Among axioms in "ethics and politics" are these: "that there cannot be an effect without a cause; [and] that the means ought to be proportioned to the end. ... " A little further on he presents "other truths in the two latter sciences which, if they cannot pretend to rank in the class of axioms, are yet such direct inferences from them, and so obvious in themselves, and so agreeable to the natural and unsophisticated dictates of common sense that ... [are] almost equally irresistible." Only disorder, strong self-interest, passion, or prejudice can refuse assent to any of this.

The Founders understood that the relationship between natural law and the institutions of the civil order is always dynamic. In *Federalist # 9* Hamilton observes, "The science of politics ... like most other sciences, has received great improvements." He identifies them, and concludes, "these are wholly new discoveries, or have made their principal progress towards perfection in modern times." He enlarges on this topic in *Federalist #14* explaining that "the people of America ... whilst they have paid a decent regard to the opinions, of former times, and other nations, they have not suffered a blind veneration for antiquity, for custom, or for names [i.e., titles]" and have brought about "numerous innovations displayed on the American theater in favor of private rights and public happiness."

Hamilton praises his fellow Founders for pursuing a "new and more noble course" that would introduce liberty to people who had never experienced it. Before the events following from Bastille Day had gained momentum Jefferson had written from France to his old tutor in law George Wythe, "If anybody thinks that kings, nobles, or priests are good conservators of the public happiness send them here. It is the best school in the universe to cure them of that folly."[35]

In making one nation out of many parts a crucial role was played by synoecism, the process in which lesser institutional units such as families and towns combine with others and with states to enlarge a civil order and make a nation with each lesser entity retaining its identity and its realm of action for fulfilling duties appropriate to it. The natural law and common law traditions of the American constitutional system seek to preserve the liberty of each individual, and synoecism serves that end. It permeates the civil order where top down authority coordinates the actions welling up from the bottom that involves myriads of institutions.[36] Civility conjoined with pluralism maintains comity, and the public good is served when citizens recognize that fulfilling duties is necessary to assure the enjoyment of their rights and secure their happiness.

At work here is the imitation of nature, which makes only three cameo appearances in the *Federalist Papers* always disguised as replication, but its implicit presence is central.[37] It plays the role of *natura naturans*, the verb that applies natural law to particular circumstances with particular attention to human nature as we found it developed earlier in this chapter. The Founders made institutions of government by imitating the always inadequate natural aspirations of men to be angels and who seek justice by establishing limits and counterforces to their failures. They also make subsidiary entities that facilitate the work of those institutions. The result is a complex ordering: of institutions that are aimed at the good; of the arrangements that facilitate the work of the institutions; and of the individuals who fulfill their civil duties as they pursue their happiness. The best constitution establishes a reasoned proportionality between these three elements that are separated and counterbalanced to address a fundamental principle of natural law, which is that justice cannot be served when a person is a judge in his own case. They also recognize the truth of the axiom Lord Acton could formulate, that "Power corrupts. Absolute power corrupts absolutely."

EDUCATING AMERICANS ABOUT ARCHITECTURE

The daunting task of the new nation's first office holders under the new Constitution was to make a functioning government. Tradition, experience, and judgment were their guides as they invented, trimmed, and recut the pieces of the new nation's fabric of law. They faced a similar task when they set about equipping the new national government with the buildings that would serve and express the purposes of the institutions that built and used them.

The new nation was impoverished in exemplary buildings and experienced builders, but its former overlord offered the greatest help now just as it had before it had won its independence.[38] The ultimate roots were in ancient Rome but with the growth and grafts of centuries. The Gothic was the indigenous architecture when Henry VIII broke with Rome. Elizabethans added something classical but distinctly English that expressed England's unique place among the nations when the Continent was using the architecture that had first grown in ancient Rome.

In England until the century that held Shakespeare's death builders saw no need to pay more serious attention to that alternative, which some were calling "regular architecture." When they did, they adopted a version Palladio had recently exhibited, not the architecture current across the Channel. When the Stuart successors to the Tudors sought to reconnect England with Rome, James I had Inigo Jones demonstrate that Stonehenge had been built as a Roman temple, and in 1619 he had Jones build the Banqueting Hall, the first conspicuous essay of classical architecture in England. In 1638 Charles I had him produce a grand plan that would have made the new hall a trinket in Whitehall Palace. Meanwhile, Jones built the noble "barn" for Saint Paul's Covent Garden in London (1630–33), the Church of England's first new church. Palladio's unelaborated architecture served well as an English contrast to the exuberant, post-Trentine architecture flourishing in Catholic lands. When building resumed after England's revolution and restoration the nation was ready for a grander public face and found it in buildings that were like and unlike those on the Continent. Examples are Sir Christopher Wren's Saint Paul's Cathedral, his (incomplete) modernization of Hampton Court Palace, the Navy's accommodation at Greenwich, and Vanbrugh's design for the nation's gift to John Churchill, Duke of Marlborough, victor over Louis XIV at Blenheim.

Before Wren had finished Saint Paul's Cathedral Palladio had achieved a new foothold. Lord Shaftsbury had censured the Cathedral and the other Wrenaissance buildings that seemed tinged with a whiff of Catholicism, Divine Right monarchy, and the Stuart dynasty. The English Milordi trouping in their numbers on the Grand Tour were not impressed by the richly molded surfaces and broken shapes that disrupted geometric clarity with variety in the buildings of Gianlorenzo Bernini and Francesco Borromini in Rome and even Baldassare Longhena's in Venice. By 1725 when Hutcheson's *Inquiry* appeared Jones' appellation as Vitruvius by his student, John Webb, was printed and Palladio had superseded Wren et al.[39] When Hume's essay of 1757 appeared taste had definitively shifted toward Palladio. By the time Kames' first edition in 1762 came out the Wrennaisance excesses were a thing of the past, although as we saw, Reynolds would find it imaginative.

By then a virtual avalanche of books supporting the taste formed on Palladio's architecture had further buried Wren's currency. Colen Campbell's multi-volume folio *Vitruvius Britannicus* that starred Jones began appearing in 1715. Although its first building was Wren's "Noble Frabric" of Saint Paul's, its stated purpose was to abolish any role for Bernini, Fontana, and Borromini with their "capricious Ornament, which must at last end in the Gothick."[40] Palladio was another antidote. Giacomo Leoni's five-year effort (1716–20) produced a translation of his *Quattro libri*, although its altered plates revealed the continuing hold of Wren et al., which Isaac Ware, in his own 1738 translation with near facsimile plates, condemned.[41] Ware dedicated it to Richard Boyle, Lord Burlington (1694–1753) whose sponsorship of Palladio changed British architecture. He "wanted to make true what Shaftesbury had propagated in his writings."[42] He had visited Italy in 1719, and in 1725–9 with William Kent designed and built his country house in Chiswick.

Based on Palladio's Villa Rotunda, it had the hard-edge linearity and stark clarity of Ware's plates rather than the soft appearance of the original's woodcut images and the building itself. Burlington's building's geometric clarity of square and circle offered to the eyes "the Square and the Circle [that] are most beautiful ..." as we saw Wren saying. When Sir Robert Walpole, a Whig and the first Prime Minister, had Colen Campbell begin Houghton Hall in 1722 Palladianism was validated for the governing aristocratic class. In 1725 Leoni published a translation of Alberti's *de re aedificatoria* based on Cosimo Bartoli's sixteenth century Italian translation. Here, more expansively than in Palladio, the British could find a position that Shaftsbury retained, which held that the visual and the moral were present in conjunction with one another in sensible and intelligible forms of things beautifully made.[43] Alberti's treatise could also support the important point concerning the role of empirical confirmation of the mind's aesthetic judgments and the role of education in informing that judgment.

Palladio's and Alberti's large, expensive books were soon supplemented by abbreviations in small, inexpensive handbooks for builders, mechanics, and workmen. The canonic orders disembodied from proportionate whole bodies were the most savory meats in these stews. Occupying the niche between treatises and handbooks were the "orders" books of models both ancient and modern. The long-popular folio that Roland Freart Sieur de Chambray published in France in 1650 reached England in 1664 in John Evelyn's translation with several later editions. The "*Orders*," he wrote, were "no other than the very *Elements* of *Architecture*," with the three Greek orders being quite enough. It was "a superfluous thing [if] we should pretend to augment their number."[44] Alberti appeared as the "most knowing in the *Art of Building*, …"[45] Among moderns, "The first of all is without any contest the famous *Andrea Palladio*," who was even "the incomparable Palladio."[46]

In 1753 James Gibbs wrote, "Palladio has given a Rule which cannot undergo any considerable change, without altering the just Proportions of Columns."[47] Palladio was supplemented but not supplanted by the new fruits emerging from Herculaneum after 1738 and Pompeii 10 years later. At mid-century exacting publications of both familiar and previously unrecorded ancient buildings added to the offerings that could be incorporated into Palladianism, with the many buildings by Robert Adam (1728–92) providing valuable lessons.[48]

Without these books there would have been no training in architecture for Thomas Jefferson. English gentlemen with their involvement in architecture were the models of culture for Virginia planters, and Jefferson, like his peers, followed their example.[49] But he took to architecture more keenly than most. He also had a deeper understanding of architecture as a civic art that facilitates the citizens' pursuit of happiness. The American architecture that he established was as important a contribution to the classical tradition as that of the ancient Romans and the masters of the Renaissance. His buildings have been well studied and little about them will be added here. Less well understood is the theory side of his architecture, which will be the subject of the next chapter.

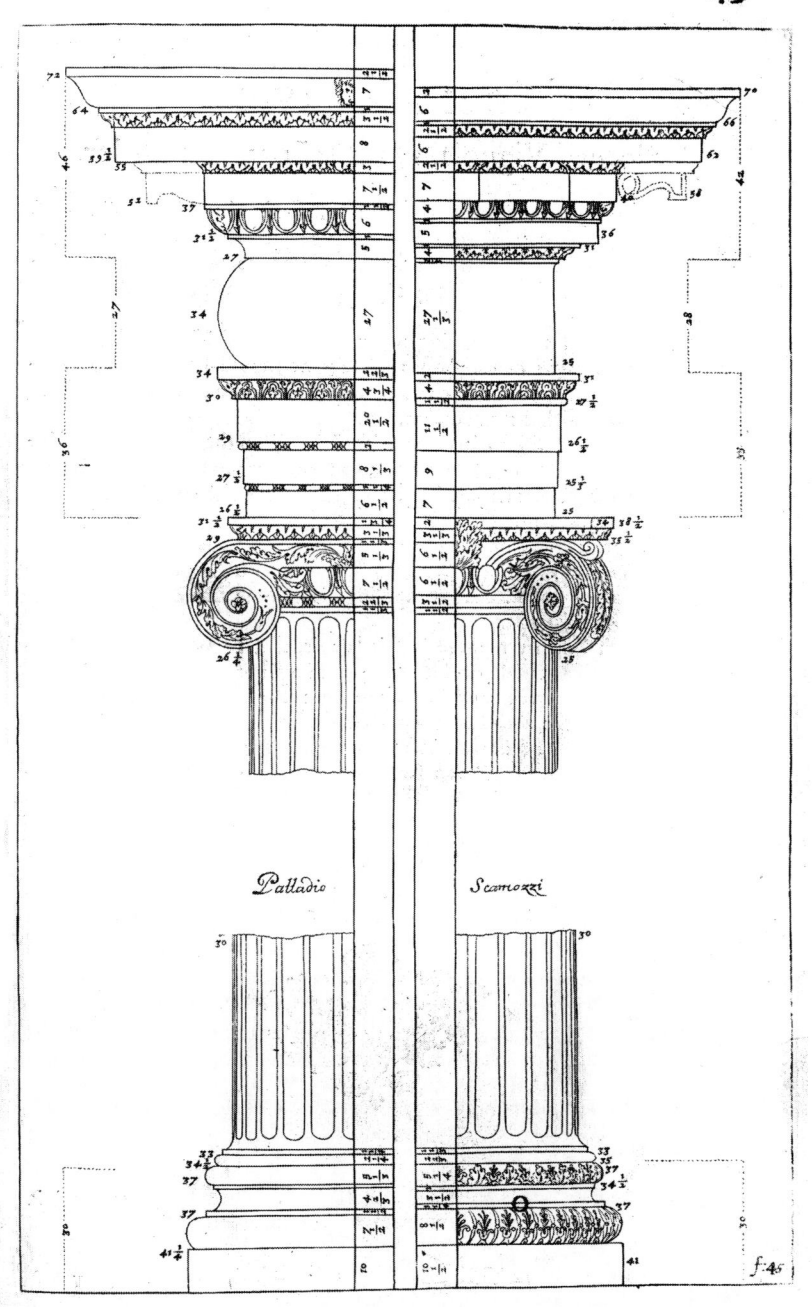

7.1 Roland Freart Sieur de Chambray, Palladio and Scamozzi, Ionic Order
Source: A parallel of the antient architecture with the modern: in a collection of ten principal authors who have written upon the five orders … Made English … By John Evelyn … 3rd edn (London: Printed by T.W. for D. Browne, 1723), 49. Image provided by the University of Notre Dame's Architecture Library.

NOTES

1. Useful reviews for the political order are Manlio Bellomo, *The Common Legal Past of Europe, 1000–1800*, trans. Lydia G. Cochrane (Washington: Catholic University Press of America, 1995), and Diarmaid MacCulloch, *Christianity: The First Three Thousand Years* (New York: Viking, 2009), Part IV.

2. Richard O'Sullivan, "The Philosophy of the Common Law," (1949) in B.A. Wortley, ed., *The Spirit of the Common Law* (Tenbury Wells, Worcs.: Fowler Wright Books, 1965), 75.

3. This is the language in its fourth form, from 1225, quoted in Theodore F.T. Plucknett, *A Concise History of the Common Law*, 5th edn (London: Butterworth & Co., 1956), 23.

4. O'Sullivan, "The Philosophy of the Common Law," 81.

5. TJ to Roger C. Wrightman, Monticello, June 24, 1826, in *Writings*, ed. Merrill D. Peterson (New York: Library of America, 1984), 1516–17.

6. Lawrence M. Friedman, *A History of American Law* (New York: Simon and Schuster: A Touchstone Book, 1973), 19.

7. See the discussion in Hadley Arkes, *Constitutional Illusions and Anchoring Truths: The Touchstone of the Natural Law* (Cambridge: Cambridge University Press, 2010), 35–6.

8. O'Sullivan, "Natural Law and Common Law," 99.

9. O'Sullivan, "Natural Law and Common Law," 103–5. My thoughts on this topic are deeply indebted to Hadley Arkes; see for example *First Things: An Inquiry into the First Principles of Morals and Justice* (Princeton: Princeton University Press, 1986), and *Beyond the Constitution* (Princeton: Princeton University Press, 1990).

10. That self-evident truths shared by a community do not have the same status relative to truth as the principles of identity and of non-contradiction is lucidly set forth in Gregory, *The Unintended Reformation*, 213ff, and passim. See Arkes, *First Things*, 51f, where he discusses what Kant called an "apodictic" or necessary truth, one that "cannot be denied without falling into self-contradiction. The proposition 'There is truth' is a proposition of that kind," as opposed to an analytic statement: "'A triangle has three sides.'"

11. When Prime Minister Margaret Thatcher attended the bicentennial July 14 celebrations in Paris in 1989 that included a celebration of the Declaration of the Rights of Man and of the Citizen, she declared that she did not see what all the fuss was about since England had done its bill of rights a century before the French got around to it, and did so with considerably less bloodshed. Her hostess gift to the French President François Mitterrand was a nicely bound edition of Charles Dickens, *A Tale of Two Cities*.

12. Daniel N. Robinson, *An Intellectual History of Psychology*, revised edn (New York: Macmillan; London: Collier Macmillan, 1981), 258.

13. For early symptoms see David Watkin, *Morality and Architecture: The Development of a Theme in Architectural History and Theory from the Gothic Revival to the Modern Movement* (Chicago: University of Chicago Press, 1977). For present-day concerns, see Gregory, *The Unintended Reformation*.

14. Wittkower, *Architectural Principles*, 3rd edn, 150. He revised his view of Shaftsbury in a later paper, "English Neo-Palladianism, the Landscape Garden, China and the Enlightenment," (1969), in *Palladio and Palladianism* (New York: George Braziller, 1974), 179. The presentation here is focused on the role of these ideas in America. For this material in the context of English architecture Henry Francis Mallgrave, *Modern Architectural Theory: A Historical Survey, 1673–1968* (Cambridge et al: Cambridge

University Press, 2005), Chapter 3, is useful. For Wittkower's Modernist historiography see Alina A. Payne, "Rudolf Wittkower and Architectural Principles in the Age of Modernism," *Journal of the Society of Architectural Historians*, 53 (1994), 322–42.

15 Christopher Wren, "Tracts on Architecture: Tract I," in Lydia M. Soo, *Wren's "Tracts" on Architecture and Other Writings* (Cambridge: Cambridge University Press, 1998), 154. Soo ignores imitation's role. She notes parallels with Alberti's ideas and inexplicably has Wren wholeheartedly embracing Claude Perrault's customary beauty, as at 135–8. For bibliography on this topic see Pierre de la Ruffinière du Prey, *Hawksmoor's London Churches: Architecture and Theology* (Chicago and London: University of Chicago, 2000), 10 and 146–7, n. 19.

16 Anthony Ashley Cooper Third Earl of Shaftsbury, "Soliloquy: or Advice to an Author," in *Characteristicks of Men, Manners, Opinions, Times*, 5th edition (London: [no publisher listed]), 1732, 1:III.iii.353; only a portion is quoted in Wittkower, *Architectural* Principles, 3rd edn, 142.

17 Anthony Ashley Cooper Third Earl of Shaftsbury, "Soliloquy: or Advice to an Author," in *Characteristicks of Men, Manners, Opinions, Times*, 5th edition (London: [no publisher listed]), 1732, 1.III.iii.354.

18 Louis Dupré, *The Enlightenment and the Intellectual Foundations of Modern Culture* (New Haven and London: Yale University Press, 2004), 109, 88. At 102 he states that Shaftsbury "vaguely intuited" Kant's theory of the beautiful, "namely, that the aesthetic experience originates in the primary awareness of harmony between the faculties of the mind and the represented object."

19 This material is especially rich in Anthony Ashley Cooper Third Earl of Shaftsbury, "Sensus Communis: an Essay on the Freedom of Wit and Humour," in *Characteristicks of Men, Manners, Opinions, Times*, 5th edition (London: [no publisher listed]), 3: 58–150.

20 Wolfgang Leidhold, "Introduction" to Francis Hutcheson, *An Inquiry into the Original of Our Ideas of Beauty and Virtue in Two Treatises*, revised edn, ed. Wolfgang Leidhold (Indianapolis: Liberty Fund, 2008), xvi.

21 Francis Hutcheson, *An Inquiry*, Treatise I, Section I, paragraph ix, 23; emphasis added. Here the counterpart to the sense of beauty is the harmony that "denotes our pleasant Ideas arising from Composition of Sounds."

22 I.VI.x.67. For the complicated role of Locke in aesthetic theory involving Hutcheson, Burke, and Joseph Priestley, see Dabney Townsend, "Lockean Aesthetics," *Journal of Aesthetics and At Criticism*, 49 (1991), 349–61.

23 I.III.viii.41; see also I.VI.v.64–5; emphasis added. Alberti's definition of beauty retains its hold here. For proportion we can read proportionality.

24 See Dabney Townsend, "From Shaftsbury to Kant," *Journal of the History of Ideas*, 48 (1987), esp. part III.

25 In David Hume, "Of the Standard of Taste," in *Four Dissertations* (London: Millar, 1757), 208. Subsequent citations in parentheses are from this source.

26 Henry Home, Lord Kames, *Elements of Criticism*, 6th edn, 1785, ed. Peter Jones, vol. 2 (Indianapolis: Liberty Fund, 2005), 706. Subsequent citations in parentheses are from this source.

27 Kames reviews the various arts' relationship to imitation and originality in XVIII, 373. Only painting and sculpture unqualifiedly qualify.

28 Kames, 705, names Perrault's "comparison of the ancients and moderns," a book from 1688 by Claude's brother Charles. Claude Perrault's *Ordonnance* was available and quoted from Chapter 13 in its first translation into English, in 1708, reissued in 1722.

29 Sir Joshua Reynolds, *Discourses on Art*, ed. Stephen O. Mitchell from the definitive 1797 edition (Indianapolis et al: Bobbs-Merrill, the Library of Liberal Arts, 1965), 204–5.

30 Richard Payne Knight, *An Analytical Inquiry into the Principles of Taste*, 2nd edn (London: Luke Howard, 1805), Intro., 6, 10.

31 Thomas Jefferson, *Notes on the State of Virginia*, ed. William Peden (New York and London: W.W. Norton, 1954), query VIII.

32 TJ to James Madison, Paris, Sept. 17, 1787, *The Papers of Thomas Jefferson Digital Edition*, ed. Barbara B. Oberg and J. Jefferson Looney (Charlottesville: University of Virginia Press, Rotunda, 2008).

33 TJ, "A Summary View of the Rights of British America," (1774) in *Writings*, 105–22, 105–6. See also "Autobiography," in *Writings*, 3–101, 9.

34 TJ, "A Summary View of the Rights of British America," in *Writings*, 105–22, 105–6.

35 TJ to George Wythe, Paris, August 13, 1786; in *Writings*, 859.

36 Do not underestimate the number of entities in the lowest realm. By one count there are 37,000 "special-purpose units of local government (transit authorities, water and sewer agencies, and community college districts, for example)" and 16,519 townships in 20 northern states; David Rusk, *Cities Without Suburbs: Fourth Edition: A Census 2010 Perspective* (Washington, D.C.: Woodrow Wilson Center Press, 2013), 127, 134.

37 In numbers 16 (Hamilton), and 41 and 63 (Madison). These are similar to imitation's appearance in the treatises on architecture mentioned in Chapter 1.

38 Louis P. Nelson, *The Beauty of Holiness: Anglicanism and Architecture in Colonial South Carolina* (Chapel Hill: University of North Carolina Press, 2008) reveals the indebtedness of that rich colony's best builders to sources, often verbal, in London in the first half of the eighteenth century. That colony's connections with the British colonies in the Caribbean are well known.

39 For Webb's term for Jones see his "Memoirs Relating to the Life and Writings of Inigo Jones, Esq.," in Caroline van Eck, ed., *British Architectural Theory, 1540–1750: An Anthology of Texts* (Aldershot, Hants; and Burlington, Vermont: Ashgate, 2003), 99. This book offers an important frame and complement to the material presented here.

40 Colen Campbell, *Vitruvius Britannicus*, 3 vols (London: printed by the author, 1715–25), I: unpaginated introduction. Quoted in van Eck, ed., *British Architectural Theory*, 231.

41 Andrea Palladio, *The Four Books of Architecture* (London: Isaac Ware, 1738), in Isaac Ware's "Avertisement," a. Ware also noted that a 1735 edition "is done with so little understanding, and so much negligence, that it cannot but give offence to the judicious." For the outpouring of Palladio editions, consult the Royal Institute of British Architects Library catalogue. See also Kruft, *A History*, 240. Leoni's publication did include the original Italian text and a French translation.

42 Wittkower, "English Neo-Palladianism," 179.

43 Retained, in the sense that Shaftsbury's aesthetic retains these four elements in the conjunction they had traditionally had, as, for example, in Alberti; see David Kipp, "Alberti's 'Hidden' Theory of Visual Art," *British Journal of Aesthetics*, 24 (1984), 231–40. See also Dabney Townsend, "Shaftsbury's Aesthetic Theory," *Journal of Aesthetics and Art Criticism*, 41 (1982), 205–13.

44 Roland Freart Sieur de Chambray, *The Whole Body of Ancient and Modern Architecture Comprehending … Ten Principal Authors Who Have Written upon the Five Orders*, trans. John Evelyn (London: J. Wilkinson et al, 1680), 8. The title within the book is given as

The Parallel of the Antient Architecture with the Modern and colloquially as *A Parallel of the Orders*. The title is slightly misleading. The ancient orders are shown one to a page, the modern ones as pairs.

45   Freart, *The Whole Body*, 23.

46   Freart, *The Whole Body*, 22; 123.

47   James Gibbs, *Rules for Drawing the Several Parts of Architecture*, 3rd edn (London: W. Innes, et al., 1753), 1.

48   Robert Adam joined in on this activity; see his *Ruins of the Palace of the Emperor Diocletian at Spalatro in Dalmatia* (London: for the author, 1764).

49   This point, made by Giles Worsley, is stressed in W. Barksdale Maynard, *Architecture in the United States, 1800–1850* (New Haven and London: Yale University Press, 2002), 59ff. Maynard's general argument is that in this period England was the major source for what Americans were building and thinking about architecture.

8

Jefferson, Architect, and the Classical Tradition

IMITATING NATURE IN AMERICA

The standing of Thomas Jefferson as a person and a statesman is fraught with contradictions: a leading figure among a band of aristocrats who founded a government based on the authority of "We the People;" a Founder who owned vast tracts where over his lifetime the hundreds of slaves he owned to work it could not produce the bounty necessary to sustain the expenditures of the life he lived but who believed that every man ought to own land in order to be a fearless critic of government; a staunch believer in the rule of law under the Constitution who exceeded its presidential authority to make the Louisiana Purchase; a cultivated, well-travelled, and learned man who trusted the moral and aesthetic judgment of ordinary people.

As an architect he is presented as a gifted amateur, as a provincial neo classicist in the French mold, as a slave to Palladio. Here it is argued that he was without doubt America's finest architect, a classical architect and successor to Vitruvius, Alberti, and Palladio.[1] He practiced architecture as a citizen who understood that the beauty sought for architecture and the justice sought by the civil order have shared foundations in nature and that they are found in the imitation of nature. In the classical tradition that he exemplifies politics, or the activities that animate a civil society, is more important than architecture, that the civic order exercises authority over what is built, that the purpose of a building is to serve and express the role its builder and user plays in the civic order, and that buildings and their accumulations in cities and the rural countryside present visible evidence of what a community values. His status as a citizen–architect far outweighs the amateurism that his buildings often exhibit, which is present partly from an excess of zeal for experimentation and innovation.

People are always fascinated by what they find in the natural world. In the classical tradition the difference was well understood between physical nature where empirical investigations lead to construing laws of nature and the human sciences where natural law manifests its presence in justice and in the good, the true, and the beautiful. The nation endorsed a brief epitome of natural law in the statement that nature has endowed us with certain inalienable rights. Jefferson provided a longer text in a well-known letter from late in his life. It includes the statement that each generation

> *may change their laws and institutions to suit themselves. Nothing is unchangeable but the inherent and unalienable rights of man. ... The Creator has made the earth for the living, not the dead. Rights and powers can only belong to persons, not to things, not to mere matter, unendowed with will. The dead are not even things.*[2]

Those rights protect our human will to pursue happiness. They reside in truth, and the role of government is to bring the facts of how we actually live together into line with what truth tells us about how we ought to life as we pursue our happiness. A truth: all men are created equal. A fact: some are enslaved. An agenda for government: bring the facts into congruence with the truth.

The tension between truth and fact is the very nature of human life. In their work the Founders sought balance by following a path different from the one being blazed on the Continent. They were steeped in English common law, and they were tutored by English and Scottish interpretations of the central tenets of the classical tradition. "It was by way of ... the diffuse influence of Scottish thought, including the useful if often irksome skepticism of Hume, that the Founders resisted metaphysical extremes and the extremes of action they often encourage."[3]

In his third year in France Jefferson, an aristocrat but an American, wrote, "State a moral case to a ploughman and a professor. The former will decide it as well, and often better than the later, because he has not been led astray by artificial rules."[4] In the previous chapter we learned that the moral sense and the aesthetic sense are parts of human nature, which allows us to formulate this corollary: state an aesthetic case to an ordinary person and a professor, and the former will decide just as well if not better.[5] Those natural endowments could be sharpened by instruction, but "artificial rules" could corrupt them. Jefferson acted on the corollary in his reform of the College of William and Mary in 1779 that "added the law of Nature & Nations, & Fine Arts to the duties of the Moral Professor."[6] Here is an instance of Jefferson's squaring the rule-abidingness of architecture with the natural law foundation of morality in the civil order.[7]

Jefferson and his American peers understood architecture as a civil art that is intimately connected with the art of governing. From Anthony Ashley Cooper, Lord Shaftsbury, they could learn the necessity of giving more authority in matters architectural to the people than to "one single Court-Architect;" he meant Sir Christopher Wren. Public buildings exhibit the grandeur of a nation, and "*the People* are no small Partrys [sic.] in this *Cause*. There can be no PUBLICK, but [i.e., except] where they are included. ..." A "*Publick Voice*" must knowingly guide and direct the artist and the workman as he strives for

> *after-Fame, and ... the approbation of his Country, and of Posterity. For with these he naturally, as a Freeman, must take part: in these he has a passionate*

Concern, and Interest, rais'd in him by the same Genius of Liberty, the same Laws and Government, by which his Property, and the Rewards of his Pains and Industry are secur'd him, and to his Generation after him.[8]

Jefferson was drawn to architecture, but the landscape of his birth had few exemplary buildings. Quite early he wrote, "The only public buildings worthy of mention" were four in Williamsburg, and he found fault with all of them; the Capitol, the Governor's Palace, the College of William and Mary, and the Hospital for Lunatics are "mis-shapen piles, which, but that they have roofs, would be taken for brick-kilns."[9]

It is commonly written that Jefferson received his most important instruction in architecture in Paris and on his three excursions elsewhere, first to England, then to the South of France and northern Italy, and finally to Holland and the Rhineland. Before his Italian journey he wrote, "Architecture, painting, sculpture, antiquities, the condition of the laboring poor will fill all my moments."[10] But the "Notes" he wrote about these excursions reveal less of Jefferson the architect than Jefferson the farmer and a person interested in assessing the lives of people under the governments on the Continent. It is not surprising that a man living on the wilderness frontier would respond more to the dramatic landscapes that would lead the picturesque into Romanticism than to gardens and their buildings, even English Palladian buildings. He found only one "superb" building, Moor Park, perhaps because it was by Giacomo Leoni, a translator of Palladio.[11]

The role of new buildings in his education as an architect is usually overstated. He wrote that in France he enjoyed "their architecture, sculpture, painting, music ... the last of them particularly. ... I am almost ready to say, it is the only thing which from my heart I envy them ... ."[12] From the south of France he wrote, "In Architecture nothing any where except the remains of antiquity ... [They] have been a great treat."[13] Early in his sojourn in France but after enough time to have had a good look at buildings comes his well-known comment that ancient models are more important than "any design which might be newly contrived."[14] Several months later he followed this with the comment that when you "leave to some architect to draw an external according to his fancy ... experience shows that about once in a thousand times a pleasing form is hit upon; the other was to take some model already devised and approved by the general suffrage of the world."[15] His nearly five years abroad surely enriched his knowledge of the art of building, but they left no traces in his ideas about architecture and proved negligible in his public buildings while they did enrich his treatment of landscape and contributed to the refinements and comfort of his domestic interiors.[16]

Jefferson always learned his architecture primarily from books. In France he could indulge his life-long "malady of 'Bibliomanie,'" and he constantly added to his already commendable library.[17] Fiske Kimball observed that his books, "reflect primarily the architectural ideas of England, with its Italian background, and its movement towards a return to the picturesque. ... [I]t was already superior not only to other collections in Virginia, but to most others in the United States."[18]

JEFFERSON'S VIRGINIA CAPITOL

Being a classical architect Jefferson put decorum in command of his activities. His best known and highest-status buildings, the Capitol of the Commonwealth of Virginia and the library of the University of Virginia, are explicitly rooted in ancient buildings, which he designed from books. For lower status buildings such as the residences he proposed for the Governorship of Virginia, the Presidency of the United States, the masterships of plantations, or the professors at the University he drew on more recent models such as those found in Palladio and Robert Morris.

In 1776 in the new (illegal) Virginia legislature he introduced a bill to move the capital from Williamsburg to Richmond, and it was passed a month before he was elected in 1779 for the first of his two one-year terms as Governor. He had been tinkering with designs for buildings in Williamsburg ever since he was a student there, and now, even as preparations for the move were underway, he made proposals for remodeling the former colonial Governor's Palace into a temple to serve as the Governor's Mansion. Kimball noted that a temple-building serving as "a domestic building was at this time quite absent abroad," and Marcus Whiffen labeled the proposal an act of *damnatio memoriae*, although its author surely also had in mind the positive political expressive content of temples.[19] In Richmond Jefferson carved an expansive precinct out of the commercial town's grid on highlands above a bluff and drew plans for three buildings in it, one for each branch of government, the first such architectural separation of powers anywhere.[20] The most complete were for the legislature's building, which he modeled on an ancient temple, a model he used perhaps as early as 1772 when he had imagined remodeling Williamsburg's colonial Capitol as a temple.[21] These are the antecedents of the design he would send from Paris for the building that still serves Virginia as its Capitol.[22]

Jefferson arrived in France in August, 1784. A Capitol in Richmond was to be begun in August, 1785, and correspondence documents the apprehension that it would not be satisfactory. Before long he was soon asked for a design, and he wrote to James Madison, "I shall send the one taken from the best morsel of antient architecture now remaining. It has obtained the approbation of fifteen or sixteen centuries, and is therefore preferable to any design which might be newly contrived." Two weeks later this followed: "We took as our model what is called the Maisonquarrèe of Nismes, one of the most beautiful, if not the most beautiful and precious morsel of architecture left us by antiquity."[23] He also noted that he had found an architect to assist him.

With construction of a different project underway in Richmond in late January 1786 and anxious to send something to get it on the right track, he shipped material that showed the "external form" that was quickly agreed on, but the press of business delayed working out "the internal distribution convenient for the three branches of government." The necessary material that included the plaster model that is today on display in the Capitol was prepared for shipment, material "absolutely necessary for the guide of workmen, not very expert in their art." He added that preparing it incurred an additional expense, but "I was sensible of its necessity."[24]

8.1 Maison Carrée, Nîmes
Source: William Henry Goodyear photo, Brooklyn Museum Archives. Goodyear Archival Collection, in public domain via Wikicommons.

The architect he selected from among all those in Paris in 1785 was Charles-Louis Clérisseau who, as Jefferson proudly informed the commissioners, "had studied this art 20 years in Rome." Palladio had given the Maison Carrée six plates, but in 1778 Clérisseau had published the definitive book on it. From the collaboration, knowledge of the inexperience of American carvers with its Corinthian order, and the expense of having capitals made in Italy forced a reluctant change to the Ionic, which Clérisseau persuaded him to take from Vincenzo Scamozzi.

Clérisseau and the antique also appealed because of "the style of architecture in this capital being far from chaste."[25] Again and again Jefferson championed the antique and the chaste, which were the qualities the Founders also favored for the new American civil order. Nothing is gained by chasing after the latest fancy when there is ample material in ancient precedents and new knowledge to assist in imitating nature.

Jefferson recognized several virtues in chastity. In advice he gave American travelers in Europe, "Pictures, statuary. Too expensive for the state of wealth among us. … They are worth seeing, but not studying." Chastity would also rebuke wastrels. Of his farthest penetration into Italy he observed,

> The Cathedral in Milan a worthy object of philosophical contemplation, to be placed among the rarest instances of the misuse of money. On viewing the

> *churches of Italy it is evident without calculation that the same expence would have sufficed to throw the Appennines [sic.] into the Adriatic and thereby render a terra firma from Leghorn to Constantinople.*[26]

Later in life he wrote that "kings, hereditary nobles, and priests" take the earnings of the laboring people and leave them with only enough "to obtain a sufficient surplus barely to sustain a scanty and miserable life. And those earnings they apply to maintain their privileged order in splendor and idleness, to fascinate the eyes of the people, and excite in them an humble adoration and submission, as to an order of superior beings."[27]

Chastity in form also made the model in ancient buildings more conspicuous, which was important because, as Jefferson would later write, this commission provided

> *a favorable opportunity of introducing into the state an example of architecture in the classic style of antiquity, and the Maison quarrée of Nismes, an ancient Roman temple, being considered as the most perfect model existing of what may be called Cubic architecture.*[28]

Chastity in form displayed the proportionality without being muddled by excessive ornament and decoration. Proportionality was for Jefferson what symmetry had been for Vitruvius and lineaments and concinnity were for Alberti and Palladio. It linked the building to the enduring beauty that nature furnishes. Late in his life Jefferson rendered the idea in his usual deft shorthand and the abbreviated language of the Enlightenment when he wrote that the Virginia Capitol

> *is on the model of the temples of Erectheus at Athens, of Balbec and of the Maison quarrée of Nismes. All of which are nearly of the same form and proportions, and are considered as the most perfect examples of Cubic architecture, as the Pantheon of Rome is of the Spherical.*[29]

The catalogue was not fixed. In his early instructions to Clérisseau Jefferson named the three non-circular buildings and added a fourth (Perrault's version of Vitruvius' peripteral temple), and he identified the books illustrating them but did not mention the Maison Carreé.[30] How can these five very different buildings, all of them non cubic parallelepipeds with pitched roofs, be cubic and "nearly of the same form and proportions"? So too the spherical, which at best is a hemisphere siting on a cylinder.

Jefferson presents them as paradigmatic models for a species, kind, or type of the geometric figures whose essence is proportionality. They are "the most perfect *examples*" of their species among which all examples differ. "Their dimensions not being sufficient for the purposes of the Capitol, they were enlarged, but their proportions rigorously preserved."[31] Cubicity and sphericity model the proportionality of his buildings even when combined to produce composites such as his much loved Villa Rotunda by Palladio, his own Monticello, and the Rotunda at the University of Virginia. Their proportionality is to truth as their proportions are to facts.

8.2 Thomas Jefferson, Capitol, Richmond, 1786, engraving, c.1840 *Source:* Courtesy of the Library of Virginia.

Proportionality, a fundamental property of the classical tradition in architecture, is made visible in the ratios of the dimensional numbers of actual material things. In an earlier age numbers resonated with external, significant or symbolic content: 3 = trinity and a perfect number; 4 = seasons and gospels; and whole-number ratios described the orderly arrangement of the terrestrial bodies that produced the inaudible music of the spheres and provided beauty in the perception of things actually seen and heard. In the seventeenth century this content was voided when the facts underlying it were found not to be factual descriptions of what experience revealed. Numbers were now employed to quantify qualities and to be operative integers formulated as laws of nature that explained change and exercised power over the forces in the physical, material world. When this new way to understand the physical sciences moved into the human sciences "The truth of the matter" gradually became "Let the facts speak for themselves."

Jefferson shunned metaphysical numerology but retained dimensional ratios within the paradigmatic cubic and spherical proportionality so that buildings could offer pleasure to the aesthetic sense. In the classical tradition proportionality had always governed innovation within tradition and imitation to protect against lapses into disproportion and into what Palladio called abuses. Jefferson did not join the French in contriving theories that were abandoning imitation and favoring archaeologically-based historical models serving as precedents and redolent with associations. Jefferson kept architecture on its classical track running parallel with law within a tradition where law was guided by precedents, architecture by models, and innovations adapted both to serve new circumstances in constantly vitalizing traditions guided by the lodestars of the good and the beautiful.

The Virginia planters had never embraced the French legal tradition or the Vitruvianism of using imperial models for institutional buildings. When the British King's imperialism become overbearing and the imperious British patricians were unresponsive the Americans responded by founding a new civil order with an enlarged scope of those who were involved in governing. Concerning too small a governing body Jefferson noted, "173 despots will surely be as oppressive as one. Let those who doubt it turn their eyes on the republic of Venice."[32] Like the other Founders Jefferson innovated inventively within the classical tradition, and his buildings made perceptible the resonance between the aesthetic and moral in their service to the new civil order.

ARCHITECTURE'S SERVICE TO THE NEW NATION

Jefferson left France toward the end of 1789 with an expanded library and not as a recently tutored French architect but as an American architect better tutored in ancient Roman architecture and Palladio. In his later years a visitor to Monticello reported to a mutual friend, "With Mr. Jefferson I conversed at length on the subject of architecture. Palladio he said 'Was the Bible.' You should get it & stick close to it."[33] Jefferson never owned the 1570 original edition and never saw a building by Palladio, but at least seven other Palladio copies passed through his hands. In them he found valued images of buildings and a discussion of architecture that conjoined the trio of reason, judgment, and nature, that incorporated the good, the true, and the beautiful, and that taught about the pairing of concinnity and imitation.

Jefferson's Palladios were large, luxurious editions aimed at an aristocratic audience, but books intended to disseminate Palladianism to English-speaking workmen with the traditional canons of proportions and of the orders became increasingly available during the eighteenth century. Their need in Virginia is found in a well-known passage about the State's private buildings in his *Notes on the State of Virginia* that he first published early in his time in France:

> *It is impossible to devise things more ugly, uncomfortable, and happily more perishable. ... [A] workman could scarcely be found here capable of drawing an order. The genius of architecture seems to have shed its maledictions over this land. Buildings are often erected, by individuals, of considerable expence. To give these symmetry and taste would not increase their cost. It would only change the arrangement of the materials, the form and combination of the members. This would often cost less than the burthen of barbarous ornaments with which these building are sometimes charged. But the first principles of the art are unknown, and there exists scarcely a model among us sufficiently chaste to give an idea of them. (Query XV)*

The next sentence expresses the hope through the curricular reform at the College of William and Mary that "perhaps a spark may fall on some young students of natural taste, kindle up their genius, and produce a reformation for this elegant and useful art."[34] The talent for the fine arts comes from a "natural taste," and it requires cultivation through education. It is an "elegant and useful art" that offers more than pleasure alone. As an adjunct to the liberal arts it is a civic art that could improve its service inexpensively by changing "the arrangement of the materials, the form and combination of the members." Chastity could benefit from economy, and economy could serve chastity.

Elevating the taste of his countrymen was a pressing concern for Jefferson. Writing from Paris to Madison about his proposal for the Capitol we read,

> *You see I am an enthusiast in the subject of the arts. But it is an enthusiasm of which I am not ashamed, as its object is to improve the taste of my countrymen, to increase their reputation, to reconcile them to the respect of the world, and procure them its praise.*[35]

Taste here refers to the capacity to recognize beauty in the imitation of the order, harmony, and proportionality of nature. This nature was manifested in a comment from yet another Founder, James Wilson (1742–98), an Associate Justice of the Supreme Court. In his *Lectures on Law* he began his chapter "Of the general principals of law and obligation" this way:

> *Order, proportion, and fitness pervade the universe. Around us, we see; within us, we feel; above us, we admire a rule, from which a deviation cannot, or should not, or will not be made.*[36]

Perched above the highest point of navigation on the James River the Capitol would be conspicuous to builders, and it would display the formal precedents and the proportionality that had its counterpart in the civic order. In other nations, at least before things changed with the French Revolution, the civil order was a familiar and traditional entity that had new laws and practices tacked on to it just as the nation's new buildings displayed recent novelty or fancy within its traditional architecture. The American nation was something new. The Founders were unencumbered by such baggage, and like Jefferson in inventing an American architecture, they drew on their experience, knowledge, and reason as they modernized the best models with indifference to where they were found, with the classical tradition being the richest source.

Other architects did differently. For example Charles Bullfinch, the well-connected stellar architect in Massachusetts, spent 20 months travelling in Europe principally in England and France and only a scant three weeks in Rome. He wrote, "At Paris I tarried sometime to view its buildings & other objects of curiosity, to which I was introduced by letters from the Marquis La Fayette & Mr. Jefferson."[37] He must have known what Jefferson intended for Richmond's Capitol, but what most attracted him were the buildings of the British architects Robert Adam, William Chambers, John Soane, James Wyatt, and Robert Mylne.[38] After returning he designed the Massachusetts State House (1787, with construction in 1795–97), which, he said, "is in the stile of a building celebrated all over Europe."

8.3 Richmond, Virginia, seen from the James River in 1817. Drawn by C. Fraser; printed by Hill
Source: Courtesy of the Library of Virginia.

That was Chambers' newly finished Somerset House begun in 1776.[39] The headquarters of the British Navy that stretched along the River Thames, Bulfinch must have decided that it had the appropriate character for his government's building, which was similarly elevated above the Boston Common. Others agreed when they emulated it or parts of it for a few of the state houses in New England and the new Capitol on Jenkins Hill (now Capitol Hill) in Washington.

Jefferson was not intending comparison with the work of other practicing architects. He wanted a beautiful building that would have four results, which he outlined in his letter to Madison. The first was that this beautiful civic building would provide instruction in taste to his countrymen. The second was to increase their reputation by elevating their taste to standards that other nations could admire. The third result had higher stakes for the countrymen because it would force the world to respect them or, in his diction, "reconcile them to the respect of the world." And in the fourth, with the taste of public and private buildings judged favorably by "the world," the international prestige of the country and his countrymen who were the country would be elevated.

Behind this program were the two criteria that allowed judgments to be made within the classical tradition. One was the proper (we might say decorous) use of conventional forms that allowed the differences between buildings old and new to be noted, especially in what Jefferson called the "externals," and most conspicuously (but not exclusively) in the five columnar orders defining the proportionality. The other was in the clarity with which the observer, both tutored and untutored, could be moved by the beauty he sees and even perceives.

HOUSING THE NEW NATION

Jefferson's emphasis on his countrymen reminds us that from the founding of the new nation they and their families occupied a fundamental place within the civil order. When people build their family residence they depend on what they know how to build, and Americans, especially Virginians, had always found the models for their residences in the colony's home country. As Americans reached prosperity in the eighteenth century and even after they gained independence they were especially attracted to the houses of the Whig oligarchy of Georgian Britain and Protestant Ireland. "Rather than personal innovation reflecting a patron's individuality, the strongest identification in these [British] buildings was to a group, a class, one portrayed as worthy of its social role."[40]

In the new nation the family residence gained a new importance among the hierarchy of American buildings because it is the seat of the individuals who are "We the People" who "ordain and establish" the Constitution. Allan Greenberg observed, "The basic building block of the new [American] architecture is not the king's palace or the church, as in England and Europe, but is instead the modest single-family house." "For the first time in history, the ordinary person's house became a work of architecture."[41] The family residence of the Medici had been given architectural treatment in Renaissance Florence, but it was less the residence of an ordinary family than an expression of that family's princely ambitions. The American residence, as with Alberti, expresses the opposite within a civic art.

Greenberg observes that a building they called a meeting house furnished the collective identity of the early Puritan settlements. He also calls attention to the peculiarity of Americans to use house in the names of civic buildings: statehouse, firehouse, schoolhouse, clubhouse, jailhouse, and so on. "Congress House and the President's House were the original names George Washington chose for the United States Capitol and the White House in Washington, D.C."[42] The proportionality of the typical American residence was not modeled on the unknowable and ungraspable gods and kings or the ambitions of emperors and monarchs but on the well-formed human figure. He also wrote that the temple exemplified by the Maison Carrée appealed to Jefferson because he believed it had been built when Rome was a republic, and a temple stands for "the principles of 'trust and inviolability.'" In American buildings, he observes, temples exist in either full fronts or in recognizable abbreviations from porches to frames for openings.

The temple was a common model for Jefferson. He toyed with it before he built the Capitol, it figures in the various large plantation houses he had a hand in as well as in his own pair, and there are 10 of them at the University of Virginia where they were to serve as models for imitation and instruction for builders.[43] Temple-derived buildings exist at both ends of the hierarchy of civil status, which calls attention to the continuity between the bottom-up and top-down authorities in the civil order that these American buildings serve. Here is decorum serving democracy.

Jefferson was always fascinated by inventions as well as by ancient models. Long after he had sent the plaster model of the Capitol to Richmond he wrote the well-known letter from Nîmes to Madam de Tessé that describes his first encounter with its model. He found himself "gazing whole hours at the Maison quarrée, like a lover at his mistress." He rhapsodizes about the "sublime" antiquities of "Roman grandeur" with which he has "been nourished." "I am immersed in antiquities from morning to night. For me, the city of Rome actually exists in all the splendor of its empire." But he also writes,

> While in Paris, I was violently smitten with the Hotel de Salm, and used to go to the Thuileries [sic.] almost daily, to look at it … sitting on the parapet, and twisting my neck around to see the object of my admiration, I generally left it with a torti-colli.[44]

Monticello II is often linked to Pierre Rousseau's building, and while Monticello owes more to Palladio, it was one of the few in Paris that he enthusiastically endorsed. Another was the Halle au Blé, not for the building but for the dramatic effect achieved by marrying old and new technology in the ribbed dome added in 1782–83. The old was in its wooden structural system that came from Philibert de l'Orme's treatise published more than two centuries earlier and Jefferson would use for his domes.[45] The new was in the glass in the dome's webs, which appeared twice in his own work. The first was perhaps sanctioned by Palladio because in the *Quattro libri* editions he consulted the Villa Rotunda had what he took to be windows added between the ribs.[46] In his anonymous competition entry for the President's House he expanded these to glazed webs. The second instance came when as President he insisted that Benjamin Henry Latrobe equip the House Chamber with the glazing that had made the Halle au Blé the "most superb thing in the world." The professionally-trained architect and excellent engineer responded that doing so posed enormous technical problems, but Jefferson insisted. It would make the House "the handsomest room in the world, without a single exception."[47] Latrobe, less dazzled, replied that small things can easily destroy the success of "the character of the work, the artist, and the government" and wondered whether the glazing would serve or undermine decorum.[48] Jefferson countered that the Chamber with this modern ceiling would express the character of the institution it served, which was a new legislative body founded on ancient principles of democracy and closest to the people whom the government served. He got the ceiling; it leaked as predicted. The chamber turned out to be an acoustic disaster as well, but not through any fault of Jefferson or Latrobe, and it was later replaced.

The national Capitol was far from finished when Jefferson assumed the Presidency. To complete it he turned to Latrobe and urged him to work energetically, but he was disappointed. Bullfinch later finished the original, which was greatly enlarged later in the century. Jefferson described it as "the first temple dedicated to the sovereignty of the people, embellishing with Athenian taste the course of a nation looking far beyond the range of Athenian destinies."[49] Athenian democracy had, after all, fallen first to tyrants and then to Roman imperialism, and that history provided lessons for statesman while the enduring beauty of "Athenian taste" remained as a beacon to architects.

That beacon was beginning to dim in Latrobe's early years in architecture which occurred in a circle that was keeping track of Sir John Soane's formal explorations in the classical tradition and architecture was developing as a professional practice.[50]

He viewed Jefferson as an old amateur who "meant every major design of his as a museum of the orders." "He was willing to go no further than mixing elements from the entablatures of established models, and then only in private buildings."[51] Latrobe was not shy in inventing in the Capitol building with the magnolia order, the "Indian Order," and "orders adorned with tobacco, corn, and other American flora."[52] But decorum governed, and he confined them to "secondary areas; that is, he did not intend them to compete with the canonical orders, which he used in major rooms."[53] Latrobe explained that the Greek orders "established *general* proportions and laws of form and arrangement, [and] all matters of detail were left to the talent and taste of individual architects."[54] For both men the orders were conspicuous ornament, decoration, emblems of the building's proportionality, and an index of taste, and both men also accepted the eye as a better judge of beauty than the caliper or measuring rod which again favored the ploughman over the professor.

The generation of architects that followed Jefferson lost contact with the common foundations of architecture and the civil order and the role of imitation in serving the good and the beautiful. Only a few generations later architecture's role as a civic art would be overwhelmed by its attachment to the Fine Arts that had formed on the Continent. It would soon push the classical tradition to near extinction except for a robust, too brief, and flawed recrudescence in the decades around 1900. Jefferson found few heirs to his role for architecture as a civic art and the role of the architect as a magistrate using his talent in architecture working with others in serving the common good.

Buildings make cities, and cities are the arena of the political life. As a classical architect Jefferson was incapable of separating statesmanship from building and architecture from urbanism. It was simple: no architecture without urbanism, no urbanism without buildings, and no service to the civil order unless decorum commands the relationship between the buildings themselves and their urban site. Furthermore, as heirs of the British the landscape always had a prominent place in both the urbanism and architecture of America. A few brief comments about a few examples of Jefferson's involvement in urbanism will complete this chapter.

Jefferson, who had reconfigured the commercial grid of Richmond to serve as the capital, found himself involved in capital-building again in 1790 as the nation's first Secretary of State. President Washington was charged with building the new federal district from scratch. He determined the 10-mile square site on land in Virginia and Maryland, a huge site where he envisaged an impressive statement of the new nation's place among the major nations of the world and where a canal to the Ohio River would make the nation's vast interior accessible. Jefferson was Washington's liaison to the commissioners who were dealing with the landowners and to Major Pierre Charles L'Enfant (1754–1825) whom Washington had commissioned "to make such a Draught of the Ground as will enable himself to fix on the Spot for the public Buildings."[55]

L'Enfant was busy with early preliminary work in bad weather in the largely untamed rural countryside when Jefferson presented a sketch plan for the capital.[56] He nestled a small, expandable, regular grid into a site poorly suited to serve commerce but suitable for the limited government of a decentralized nation.[57]

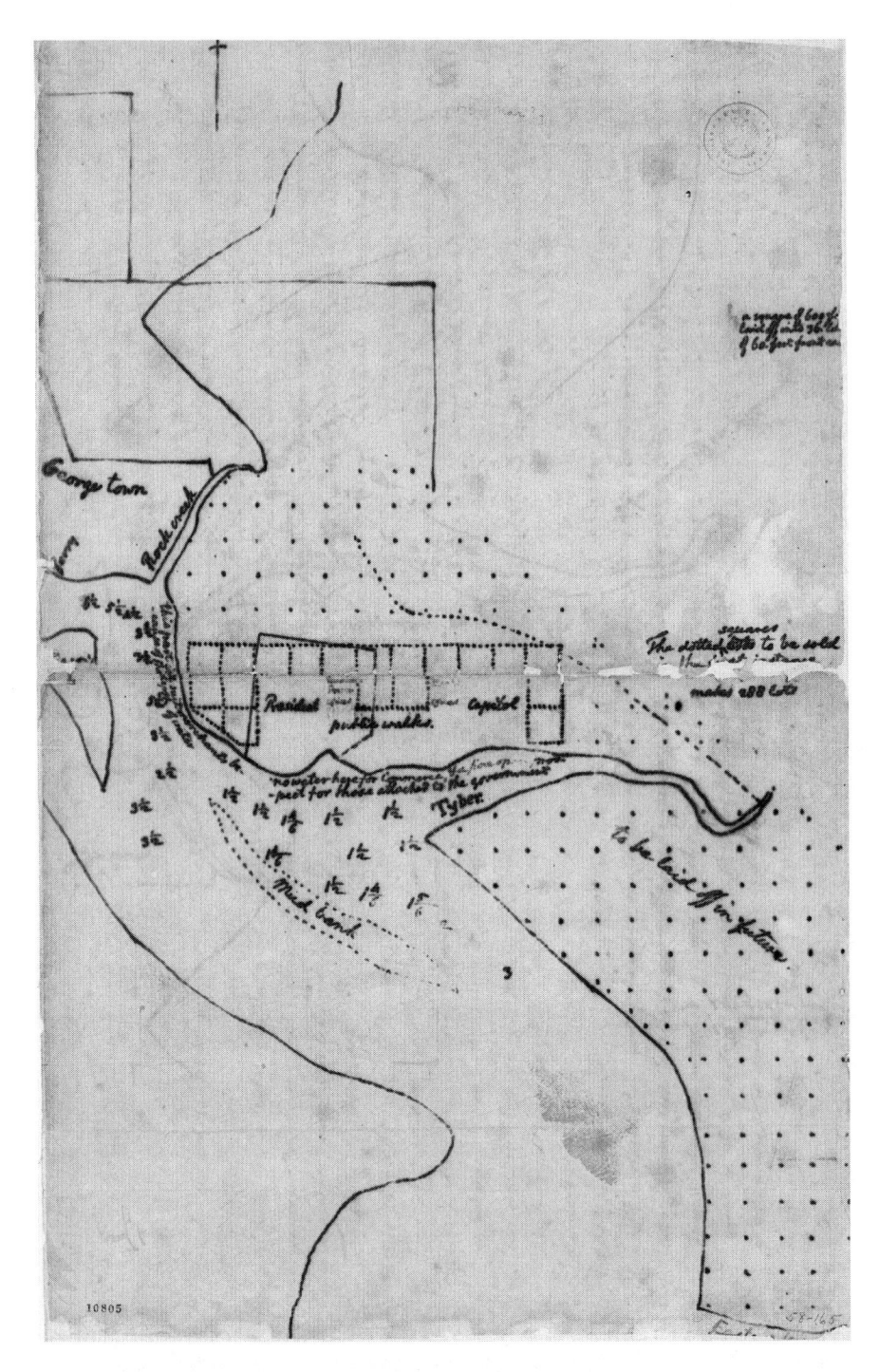

8.4 Thomas Jefferson, sketch plan for national capital, made between March 10 and 21, 1791
Source: Library of Congress. Often cited as Thomas Jefferson Papers, 80:10805, it is image 210 in The Thomas Jefferson Papers Series 1. General Correspondence, George Washington, March 31, 1791, Proclamation of Federal District with Map, http://hdl.loc.gov/loc.mss/mtj.mtjbib005334.

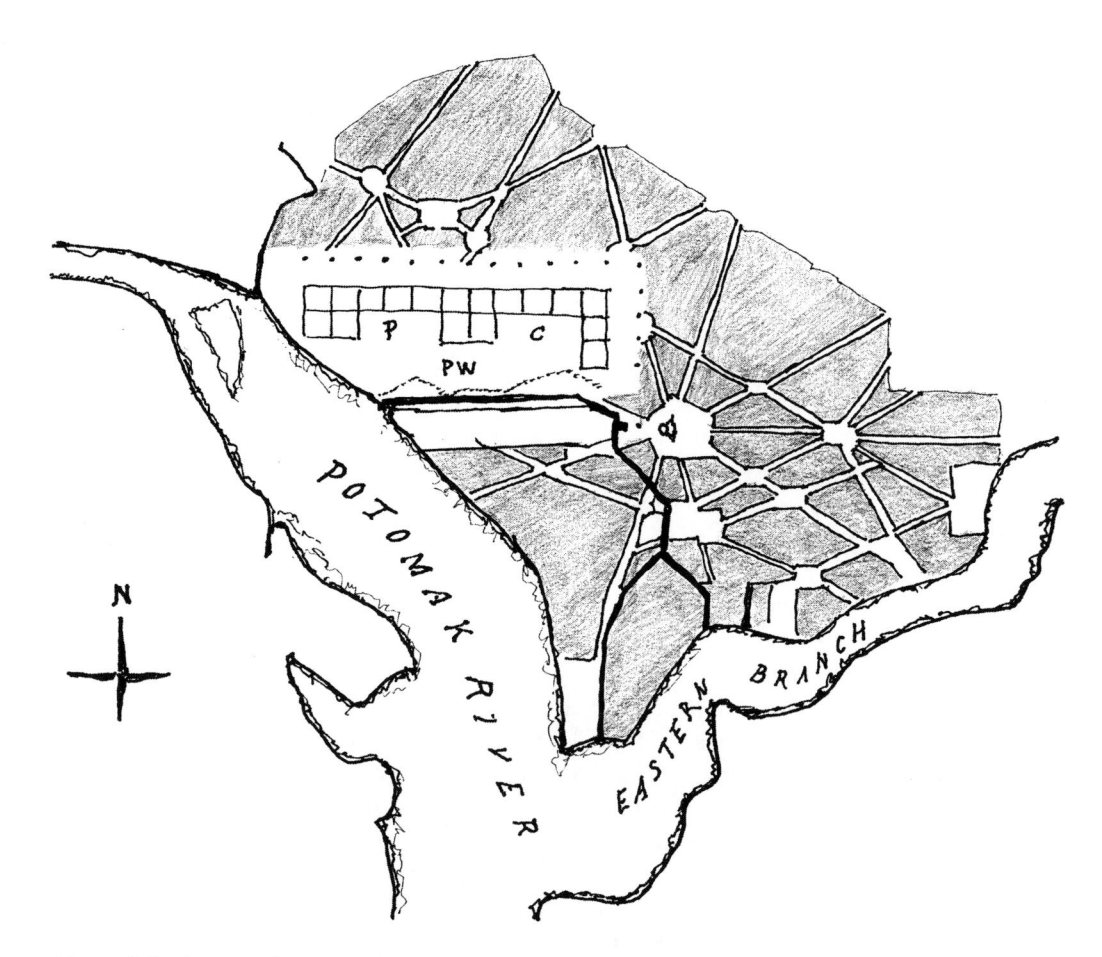

Meanwhile the President and the Major spent months working out the much larger and grander city that is the heart of the metropolitan area we know today.

Overlaying the central kernel of Jefferson's sketch on the earliest published plan of the present city makes clear the great difference between two very different ideas about what the image of the new nation's new capital city ought to be. When the entire area of each is compared we find that both fill roughly the same fraction of the 10-mile square, but Jefferson's plan puts at its center what appears to be a large market town. He outlines 18 full blocks that would accommodate the initial residential settlement and anticipates future expansion into a grid defined by dots. The Washington/L'Enfant scheme spreads the institutions of government broadly through the city anchored within an axial scheme of broad avenues, many connecting with existing roads and other topographic features, sprinkled with squares that the various states were to decorate. Here is the federal order, which is laid over a municipal grid with nominally rectangular residential blocks differing in size according to the requirements of that federal order.

If Jefferson's sketch found a place in this grand design it is in the orientation of the President's House (P in Figure 8.5, which covers over the building's actual site that is larger and slightly to the northeast) to look down the Potomac River.

8.5 Central section of Jefferson's 1791 sketch superimposed on the Washington/L'Enfant scheme
Source: Jefferson image: as Figure 8.4. Ellicott image engraved in 1792, the first printed version of the Pierre Charles L'Enfant plan, 1792. Both in public domain. Drawing by the author.

It may also have been the seed that grew into the location of the other major institution of government, the Capitol (C) sited relative to what would become the Mall that Jefferson had called the Public Walk (PW). The Mall occupies part of the sluggish Tyber that has been regularized as part of the canal running through the city with its two southern branches serving the commercial, industrial, and naval facilities along the East Branch (present-day Anacostia River). Later abandoned and covered, its Tyber stretch is now Constitution Avenue NW.

It is likely that both schemes have a common origin in a capital city that all three men knew well, Williamsburg, where the Governor's Mansion looks down a mall to the principal street running at right angles and anchored at opposite ends by the Capitol and the College of William and Mary. Virginia's colonial capital must be considered at least as important a precedent as Versailles, where L'Enfant grew up, and the many colonial and European cities and gardens where a geometric pattern connected and set off important elements against a subordinate background.[58]

The Washington/L'Enfant scheme is no mere sketch but a fully realized plan. It ingeniously exploited the picturesque potential of the site as a display of a central government's authority. It interweaved landscape and urbanism, it was receptive to commerce, it envisaged a large population, and it satisfied decorum with special prominence for the buildings serving and expressing the purposes of a truly federal government. It expressed a conception of government that was poles apart from the one expressed in Jefferson's little sketch. The extremes the two schemes express convey the poles that the political life must always reconcile between people gathered in urban concentrations and others in small communities across the land. Jefferson feared that if the large commercial and industrial cities that were emerging in Europe were to appear in America mobs and top-down threats to liberty would emerge as well. He always favored the farmer and the local community as the bottom-up counterweight while his urban proposals always used decorum and geometry to express the control of the civil order's authoritative institutions. And they always shy away from embracing the federalism that Washington and Alexander Hamilton believed were essential for security.

Despite Jefferson's best efforts L'Enfant's character caused the implementation to go awry rather quickly, and he was dismissed. Jefferson, tired of fighting Alexander Hamilton and other Federalists, resigned as Secretary of State at the end of 1793 and retired to Monticello. The President, eager to have an inhabited city expressing the welding of the many states into a strong and prosperous federal union, pressed on. On schedule in 1800 his successor John Adams and the rest of the government moved from Philadelphia to the unfinished city that was both unique in the world and a statement about the new nation's ambitions. This great city in the classical tradition would eventually, to paraphrase Jefferson, earn the nation's citizens the respect of the world and procure them its praise.

The public buildings' construction dragged well into the new century. These anchors in the urbanism present the character of proportionality, chastity, and participation in the classical tradition that Jefferson had believed made buildings distinctly American. They, and their now enlarged successors, powerfully command the city's decorum, and with the urban order holding them they express the purposes that the Constitution entrusted to the institutions that use them. Jefferson's sketch for the little capital on the "Tyber" is of a piece with other proposals that range from village-like Monticello to Jackson, the capital of Mississippi.[59] They illustrate the pattern found in the earliest English settlements that were always loosely defined within a landscape whose uses move easily out into the surrounding rural land and wilderness. Whether scattered or corralled, residences that occupy their own plot of land constitute the broad blanket on which the institutional structures are set. A very different pattern existed on the Continent where Roman law with its different legal status for urban and rural land had deep roots. In America before the full force of the commercial and industrial revolutions was felt the land provided the sustenance necessary for citizenship. The citizen was the basis of the civil order, and the urbanism serving it always rested gently on the land. This is well illustrated by Monticello, which is well known and much studied. It sits atop the little mountain with its service wings nestled into the brow. The approach up the hill from the east and landscaped setting stretching out to the west are carefully considered, and the slave quarter is on lower land where it is excluded and partially obscured. The principal axis anchors the main dwelling to the land. The entrance temple front opens to a reception room stocked with displays that testify to the abundance of America's natural world, its floor painted green. Its complement is the half-octagon sitting room opening to the temple front with its exterior turf floor, beyond which is the garden extracted from the wilderness.

A VILLA AND A VILLAGE

In 1806 Jefferson was looking forward to the solitude that the end of his public duties would bring. Aware that Monticello could not offer it he began constructing a retreat in his extensive land holdings 90 miles southwest of Monticello. Monticello was named for the little mountain it occupied. This one was set in a Poplar Forest and hence its name. It would be "the best dwelling house in the state, except that of Monticello; perhaps preferable to that, as more proportioned to the faculties of a private citizen."[60] Habitable when he left the Presidency in 1809, here as at Monticello he constantly made additions and modifications. In 1822 when he was preparing "to mix the faces and ox skulls" in the central room he wrote that he would follow "a fancy which I can indulge in my own case, altho in a public work I feel bound to follow authority strictly."[61]

Like the normative American residence it occupies a defined place in a plot of land, but here it is much larger than the modern suburban eighth of an acre. The grounds that the house occupies are set apart from the productive rural tracts with a curtilage fence beyond the area shown in Figure 8.6 that excludes livestock and describes a parallelogram. Within it a circular drive lined by a parallel row of trees encloses the garden landscape of the residential precinct with roughly 60 acres where the landscape distills the wide range of modern French, English, German, and American ideas.

8.6 Thomas Jefferson, Poplar Forest, view of the site, 1806f
Source: Courtesy, Thomas Jefferson's Poplar Forest, L. Diane Johnson, artist.

The principal axis carries the approach from due north that runs through a boscage of local poplars to reach a circular termination before the temple-fronted entrance. The axis projects through the house to the twin of the entrance's temple front that the sloping land allows to be set on an arcade that gives access to the basement. It continues southward across land excavated to form a parterre whose level ground meets the original grade just short of the circular drive. On the cross axis the extension to the east has the wing of offices added in 1814. The slope obscures its presence from the entrance side but on the downhill side provides access through an arcade. Its flat roof offers a terraced platform reached by one of the pair of stair enclosures added to the original scheme to provide access to the basement. That wing's complement on the west is an enfilade of paired trees. This axis extends in each direction to a forested mound and finally terminates in an octagonal "necessary" set at the octagonal perimeter fence.

Pinioning similar elements along cross axes was not uncommon in the grounds of plantations; Monticello had something similar, and a variation was proposed for the President's Mansion, probably by Latrobe with Jefferson's involvement, when Jefferson was its occupant.

As at Monticello, the retreat house occupies the highest land in the area that here provides views to the mountains beyond. Jefferson described "the order in which they are seen from Poplar Forest" through various windows in the central octagon house. This late essay illustrates Jefferson's own life-long fascination with the octagon

8.7 Thomas Jefferson, Poplar Forest, from the garden, 1806f
Source: Photo by author.

and its mate, the circle that had been features of house plans from Palladio forward, and with the mathematics and geometry that had always fascinated him; he had used them adroitly in calculating volumes of materials needed for building to proposing a decimal coinage. Throughout Poplar Forest spherical and cubic geometry and proportionality obey Jefferson's "fancy."[62] The control begins in the surrounding circular roadway with a 500 feet inner diameter just beyond a fence (not shown in Figure 8.6) on an octagonal plan of about 200 feet on each side. The entrance roadway penetrating the circle from the north comes to a circular drive with a 100 foot outer circumference and a 50 foot inner circle that was originally planted with five concentric circles of dwarf boxwood around a 20 foot planting bed. On the east–west cross axis the wing of offices and the enfilade of trees run 100 feet to reach another 100 foot square holding the mound 75 feet in diameter with a base surrounded by plantings and a top diameter of 20 feet. The main axis projecting 200 feet southward across the parterre has splayed sides planted with heavy foliage and would, according to a garden book that Jefferson consulted, have approached the appearance of a double square when viewed from the villa house's south portico.

Nestled in the center of this geometric nexus is the octagonal villa house with 50 foot sides. We have already noted the half-square porticos projecting from each face along the principal axis. Inside, the perimeter has four double cube rooms with half octagon terminations. These surround the larger, central, sky lit, 20 foot cube, the sanctorum of the entire complex that is talismanic of reason that orders the inner garden, that cultivates nature to produce its bounty in the plantation lands, and that west of the Ohio River was taming the vast untapped American wilderness to make the great Jeffersonian Northwest Ordinance grid where settlers would cultivate their lands and their civil orders.

At his leisure in the central cube and the elongated octagon library opening to the south portico Jefferson enjoyed "the delights of classical reading and of mathematical truths, and … the consolations of a sound philosophy" while developing the plans of "the Hobby of my old age," the University of Virginia.[63] There and in Poplar Forest are his, and America's, best illustrations of the classical tradition's reciprocity of architecture, urbanism, and landscape supporting America's civil order.

The University was completed just before his death as the summit of his lifelong endeavor to provide Virginians with the education necessary to protect their liberty and pursue their happiness. Not a market but an "academical village" that markets sustain, it was intended to play its particular role in the larger civil order.[64] Jefferson had sought a system of public education from his earliest involvement in public affairs.[65] The sons of the privileged had tutors while the rest depended on what came from the pulpit of the established Church of England. His proposed graduated system of preparation for citizenship began with three years of universal education in the hands of wards or townships of five or six square miles that administered local public affairs. "Where every man is a sharer in the direction of his ward republic he will let the heart be torn out of his body, sooner than his power be wrested from him by a Caesar or a Bonaparte."[66] At the other end was the University that was to form youth "to habits of reflection and correct action, rendering them examples of virtue to others, and of happiness within themselves."[67]

The education system shows his devotion to the reciprocity of bottom-up and top-down and the role of synoecism in the civil order. A person enters a family or state by birth, and his natural talents and education elevate him to ever more specialized and responsible duties within the civil order. As in a civil order of any extent, from family to nation, its members and the buildings serving their various purposes within the "academical village" are given their ordered place in the landscape with a much-studied geometric order and the character that expressed their purposes within the whole.

Here as in building the national capital, the University came into being through the long, political efforts of a number of people, and its form benefited from the collaboration of others, most notably William Thornton and Latrobe playing more than Clérisseau's role. The physical plan built between 1817 and 1825 has its roots in the typical large Virginia plantation such as Monticello, enlarged, transformed, and regularized. On the highest land stands the Rotunda, its sphericity presenting the perfect proportionality of unity with its model in the Pantheon pointing to the ancient beginnings of the classical tradition. As a library it serves and expresses the role of reason, experience, and knowledge in the affairs of the civil order that seeks the good and facilitates the pursuit of happiness of each individual. Presiding like a head over a well-proportioned body, its dominant size and position at the top of the central axis governs the disposition of the subordinate units. The two rows

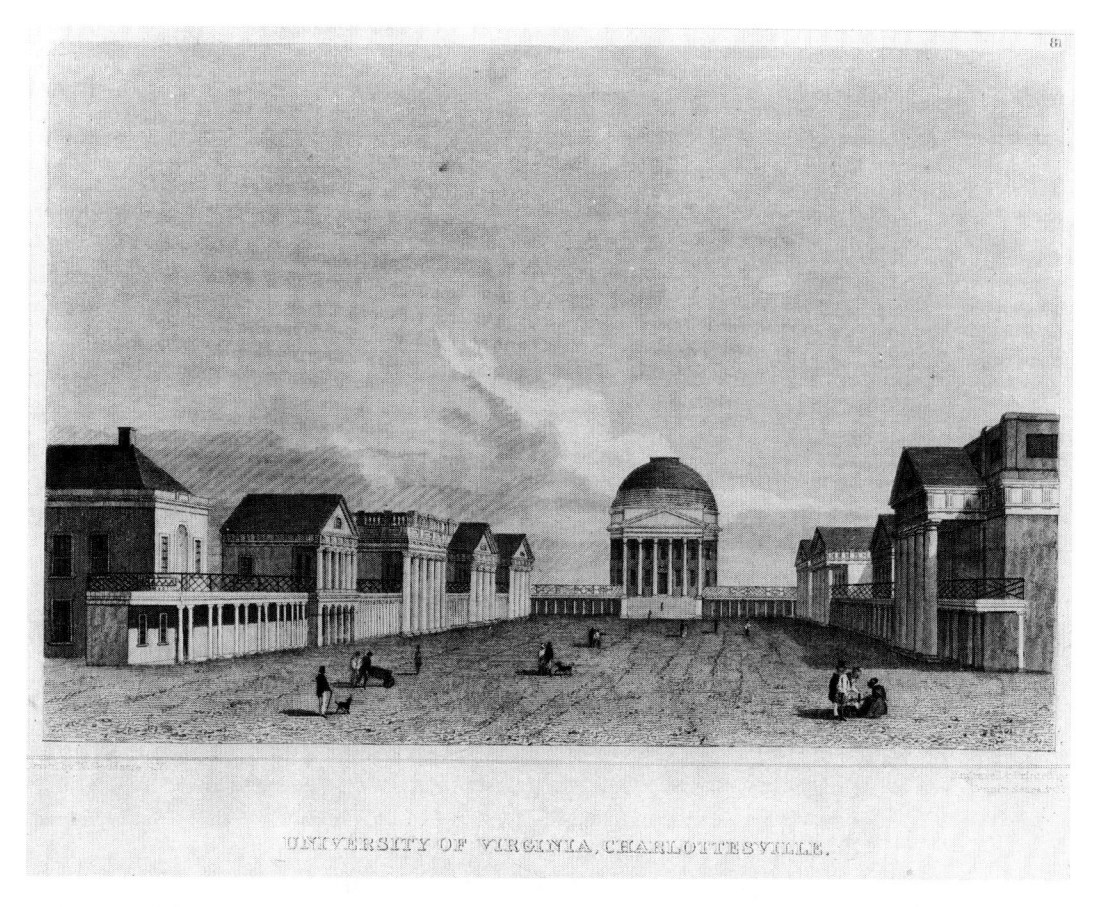

UNIVERSITY OF VIRGINIA, CHARLOTTESVILLE.

8.8 Thomas Jefferson, University of Virginia, Charlottesville, 1817–25
Source: Drawn by W. Goodacre, printed by Fenner Sears & Co., 1831. Courtesy of the Library of Virginia.

of the ten pavilions where professors taught students and lived with their families are disposed in increasing distances from one another and are interspersed with student rooms fronted by a colonnade which itself has trees lined along it (not shown in Figure 8.6; see Figure 1.2). The arrangement is repeated on the flanks down the slopes beyond the intervening gardens where the larger buildings interrupting the rows of student room serve as refectories, dispensaries, and so on (this area is not shown in Figure 8.6). They also house staff who, with the slaves, counted for probably half of the academical village's population.

The buildings produce an easily decipherable gradation from public to private uses and places within the landscape. The lawn stretching before the Rotunda and framed by the pavilions and student rooms is a kind of public common; here I come together with others. The student rooms are private; their residents may be alone there. The colonnades facing the lawn or the arcades in the ranges down the slopes and beyond the gardens offer protection from inclement weather and, more importantly, are like streets that mediate between the public realm in the commons and the private realm of the rows of student rooms that are miniatures of the row houses lining urban streets all through the period's cities, although, the uses that the modern era imposes on streets make it impossible for streets to render that service now.[68] Among the gardens some, or some part of some of them, are preserves of the contiguous pavilion's family, demonstration plots for professors, or gardens for produce or pleasure.

The disposition of the buildings within the landscape illustrates the proportionality endemic to the classical tradition.[69] The whole is demarcated into separate, discrete units in a rational disposition whose geometric and proportionate control make visible the result of imitating nature's proportionality. The material elements of building are assembled from a limited range of configurations and membratures that draw from the classical tradition and display innovations that fit them in their time, place, and purpose. The entire apparatus is a model for the University's graduates who are both alike and different and are destined to become leaders and models for others in both governing and building. Jefferson explained that the ten cubic professors' pavilions with "no two alike [are] to serve as specimens for the architectural lecturer" and present a syllabus of ancient and modern examples of the columnar orders.[70] In the complex any visitor can discern the relative importance of the purposes the different buildings serve, and knowledgeable visitors can easily recognize their parentage in the Pantheon and in Palladian villas and Virginia plantation houses as well as the dilution to make the student rooms.

Cities and their surroundings inevitably must find a place for things that are necessary but whose conspicuous presence would disrupt decorum. At the University barnyards, a dissecting theater, and shacks for the service personnel and slaves were tucked in here and there, all of them subsequently erased. They presented a reality as inconspicuously as possible; more conspicuous, and intended, was Jefferson's understanding that commerce, industry, and the market are necessary to sustain the city but are not themselves the city and need to be controlled by the city. He kept them accessible but at a distance, a mile away in Charlottesville, the county seat that a canal connected to the outside and Jefferson had helped bring into being.

Jefferson had taken up residence in the Piedmont more than a half century before the University opened. In that interval the frontier wilderness had moved well beyond the University's Piedmont site. Nearer to hand and won from the wilderness rested the cultivated, rural, agricultural landscape holding the civil landscape of villages and cities and the specialized gardens, a landscape that reaches its ultimate refinement in a trimmed, turfed, public common often surrounding a courthouse, the seat of justice. All this except wilderness is found at the University with the rural tracts beyond the lower ranges, the gardens enclosed within the serpentine walls, the Rotunda, pavilions, and student rooms and colonnades defining the civil landscape and the public common. The common or civic forum of the village is most intensely present in the Lawn where twin rows of trees parallel the colonnades and bring the material of the sylvan wilderness into the disciplined urban center. Connecting and unifying the village's different landscapes are pathways and alleys reached by a subtle arrangement of gaps in the rows of student rooms and ranges that reveal a wonderful sensitivity to both routes and views within the complex. At Poplar Forest we saw a place "proportioned to the faculties of a private citizen." Here we find an epitome of the American civil landscape, a diverse landscape that makes a visible setting for the second nature where people united in a civil order pursue their happiness together with others.

NOTES

1. Despite later studies the definitive book remains Fiske Kimball, *Thomas Jefferson, Architect* (Boston: Riverside Press for Private Distribution, 1916; reprinted New York: Da Capo Press, 1968); his sections on Jefferson in *American Architecture* (Indianapolis and New York: Bobbs-Merrill, 1928) have not been improved upon. Useful is Hugh Howard, *Dr. Kimball and Mr. Jefferson: Rediscovering the Founding Fathers of American Architecture* (New York: Bloomsbury, 2006). Unfortunate are amateurs' studies such as Ralph G. Giordano, *The Architectural Ideology of Thomas Jefferson* (Jefferson, North Carolina, and London: McFarland & Company, 2012) with a reach that far exceeds the grasp.

2. TJ to Major John Cartwright, Monticello, June 5, 1824, in *Writings*, 1490–96, emphasis added. In citing TJ's letters I have striven to cite the most easily accessible when there are multiple sources.

3. Daniel N. Robinson, "The Scottish Enlightenment and the American Founding," *The Monist*, 90:2 (2007), 180.

4. TJ to Peter Carr, Paris, August, 10, 1787, in *Writings*, 902.

5. Kenneth Hafertepe, "An Inquiry into Thomas Jefferson's Ideas of Beauty," *Journal of the Society of Architectural Historians*, 59 (2000), which supplies material to correct the flaws of the stylistic approach in the nonetheless useful article by Buford Pickens, "Mr. Jefferson as Revolutionary Architect," *Journal of the Society of Architectural Historians*, 34 (1975), 257–79.

6. TJ, "Autobiography," in *Writings*, 3–101, 45.

7. In a later letter Jefferson wrote, "We have indeed an innate sense of what we call beautiful, but that is exercised chiefly on subjects addressed to the fancy, whether through the eye in visible forms, as landscape, animal figure, dress, drapery, architecture … " etc. This followed the statement, the "criticism of taste" concerns "a faculty entirely distinct from the moral one." The "faculty of taste … is not even a branch of morality." TJ to Thomas Law, Poplar Forest, June 13, 1814, in *Writings*, 1336. We will find fancy in TJ to Buchanan and Hay, Paris, January 26, 1786, in *Writings*, 845, and discussed a little later here. The taste that fancy addresses is imagination, not the taste that gives access to the beautiful that is the counterpart to the good.

8. Anthony Ashley Cooper, Lord Shaftsbury, "A Letter Concerning Design," 1714, in (1714) in *Characteristics of Men, Manners, Opinions, Times*, 5th edition (London: [no publisher listed]), 1732, 3: 41–2.

9. Jefferson, *Notes on the State of Virginia*, query XV.

10. TJ to William Short, Lyon, March 15, 1787, *Papers*, vol. 11, 215.

11. TJ, "A Tour to some Gardens in England," in *Writings*, 627.

12. TJ to Charles Bellini, Paris, September 30, 1786, *Writings*, 834.

13. TJ to William Short, Aix, March 29, 1787, *Papers*, vol. 11, 253–4.

14. TJ to James Madison, Paris, September 1, 1785, *Writings*, 822.

15. TJ to Buchanan and Hay, Paris, January 26, 1786, *Writings*, 845–8.

16. See for domestic comfort Frederick D. Nichols, "Jefferson: The Making of an Architect," in William Howard Adams, ed., *Jefferson and the Arts: an Extended View* (Washington: National Gallery of Art, 1976), 159–85.

17. Richard Guy Wilson, "Thomas Jefferson's 'Bibliomanie' and Architecture," in Kenneth Hafertepe and James F. O'Gorman, eds, *American Architects and their Books* (Amherst:

University of Massachusetts Press, 2001), 59–72; William Bainter O'Neal, *Jefferson's Fine Arts Library: His Selections for the University of Virginia Together with His Own Architectural Books*, 2nd edn (Charlottesville: University Press of Virginia, 1976).

18 Kimball, *Jefferson Architect*, 1916, 34.

19 Fiske Kimball, *Domestic Architecture of the American Colonies and of the Early Republic* (New York: Charles Scribner's Sons, 1922), 159; Marcus Whiffen, *The Public Buildings of Williamsburg, Colonial Capital of Virginia* (Williamsburg: Colonial Williamsburg, 1958), 179–81, whose analysis refines Kimball's dating for the drawing.

20 See Fiske Kimball, "Jefferson and the Public Buildings of Virginia, II. Richmond, 1779–1780," *Huntington Library Quarterly*, 12 (1949), 303–10. He dates the drawings of the Capitol to the spring and early summer of 1780.

21 The drawing is in the Huntington Library, San Marino, California, HL 9373. It lacks stairs and podia. See Douglas L. Wilson, "Dating Jefferson's Early Architectural Drawings," *Virginia Magazine of History and Biography*, 101 (1993), 59, who depends on dating the handwriting; see also Mark R. Wenger, "Thomas Jefferson and the Virginia State Capitol," *Virginia Magazine of History and Biography*, 101 (1993), who earlier had dated it to 1774–July 1776, 82–7, on the basis of the room uses.

22 The basic material concerning the Capitol are Thomas J. McCormick, *Charles-Louis Clérisseau and the Genesis of Neo-Classicism* (Cambridge, Mass., and London: MIT Press, 1990), Chapter 9; and Fiske Kimball, "Thomas Jefferson and the First Monument of the Classical Revival in America," *Journal of the American Institute of Architects*, III, (1915), 375–6. Fiske Kimball, *The Capitol of Virginia: A Landmark of American Architecture*, revised and expanded from a 1989 republication edited Jon Kukla, with a new introduction by Charles Brownell, (Richmond: Library of Virginia, 2001), where, at 9, we find that commissioners in Richmond also "requested a draught for the Governor's house and a prison," but said there was no hurry on these; James Buchanan and Wm Hay, to TJ, Richmond, March 20, 1785.

23 TJ to James Madison, Paris, September 1, 1785; and September 20, 1785, Kimball, *Capitol of Virginia*, 5–6. The parsimonious commonwealth required that it include the judiciary.

24 TJ to Buchanan and Hay, Paris, January 26, 1786, *Writings*, 845–8.

25 TJ to Buchanan and Hay, Paris, August 13, 1785, in Kimball, *Capitol of Virginia*, 10–11. Roger G. Kennedy, *Orders from France* (New York: Alfred A. Knops, 1989), 433–5, notes that he later went out of his way to visit Nîmes not to see the building but to rendezvous secretly with a Brazilian insurrectionist.

26 "Jefferson's Hints to Americans Travelling in Europe," *Papers*, 13: 264–75; 269, 272.

27 TJ to Justice William Johnson, Monticello, June 12, 1823; in *Writings*, 1470.

28 TJ, "Autobiography," *Writings*, 3–101, 41. This passage, placed in a discussion of his proposed revisions to penal statutes, also refers to the new ideas he had for the prison that the commissioners also requested.

29 From 1821, "An Account of the Capitol in Virginia," in Albert Ellery Bergh, ed., *The Writings of Thomas Jefferson* (Washington: The Thomas Jefferson Memorial Association, 1904) vol. 17, 353–4; quoted in Fiske Kimball, *Capitol of Virginia*, 7.

30 Charles Brownell publishes material about these "Notes explicatives" to Clérisseau in his "Introduction to the 2002 Edition" of Kimball, *Capitol of Virginia*, xxi. His comment that the note suggests a departure from his initial scheme based on the Maison Carrée through "the impact of newer archaeological literature," and that Clérisseau returned

the scheme to the model of the Maison after having acquired the books of Woods (1757) and LeRoy (1758) soon after he arrived in France is doubtful. Kimball, *Jefferson Architect*, 35 notes that he listed those books as desiderata when he left for France; he had probably acquired the Perrault before 1775.

31 From 1821, quoted in Kimball, *Capitol of Virginia*, 2001, 7; emphasis added. Charles E. Brownell, in Brownell et al., *The Making of Virginia Architecture*, (Charlottesville and London: University Press of Virginia, 1992), 214 noted that his "thinking obviously belongs to the family of square and circular proportional systems of which both Vitruvius and Palladio had written, and that the [Inigo] Jones circle and his eighteenth-century followers had employed in Britain." Kruft, *A History*, 346, misleadingly links the geometric origins to the "French revolutionary architects whom he encountered during his stay in Paris."

32 Jefferson, *Notes on the State of Virginia*, query XIII, 4. See also Ackerman, *Palladio*, 1966, 75–80; and Robert Travernor, *Palladio and Palladianism* (London: Thames and Hudson, 1991), Part VI.

33 Often cited, from a letter of Colonel Isaac C. Coles to General James Hartwell Cocke, February 23, 1816, University of Virginia, Special Collections, Cocke Papers, no. 640, box 21.

34 Thomas Jefferson, *Notes on the State of Virginia*, query XV.

35 TJ to James Madison, Paris, September 20, 1785, *Writings*, 828–30. Similarly TJ to Edmund Randolph, Paris, September 20, 1785, *Papers*, 8: 538.

36 James Wilson, *Lectures on Law* in Bird Wilson, ed., *The Works of the Honourable James Wilson, L.L.D.*, 3 vols (Philadelphia: Bronson and Chauncey, 1804), 1: 55. Note that he does not include what we hear.

37 Remarks to the legislative committee in charge of the State House project quoted in Harold Kirker, *The Architecture of Charles Bulfinch* (Cambridge, Mass.: Harvard University Press, 1969), 7; see also 11, and Harold & James Kirker, *Bulfinch's Boston, 1787–1817* (New York: Oxford University Press, 1964), 43.

38 See Harold Kirker, *Bulfinch*, 10ff. See also Harold Kirker, "Charles Bulfinch," in Adolph K. Placzek, ed., *Macmillan Encyclopedia of Architects*, 4 vols (New York: The Free Press, 1982).

39 Kirker, *Bulfinch*, 103.

40 Jeffrey A. Cohen, "Forms into Architecture: Reform Ideals and the Gauntlet of the Real in Latrobe's Surveyorships at the U.S. Capitol, 1803–1917," in Donald R. Kennon, ed., *The United States Capitol: Designing and Decorating a National Icon* (Athens, Ohio: Ohio University Press, 2000), 33, and passim stresses the Irish connection.

41 Allan Greenberg, *The Architecture of Democracy* (New York: Rizzoli, 2006), 30.

42 Greenberg, *Architecture of Democracy*, 72; 86–90.

43 For the role of Jefferson's buildings as teachers see for example Bryan Clark Green, *In Jefferson's Shadow: The Architecture of Thomas R. Blackburn* (Richmond: Virginia Historical Society and New York: Princeton Architectural Press, 2006).

44 TJ to Madam de Tessé, Nismes, March 20, 1787, *Writings*, 891–3, emphasis in original.

45 Philibert de l'Orme, *Architecture* (Rouen: David Ferrand, 1648), 306 et seqq; see Mark Deming, *La Halle au Ble de Paris, 1762–1813* (Brussels: Archives d'Architecture Moderne, 1984), 175–84. The dome's parentage in de l'Orme, by Jacques-Guillaume Legrand and Jacques Molinos, was proudly acknowledged in a plaque.

46   Figure 5.6 presents the original image that Jefferson never saw; it lacks the "windows."

47   Paul Norton, "Latrobe's Ceiling for the Hall of Representatives," *Journal of the Society of Architectural Historians*, 10 (1951), 5–10, with quotations from TJ to Maria Cosway, October 12, 1786, and TJ to Latrobe, September 8, 1805. A clear description and Latrobe's drawing of the solution is in William C. Allen, *History of the United States Capitol: A Chronicle of Design, Construction, and Politics* (Washington: U.S. Government Printing Office, 2001), 63–4; TJ to Latrobe, Monticello, April 22, 1807, in John C. Van Horne, ed., *The Correspondence and Miscellaneous Papers of Benjamin Henry Latrobe*, 3 vols (New Haven and London: Yale University Press, 1984–88), 2: 410–11.

48   Latrobe to TJ, Washington, August 31, 1805, in *Papers of Latrobe*, 2: 137.

49   TJ to Latrobe, Monticello, July 12, 1812, in *Writings*, Bergh, ed., 1905, 7: 179.

50   For England see Frank Jenkins, *Architect and Patron* (London: Oxford University Press, 1961), Chapters 4–6.

51   Charles Brownell, "Thomas Jefferson's Architectural Models and the United States Capitol," in Donald R. Kennon, ed., *A Republic for the Ages: The United States Capitol and the Political Culture of the Early Republic*, (Charlottesville and London: University Press of Virginia, 1999), quotations from 401, 371.

52   Damie Stillman, "From the Ancient Roman Republic to the New American One: Architecture for a New Nation," in Donald R. Kennon, ed., *A Republic for the Ages: The United States Capitol and the Political Culture of the Early Republic*, (Charlottesville and London: University Press of Virginia, 1999), 290 and Figs 13, 14; see this also for L'Enfant's inventive America-themed orders.

53   Brownell, "Architectural Models," quotations from 369.

54   Latrobe to John Lenthall, Philadelphia, August 5, 1804, in Latrobe, *Papers of Latrobe*, 1: 527–8, original emphasis; see also Cohen and Brownell, *Drawings of Latrobe*, 11.

55   For a recent general treatment see Scott W. Berg, *Grand Avenues: The Story of the French Visionary who Designed Washington, D.C.* (New York: Pantheon Book, 2007). For the proclamation, see *Papers*, vol. 19, 65–6; for L'Enfant, see "The Secretary of State to the Commissioners of the Federal District, Philadelphia, 18 January, 1791," *Papers*, 19: 67–8. Also informative is Julian P. Boyd, "Editorial Note: 'Locating the Seat of Government,'" *Papers*, 19: 3–58.

56   It exists as a press copy of the original that President Washington gave to L'Enfant and is now lost. Jefferson made his sketch before he knew that the President had obtained a vastly larger site that could include 3,000 to 4,000 acres for public uses and land for streets, alleys, and public buildings, which together could occupy more than 12 percent of the district's land; Washington to Jefferson, Mount Vernon, March 31, 1791, *Papers*, 20: 81–2.

57   Recent publications show that the usually reliable John Reps in *Monumental Washington: The Planning and Development of the Capital Center* (Princeton: Princeton University Press, 1967), 2–4, misidentified the sources for one of two Jefferson sketches, neither illustrated here. The one that shows a typical block is in TJ [29 August, 1790]. "Jefferson's Draft of Agenda for the Seat of Government," *Papers*, 17: 460–46. This is not, as Reps suggests, the source for the 4×7+ block grid in the acute junction of the Potomac and Tyber, which is instead in "Jefferson's Report to Washington on Meeting Held in Georgetown" from 14 September 1790, in *Papers*, 17: 461–3.

58   Note also that Jefferson found no place for Versailles, which he knew well, in his sketch. Versailles is tirelessly evoked as L'Enfant's model. But see Allan Greenberg, *George Washington Architect* (London: Andres Papadakis, 1999), Part 2, that sensibly

argues that the "'Sun King's symbolism … would not have appealed to Washington, or to most Americans, as a model,'" and instead stresses Annapolis and Williamsburg and Christopher Wren's 1666 plan for London. Note that these, congruent with English tradition and the American Constitution, separate both the powers and localities of the authoritative institutions.

59   See for these John W. Reps, "Thomas Jefferson's Checkerboard Towns," *Journal of the Society of Architectural Historians*, 20 (1961), 108–14.

60   TJ to John Wayles Eppes, September 18, 1812, quoted in C. Allan Brown, "Thomas Jefferson's Poplar Forest: the Mathematics of an Ideal Villa," *Journal of Garden History*, 10 (1990), 119, which, with S. Allen Chambers, *Poplar Forest and Thomas Jefferson* (Forest, Virginia: The Corporation for Jefferson's Poplar Forest, 1993), are the sources for much of the material here.

61   TJ to William Coffee, July 10, 1822, quoted in Timothy Trussell, "A Landscape for Mr. Jefferson's Retreat," in Barbara J. Heath and Jack Gary, eds, *Jefferson's Poplar Forest: Unearthing a Virginia Plantation* (Gainesville et al: University Press of Florida, 2012), 83.

62   For the Geometry see Brown, "Mathematics," 126, 129, and Figure 13.

63   The first quotation is TJ to William Short, October 31, 1819, in Brown, "Mathematics," 131; the second is TJ to A.C.V.C. Desutt de Tracy, Monticello, December 26, [18]20, in *The Writings of Thomas Jefferson*, ed. Paul Leicester Ford Paul, x: 174.

64   Jefferson used the phrase in 1785 to refer to Williamsburg's reduction to "a mere academical village" after the capital was moved to Richmond. TJ to Samuel Henley, Paris, Oct. 14, 1785; *Papers*, 8: 634–5, and again in 1804–6 and 1816–17. See Kimball, *Jefferson Architect*, 74ff; and Richard Guy Wilson, "Jefferson's Lawn: Perceptions, Interpretations, Meanings," in R.G. Wilson, ed., *Thomas Jefferson's Academical Village: The Creation of an Architectural Masterpiece* (Charlottesville and London: University Press of Virginia, 1993), 68.

65   "A Bill for the More General Diffusion of Knowledge," from 1779, in *Papers*, 2: 526–33; a reference to "a log school house" is in Jefferson's letter to Joseph C. Cabell from February 2, 1816, published in James B. Conant, *Thomas Jefferson and the Development of American Public Education* (Berkeley and Los Angeles: Univ. of California Press, 1963), 118.

66   TJ to Joseph Cabell, February 2, 1816, in Conant, *Jefferson and Education*, 118–19.

67   "Report of the Commissioners for the University of Virginia," in Merrill D. Peterson, ed., *The Portable Thomas Jefferson*, (New York and London: Penguin, 1977), 335.

68   See David E. Nye, "Energy," in Miles Orvell and Klaus Benesch, eds, *Rethinking the American City* (Philadelphia: University of Pennsylvania Press, 2014), 5–10.

69   I have discussed these principles elsewhere; see "Classical American Urbanism," in Andreas Papadakis and Harriet Watson, eds, *New Classicism: Omnibus Volume* (New York: Rizzoli, and London: Academy Editions, 1990), 73–5.

70   TJ to Latrobe, June 12, 1817, LC, quoted by Wilson in Wilson, ed., *Jefferson's Academical Village*, 70.

9

Imitation and Architecture's Restoration

RESTORING ARCHITECTURE ON ITS TRIPOD

Thomas Jefferson's role in the architecture of the classical tradition is important enough to deserve the term Jeffersonianism. The roots it sank were not as deep as those of the civic order that still guides our political life. The architects and builders in the next few generations in America became entrapped by a culture that had quite different ambitions from those that animated the Founders. The nation's centennial celebration reminded Americans of the unique place the nation occupied in the world, and in the next decade the forms that appealed to the Founders gained a new birth of freedom. In the decades after the First World War that episode was undermined by a doctrine that rejected the reasons that validated the traditional forms that had been brought back into play. An inquiry into the inadequacies of the revival will help us understand why it was rejected, after which we can turn to suggestions about how to restore Jeffersonianism to American architecture.

The buildings that illustrated America's self-confident stance in the world in the decades around 1900 had their sources in the education offered in the Ecole des Beaux Arts in Paris. After the American Civil War increasing numbers of Americans went there, and in the first three decades of the twentieth century most American architects were trained there or in an Americanized version offered in offices and most universities. The professionalization of architecture coincided with the dominance of what came to be called Beaux Arts architecture, and the culture of architecture absorbed the understanding of what an architect is and does from this import from the Continent. The contributions of these architects and builders to American cities can hardly be overstated.

The Ecole had been established in the wake of the French Revolution to train architects to build in post-Revolutionary France. Students joined ateliers of approved masters where they learned how to compose formal configurations and membratures and make convincing graphic representations of their designs.

The program had been adapted from the one invented to train Napoleon's engineers to build utilitarian buildings whose form follows their functions. For the important buildings that the Ecole architects would build the form follows function formula was expanded to invest the integument with the character that testified to the government's Frenchness and thus to the legitimacy of its authority. Governments came and went, but the role of their Frenchness remained. This put the focus on the formal properties and allowed the actual tectonic, material structure to be quite separate from the actual membrature's actual tectonics. The tectonic structure exploited the structural potential of the new materials and technologies but it was not allowed to detract from the Frenchness or welcome them as part of the formal expression, particularly in the later years when Americans were abundant in the Ecole. In Berlin and Vienna the tectonics played a larger role in the formal character.

Beaux-Arts planning is the name given to the large-scale, comprehensive planning that Paris taught the world, but urbanism was not taught at the Ecole. Its attention was on the formal properties of high-status, stand-alone set pieces that could fill the sites prepared for them in the urban matrix that Napoleon III and Baron Haussmann were planting in Paris; Ecole professors and graduates were hardly otherwise involved.[1] The affluent Americans haunting Paris and American students studying there absorbed this urbanism while the architects also learned the classical styles that the Ecole taught. They then de-Frenchified and polished them with a close study of the ancient Roman models and their chaste Renaissance successors that Jefferson had so valued. Charles Follen McKim helped found the American Academy in Rome to give them access to buildings that Jefferson knew only through books.

Instruction at the Ecole was long on practice and very short on theory despite the devotion to theory by its long-time director, Antoine Chrysostôme Quatremère de Quincy (1755–1849). Quatremère was resuscitating the doctrine of imitation, but those around him in the Ecole were smothering it. His extended essay concerning the representational arts, *Essay … [on] Imitation in the Fine Arts*, came in 1823 before he moved on to the very different topic of imitation in architecture.[2] It was among the topics that he had broached 40 years earlier, developed subsequently, and spread through a sprawling dictionary published in 1832. Largely ignored until a few decades ago, his ideas have now become accessible in a masterful translation and discussion.[3]

Quatremère's ideas opened up useful, new understandings of type, character, style, and other important terms with imitation at the center. Quatremère's type addresses architecture's lack of a model or real thing to imitate. To supply the want he offered types that are found in the nature of things that men have built. These models are not things nature has made, such as the trees or the human figure cited as models for the columnar orders. Types belong to architecture, and they are universal in the sense that they belong to no particular time or place; instead, they link architecture in all times and places to what is true in nature about the art of building and serve as "an originating reason accessible to the intellect."[4] In Chapter 1 we reviewed the extension of this idea in Demetri Porphyrios' discussion of tectonics. Here we will go farther.

Here we can make use of the tripod that supports architecture with its three legs of the tectonic, the formal, and the urban. A building may emphasize one or two, but to be elevated to architecture all three legs must play their roles as members of the whole body of the building.

In addressing the formal leg the type becomes useful to the architect as an image that will become the representation of the type in the real, actual building. One essential workman bridging between image and representation is the fiction in the building's membrature: this thing you see is the fictive, truth-telling image of the type. One truth that it makes visible is the building's capacity to endure as a material entity and assure you of its enduringness and stability, as Porphyrios explained. That assurance is true in the image, and it is legible to you because its representation in the real building belongs to your culture of building. That culture of building exists within a tradition that the new building will join and that provides the models that guide architects in finding the fiction that makes visible the qualities of what he calls the essential, distinctive, and relative characters.

Character is extracted from models, which are always in the plural. *Essential* character, most evident in the formal properties of paradigmatic models, reveals the universal type that is true of all buildings that become architecture. *Distinctive* character is learned from canonic models that are part of the tradition of building to which the new building will contribute. That tradition also furnishes the *relative* character that uses visual qualities to identify the building's particular use and to honor decorum.[5] Style completes Quatremère's trilogy. It identifies the manner that is unique to the architect, the workmen, the place, and the time. Other theorists and the current dominant narrative use the word to refer to the all-important formal identity produced by the influences that make a building "of its time" and insert it in a narrative of sequential, irreversible change. For Quatremère style is much less important and quite different. It is merely, but importantly, the final finishing touches of a building; type and character that prevail across time within a tradition are much more important.

Quatremère's method of imitation stands clear of collapsing into emulation. The difference is in what sets precedents apart from models. Emulation uses precedents, more often singular than plural, to provide the point of departure for a new design, which turns out to be an adaptation of the precedent. Quatremère's imitation uses models as the visible material that gives access to the universal type's image for the kind of building that the building is. That image is then translated through fiction to the representation made visible in the material building's character and style. Emulation can hover around copying while imitation defies copying or transcribing with a pantograph, tracing paper, dividers, a light table, a photocopy machine, a computer, or even a hand deft at making descriptive sketches.

When type, character, and style work together, when the building is beautifully and marvellously made, it will embody the universal truth that is cross-cultural and timeless and also display the particularities of time and place within a tradition of building. It will identify its specific purpose and its place in the civil order. Beauty is there to be perceived, and its response to decorum can be recognized by anyone with eyes capable of making comparisons between things they see. Clear here are the similarities of architectural expression to a legal order's dual allegiance to *jus naturale* and *jus civile*, although Quatremère does not make that connection. His framework is more Platonic than Aristotelian, and it is apolitical. He presents architecture as a fundamentally aesthetic undertaking that offers unquestioned support to the civil order that uses it to express its authority. Quatremère's teaching therefore stands apart from that of others we have met: Vitruvius, various medieval authors, Alberti, Palladio, and Jefferson, although we will soon review its utility in serving their purposes.

SOME RESTORATIONS OF THE FOUNDATIONS

The hope of those who sought a bridge across the abyss between the present and the classical tradition was kept alive by the flame that Henry Hope Reed tended at the shrine of America's Beaux Arts architecture and the continued practice of a small number of Other Modern architects who simply avoided Modernism.[6] Eventually some Modernist architects became bored by minimalism and spent a few years raiding traditional buildings for forms before moving on to other entertainments. Meanwhile, those who were dissatisfied with Modernism's justificatory theories began investigating theories concerning types, although they too soon wearied, except for two young architects who refused to come under Modernism's heel. They found material in Quatremère, who had receded into near total obscurity, that provided their points of departure for their modernization of classical architecture's foundations.[7] One, Demertri Porphyrios (b.1949), we encountered earlier; here we will concentrate on the other one, Léon Krier (b.1946), who was the first laureate of the Richard H. Driehaus Prize with Porphyrios being the second.

Krier's goal is to restore the urban and formal legs to their former roles in a renewed tripod of classical and traditional architecture and urbanism.[8] A native of Luxembourg, after a few months in architecture school in Germany he became repulsed by the teaching and by Modernism's hold on the rebuilding of war-ravaged Europe proclaiming, "Because I am an architect I do not build." Instead he polemicized with witty and trenchant diagrams and texts and with competition entries and counter proposals to bring into existence a culture of traditional and classical architecture and urbanism in which he could build. In the 1970s his clear diagrams of the roles of public and private uses in cities in the landscape and the traditional formal types for the buildings serving them gained attention. He observed that the healthy city does not grow by segregating functions and enlarging buildings in monocultural zones but by adding identifiable, walkable, mixed-use neighborhoods whose buildings draw on local traditions. He taught that rooms make buildings and buildings make blocks and define public places that are streets and squares that clearly serve the diverse activities of a civil life.

Krier's now-extensive corpus of urban schemes, buildings, and books has become a persuasive reminder that a good civic architecture is a sustainable architecture based on an artisanal art of building that begins in the vernacular. Proportionality based on metaphoric relationships to the human figure and to mankind's needs must

CIVITAS

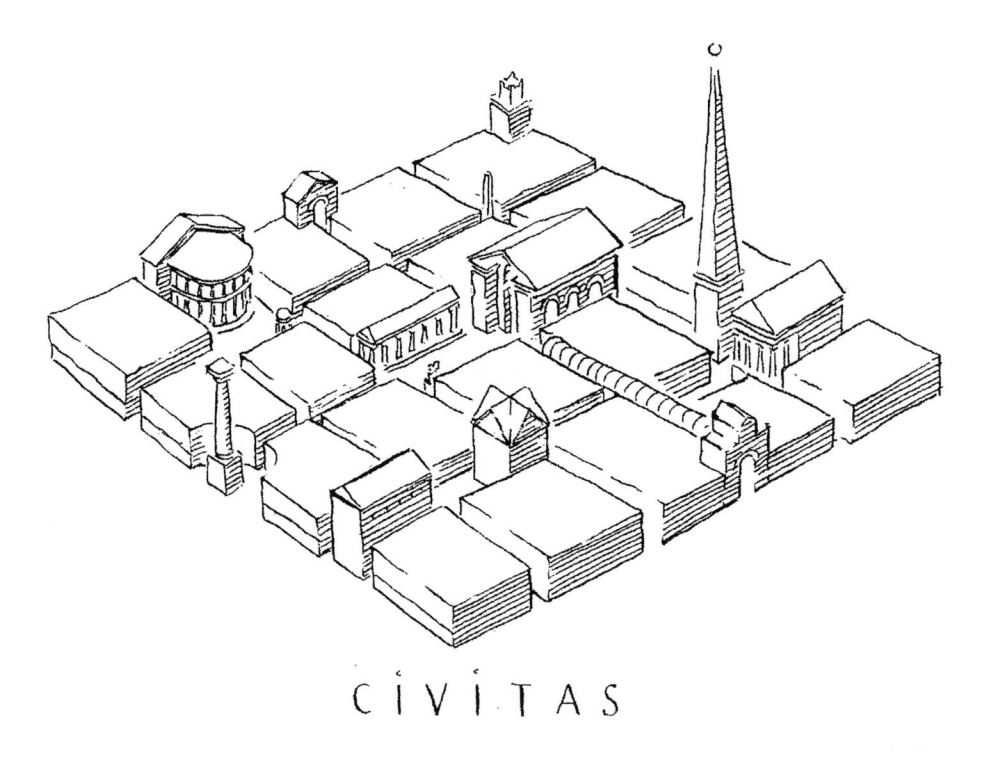

govern the right-sizing of the building's members, their assembly into a membrature, the configuration's composition, and the relationships between built-up and open public and private urban and rural realms. His is a traditional civic architecture, one in which the city is for its residents and aimed at facilitating their public and private activities. He favors ploughmen over professors. He has never defined what the ends of those activities are or ought to be but insists that they must be in the hands of citizens and free from the control of the nearly hegemonic destructive Modernist ideologies. One that is prominent is in the unrecognized forces of *technique* that the French philosopher Jacques Ellul had identified. Another is the snare of mimetic rivalry that prevents architects from looking after the public good.[9]

A notable recent contribution to theory has come from Nikos Salingaros, a mathematician who brings his knowledge of fractals, physics, and neurophysiology to his critique of Modernist architecture.[10] Salingaros exposes the Modernists' fraudulent use of modern science and mathematics to support their theories and to justify their buildings' incoherent compositions and banal minimalism. He documents Modernism's success in duping people into accepting easily produced and easily remembered superficial "memes" (clichés) as the basis of the architecture of the new era in history that has overwhelmed the life-enhancing formal richness of traditional buildings. His antidote would apply a formal ordering to the composition of buildings that uses fractals, "scaling," "modularity," and so on in architecture's "form language" and "pattern language." Success would undercut the Modernists' claim to a method that exploits the most modern of modern science's techniques, and it would implement a method for restoring traditional

9.1 Léon Krier, Civitas: res publica and res private; monuments without streets and squares, streets and squares without monuments
Source: Demetri Porphyrios, guest ed., *Léon Krier: Houses, Palaces, Cities*, (London: AD Profile 54, 1984), 41. Used by permission.

architecture's relationship to the order of nature by enriching the proportionality of buildings' symmetry (that is, *symmetria*) which, like Vitruvius' *venustas*, would pay their inhabitants with good feelings and comfort and replace the derring-do of Modernists' technologies.

Salingaros' concern is with the tripod's formal leg, and his attention to *venustas* tends to neglect a commitment to the public realm and the common good. That commitment's counterpart in the civil order is the pursuit of individual comfort and abundance, which does not quite square with the highest purposes of the Founders' modernization of the classical tradition. In that new program architecture retained the foundation it shared with the civil order in which each imitated its origins in the universal and timeless standards for justice and beauty to "secure the Blessings of Liberty to ourselves and our Posterity." This is the classical architecture that seeks beauty as the counterpart to justice and serves and expresses the authority that the civil order exercises to seek justice. And it is the architecture that has always recognized that to be successful it must accept the civil order's authority over the ends that it seeks.

Those who are comfortable in Plato's cave and take the images that they see to be reality are indifferent to this goal and role. From there they cannot see heaven's illumination or the horizon that orients them in the larger world.[11] Vitruvius would tell them that they "have chased after the shadow, not something real" (1.1.2). In our age we will find them on *technique*'s train, that potent symbol of the power of technology that first enthralled the world but whose passengers are unable to see the direction it is taking. They present their buildings as symbols of the *Zeitgeist*, but to the extent that they are symbols they symbolize the influences whose tyranny they willingly accept, which, in a "vicious circularity," symbolizes only its own content. "A symbol that symbolizes itself is a condition of no sense."[12] They remain oblivious that the visible and perceptible content of the symbol that serves the highest aspirations of mankind, which is the concinnity that binds the good, the true, and the beautiful in buildings that attain the status of architecture.

Concinnity serves the classical tradition that reaches into the timeless cosmos to find the universal and enduring standards for justice and beauty that across three millennia have taken a variety of forms in the variety of particularities of times, places, and people. The theorists we have reviewed in this chapter have led fifth-column assaults on Modernism. They and others have sought to reunify architecture and urbanism, and they have initiated the modernization of imitating nature with innovative knowledge, materials, and techniques that have enriched the classical tradition. But they have not yet brought down the Modernists' wall that separates denatured nature from the whole of nature, and so material nature remains isolated from its better part, which is the moral order in which humankind alone has been allowed to dwell. The ideologies of political and architectural theory remain in power, which leaves the civil order impotent in the face of Modernist architecture, and it leaves architects in the *Zeitgeist*'s tyrannical control. The rest of this book will explore some ways to restore the role of citizen–architects in using their art to protect the liberty of free people to live nobly and well in a just civil order.

PUTTING THE CIVIL ORDER IN COMMAND

We begin with a brief review of the structure of a civil order and then move to the buildings that serve it. A civil order is organized with a constitution whose building blocks are institutions and arrangements that serve its goals. These organize the political life of citizens. Each one has a particular purpose or role to play. They use buildings that they build or take over to serve and express that purpose or role, and these serve as the physical blocks of the urban order that the civil order inhabits. In traditional architecture and urbanism, that is, when architecture is practiced as a civic art, the public buildings that serve and express the purposes of the major public, civil institutions always look appropriate for the role they play and display their superiority over the lesser arrangements that serve them or that they supervise.[13]

The word "institution," which is now often used with abandon, will be constrained for our purposes. An *institution* is the enduring form given through custom, practice, tradition, or law to a principled activity that a community undertakes; its most distinctive characteristic is that it accounts for the moral character of the community's members.[14] Institutions serve purposes that are as unchanging and enduring as human nature and its needs. Not all entities are institutions. Some are what can be called *functional arrangements*, or simply arrangements, that fill out the civil order. Some arrangements assist institutions in their work by providing services that predictably will change over time, and others pursue their own ends, but how the arrangements do their work will be subject to constant revision as better means for doing so present themselves. More about them in a moment.

It may be that the several institutions that compose the constitutional order of any civil order fall into only four categories, primary, political, religious, and cultural. Among the *primary institutions* the family surely occupies the first rank because it precedes the city. To paraphrase Aristotle and recall the role of synoecism: no family, no tribe or village; no village, no city. Common law traditions confer on the American family nearly complete autonomy concerning its way of life and expect it to contribute to the public good from its foundational or bottom-up position. It is an institution. A market, necessary as it is, is no kind of institution. It is an arrangement that facilitates the work of the institutions it serves, which are the family at one scale and the city at another and every institution in between. A market, and the vast array of commercial-industrial-financial arrangements that assists it, can easily overwhelm a city founded on the classical tradition.[15] But deeply embedded in the classical tradition is the understanding that the market justice that seeks fairness in the market is not the justice that serves the public good and the highest aspirations of the individual citizen. The market serves the institutions that constitute the city, but market justice is a lesser thing than civil justice, which is a species of universal justice. In order that the market remains the city's servant and does not become its tyrannical master its operations and its justice require the supervision of the city's institutions.

That supervision comes from the *political institutions* that come into existence when the city does and remain authoritative so long as the city seeks justice, moral well-being, and happiness for all of its members. The modern civil order has three institutions at its heart, the legislative, the executive, and the judicial. Each of these establishes the various arrangements it needs to reach its purpose, running from police departments and military forces to social welfare agencies, from market inspectors to economic councils, from chambers of commerce to departments of planning and building, from agencies that build roads and those that protect against and render assistance after natural catastrophes.

In the American civil order these institutions and their arrangements are found at all levels of government, from the three branches of the federal government down to the municipal waterworks. In all of them the people enjoy several protections from government intrusion, among them the government's "abridging the freedom of speech, or of the press, or the right of the people peaceably to assemble, and to petition the Government for a redress of their grievances." The civil order also contains many other institutions among which the most important are those devoted to education, and these too are in the hands of the variety of subsidiary levels, principally states, cities, and rural districts.

Religious institutions are the third class. In the United States and in many other modern states these are given independence from the institutions that serve the political activities. The Founders recognized the fundamental incompatibility of the ordinances that arise from the nature of the city of man and the nature of a religious community united by an act of will and following divine instruction. Religious institutions often make subordinate arrangements to facilitate their purposes, and the nexus they spin can be every bit as complex as those that organize civil activities, but in a modern civil order institutions of neither one may without reason intrude into the affairs of the other.

The fourth category holds *cultural institutions*. These enhance our lives. While the word used to be understood as artifice's transformation of nature to make something useful to people it now has a much broader compass. When true to their name cultural institutions allow individuals to gain an enhanced sense of the richness of their human nature and its moral content whether through active involvement or otiose leisure. Some entities are not institutions but only harmless arrangements offering transitory pleasure with no promise of happiness. Others nourish only the vicious in human nature. And yet others nourish the best in some people while providing only pleasure to others. The anchors at the ends of the spectrum between obvious institutions (for example, liberal arts colleges) and vicious arrangements (for example, dog fights) are clear, but the range in between holds many shades of gray. Consider the following, in no particular order, and note that different people would place them in different places on the spectrum: national parks, professional sporting events, art museums, circuses, symphony orchestras, hospitals, barber-shop quartets, rock concerts, pornography, active and lively main streets, county fair midways, legitimate theater, opera, movies, and on and on.

A constitutional order's institutions and arrangements flourish in a culture in which people share their understandings, some of them implicit and others explicit, about how to strive for justice. Cultures come into existence across time and through synoecism in which each unit, whether individual, family, city, state, or nation and among the various institutions and arrangements retains its identity as it makes its contribution to the public common good. Command must always be reserved for the institutions in the civil order that govern by majority rule while protecting the natural rights of each individual. Those institutions may extract duties from lesser entities and individuals whether they are as minimal as enforcing public decorum and paying reasonable taxes or as intrusive as responding to military drafts to "provide for the common defense" or taking private property for public use through due process of law.

Institutions and arrangements build the physical components of the public and private realms. They build in both the rural and urban realms to serve the purposes and functions of the civil order that commands the land. They build examples of the typical and the particular characteristic buildings that will serve and express the purposes their builders have for them. This congruity between types and purposes is embedded in the classical tradition; to depart from the traditional congruity, as Modernism does, is to depart from that tradition, as Modernism willfully does. Distinctive types serve distinct activities. We must note that a type as used here exists only in the mind, as an idea, and that it contains within it all possible variations of ways to serve the activity that have existed or ever will exist. It is as enduring and universal as human nature itself, as the good that the building it generates seeks to serve and, as we shall see, as the beautiful that a marvelously made example of the type makes perceptible. We can consult *natura naturata* and *natura naturans* to find the types. In doing so we will follow the method that allowed Alberti to include existing buildings as part of *natutra naturata* and recall that Quatremère did as well. This observation leads us to consult the outflow of traditional buildings across all times and places and distill from them the congruity of type and purpose. Doing so we find probably only seven building types. Each type belongs to the reason and the nature of the action that serves the purpose of a particular institution or the functions of an arrangement. In other words, type follows either purpose or function.

Each type is known through a distinctive image or a building idea type that makes visible the ultimate distillation of the pattern of people's activities as it facilitates their pursuit of the purpose or the fulfillment of the function. When the visible image moves toward a building people in different times and in different places give greater specificity to that pattern and thereby produce an actual preliminary drawn diagram that can guide the steps that will lead to the configuration that will join with the membrature to make the character of the real building. Here we are at the beginning of all that. At this point in the explanation the diagram amounts to little more than an image that provides the first of the many steps toward arriving at the character that plants it firmly in the culture that builds it and that it serves.

The seven types (if that is their proper number) can be identified by the gerunds that describe the activities of the purposes or functions they entail and thereby produce the idea type images.[16] Any, or all, of the seven idea types operate at the level of either an institution with ancillary, facilitating arrangements or as an arrangement under institutional supervision. Among the seven types five can be called primary, that is, necessary for the civil life.

9.2 Images of the seven building idea types:
1, tholos;
2, temple;
3, theater;
4, regia; 5, domus;
6, taberna;
7, hypostyle
Source: Drawn by the author.

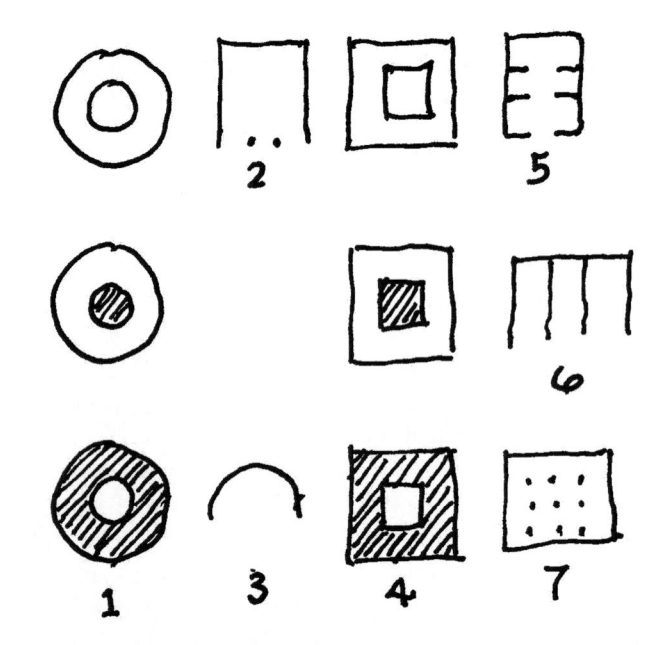

We can begin with *venerating*, which involves public, communal, or private pious devotion to something of transcendent importance. The activity normally occurs at a shrine of some sort. Its building idea type's name is *tholos* whose image is a circle or some other centralized geometric shape, normally with another, like shape within it.

Celebrating brings people together to share their joy or sorrow in some event. Liturgical Christians process, and so do graduates, sometimes toward a tholos, while winners are celebrated by marches and by large gatherings. Both institutions and arrangements organize celebrating. The name of the building idea type is *temple* to refer to a place set apart from, or within, the profane world. Its image has an open end celebrated with a pair of supports followed by an axis organizing the celebration and focusing attention on the thing being celebrated, perhaps something deserving a tholos that produces a composite type.

Imagining describes people reasoning together to achieve a closer congruence between the ideal and the real or the true and the factual. Usually an institutional activity, it occurs in the face-to-face activities in seminars, in spontaneously formed groups, in legislative bodies, and in the invisible but felt interaction between an audience and performers in an opera, a play, or a concert performance. Named *theater*, its image is a half-circle, perhaps as evanescent as a temporary arrangement of people on a lawn or as permanent as a Greek theater, and even open to being divided into facing halves as in the British House of Commons.

Exercising authority involves governing or projecting lawful power over others in the interest of the common good, which only institutions may do and all institutions must do. These are the primary institutions of the family and the various institutions of the civil order and their mates and allies. Religious institutions exercise authority over their willing members, and assisting and supplementing both kinds of institutions are libraries, universities and colleges, museums, art academies, philharmonic societies, and so on when they add to their charge the quest for the true and the beautiful. The state may operate these or license individuals or corporate bodies to pursue them, even at a profit.

These, more obviously than the other institutions, generate arrangements that prepare people for what institutions offer or to extend their reach into important but facilitating activities. The schooling of the young prepares children to pursue the fullness of their nature in citizenship and in higher education or rewarding work. Many other arrangements are often confused with institutions even as they support desired and even necessary activities: providing transportation for people; offering goods for sale; handling money and selling stocks and bonds; distributing gas, electricity, water, and other public services; entertaining with shows and sports; staging participatory sporting activities, and so on. All arrangements require the governance of institutions, and institutions themselves require protection from those who would assault them, which suggests its name, *regia*, and its image, a square doughnut whose character can have either a hollow or a solid core.

A much less specific activity is *gathering*, which identifies diversity running from transient picnics to long-term investment in commerce. A gathering might have religious institutional content (a wedding overlooking a lake; Muslim prayer services), be a cultural institution, or serve a mere arrangement (banking; commerce). Its building idea type is the *hypostyle hall*.[17] The term is elastic encompassing a mosque's forest of regularly spaced columns rising from a defined area and supporting a covering, or an open hall produced by modern engineering that renders columns unnecessary as in a convention hall or sports arena, or in a stack to produce a skyscraper. When these serve arrangements they require governing by an institution, and so a regia will commonly find its way into its character.

The final two activities are fundamental arrangements that, like all arrangements, require institutional supervision. In a perfectly prosperous democracy with no poverty among its perfectly healthy and law abiding members with perfect access to social, political, and economic participation for the "whole body of citizens" everyone would be a member of a family and every family would live in a regia. But our world is imperfect and peopled by imperfect individuals, and so there must also be accommodation for an additional kind of residence. Its need may be occasioned by a defective constitution that excludes universal suffrage, or an individual may opt out of the political life (the hermit; the traveler), or individual debilitation might require the assistance of others to sustain life, or a legitimate authority might force the exclusion (the incarcerated). For these and others like them the *dwelling* will serve. Its building idea type is a *domus* whose image is a rectangle with interior cells reached through gaps in the divisions aligned with a gap in one narrow end. Domuses are flats above the store, the units in apartments stacked in Modernist warrens along city streets and disengaged from the public realm, the cells in jails, hotel rooms, hospital rooms, and so on.

The final activity is exemplified by the shops below those flats and the successors in strip malls, other malls, market stalls and supermarket aisles, and so on. They and their like provide *sustaining*, an arrangement devoted to making, storing, and exchanging goods whether physical as in actual markets of in the virtual markets in commercial office buildings. Its building idea type is a *taberna* that may be collected into hypostyle halls holding malls or stacked in commercial towers. A variation of the domus, its rectangle holds cells open along the long side.

MAKING CIVIL BUILDINGS

So far the building idea types, the images they shepherd, and the material buildings that will be developed from them can take us only to the buildings' configurations. These are known through what Alberti called their lineaments and we can recognize in line drawings. They are minimalist abstractions and not yet buildings that can be seen. To become real, actual, visible buildings the membrature must join the configuration, and with that conjunction it receives its tectonic leg and eventually its formal leg as well. Here imitation again comes into play.

We saw in Chapter 1 that Porphyrios argued that architecture is the imitation of the art of building. That is, a building's membrature is a perfection of the traditions that first arose, and continue to develop, in vernacular buildings. The perfection requires the translation of materials and attention to refined craftsmanship and ornamentation that enriches the sense of stability and carries the mythic content that a culture of building possesses. We move from seeing to perceiving and thereby enjoy the security of its capacity to withstand nature's entropic forces, and we celebrate its evident resistance to the seven directions of motion that the ancients and common sense today can identify: left and right; back and forth; up and down; and around. Entropy, gravity, wind, and other forces, and those seven directions describe the activities of *natura naturans* at work, and *natura naturata* and the traditions of sound tectonics in the art of building describe the limited number of countervailing tectonic means that resist them. Those countervailing means can be found in *structural idea types*, which are the membrature's counterpart to and completion of the configuration's building idea types.

There are three of them, each with ramifications, each with an imaginable image that can easily be described in words, and each can take real, material form in the building.

1. Wall: a line;
2. trabeation involving post and beam or lintel: two uprights and a topping cross bar;
3. arcuation involving an arch and its supports: two uprights carrying a half circle or a segment or variation of a circle.

Extending a lintel makes a floor slab; extending an arch makes a vault; a dome is an arch spun; and a truss might be considered a variation on an arch or a more abstract composite of trabeation and arcuation.[18]

These are easily identified in vernacular construction, which as Krier has pointed out always involves building materials that can be put in place by two workers and leads to sustainable construction. These materials, often available locally, when properly handled, fabricated, and put in place consume little energy, and when properly maintained they resist deterioration. They constitute a membrature that is built up of individual *pieces*, or the smallest material units of the assembly (stone shaped as ashlar, rubble, or other stone shapes; bricks; column bases; column shafts or drums; capitals; the several pieces of entablatures and gables; voussoirs; and so on). The traditions of the art of building assemble these into certain familiar vernacular patterns, which we can call *elements*, or canonic assemblages of pieces (wall with mudsill and cornice; pier or column with base, shaft, and capital; arch with base, mid-section, and usually with spring block and keystone; entablature with architrave, frieze, and cornice, and so on). And these in turn are assembled into larger *motifs*, or one complete structural element (colonnade or arcade bay; Serliana; tabernacle, and so on). The structural idea types cannot work alone; they always work in coordination with one another in the various canonic forms they assume. That is, a column without an entablature is not a motif; it is an ornament without a building. Similarly, walls without a floor or roof belong to a garden but not a building. The art of building requires modifications to achieve the art of architecture, and those modifications are found not in conventions that lock assemblies into straitjackets illustrated in pattern books but in the innovations to the traditions that the building culture of a place carries. Tradition and not convention also guides the collocation of elements and motifs to produce the membratures that make façades and other "externals," to use Jefferson's word.

In a membrature ornament plays a fundamental role in elevating a building from the conventional routine of the art of building to the status of architecture. Ornament's natural home is wherever there is a change of material and any sensible change in the direction of the flow of stabilizing resistance to destructive forces, for example where the load moves from horizontal to vertical as when an abacus caps the capital and the capital caps the column. Fiction introduces the enhancement that calls attention to the actual work being done. It is as essential in architecture as it is in the human figure where we can see the body's actual enclosure as the fictive expression of the underlying elements that make the body a live, mobile, stable, balanced, proportionate whole. We are not presented with the bones, muscles, tendons, and entrails that are inside but the rippling of the skin over the joints and the presence of musculature under the flesh, such as that which art makes visible in the *Apollo Belvedere* and Michelangelo's nudes. Here *natura naturata* reveals *natura naturans* through the fiction that is a necessary constituent in imitation where fiction reveals truth in a way that facts cannot. Visible and convincing structural stability takes different forms in different building cultures. In something that is beautifully and marvellously made the particularities transcend the facts and reveal the universal. The universality in building cultures such as the triplet of beginning, middle, and end in the columnar orders, in the moldings that ornament them, and in the compositions of whole membratures establishes a metaphoric connection to the life spans of people and the stories in the narrative history of the civil orders that the buildings serve.

Ornament has another important role: it gives evidence that a building is loved.[19] Ornament and its mate decoration are intertwined in all three legs of architecture's tripod. Ornament enhances tectonic clarity and shows off materials, while decoration serves decorum by garnishing the particular and relative character and style of buildings according to the status of their role in serving the civil realm. The principal ornaments are the columnar orders, which are not mere add-ons that taste or whim supply and can be varied at will. They are the visible evidence of the ascent of building to architecture, the emblematic index of the building's proportionality, and the decoration that establishes its role in a civic art. In a well-proportioned building they are perceptible even when not present to sight.[20] As Porphyrios observed,

> *The Order sets form over the necessities of shelter; it sets the myth of the tectonic over the contingencies of construction. ... Classical architecture constructs a tectonic fiction out of the productive level of building. The artifice of constructing this fictitious world is seen as analogous to the artifice of constructing the human world.*

As he explains, such a building replaces "mere extension of production" with "disinterested contemplation."[21] Ornament portrays the union of mind and hand in the material tectonics of architecture as it imitates its sources in nature just as decoration strengthens the building's expression of the purpose of the institution it serves. It is worth mentioning that the machine analogy neither wants to do this nor is capable of doing so. It cannot elevate building to architecture.

In a vigorous tradition new buildings enrich the legacy they draw on and transmits it to successors. Its content includes two kinds of models. One kind consists of paradigmatic models that embodied what Jefferson called the cubic and the spherical and came in a variety of different incarnations. For him they were most clearly portrayed in the Maison Carrée in France and the Pantheon in Rome. Palladio's were less specific, Alberti's included the triumphal arch and the temple front, and Quatremère found their essential character in specific building traditions. Their most important presence is in what Jefferson called the externals for the most important buildings of the most important institutions where the stability of their expression is more important than the actual work their interiors perform. The other kind of model is the canonic model that assists in addressing the contingent circumstances that the new building must address. They assist in coming up with the configuration and for translating the building idea image and paradigmatic model into the configuration and membrature that will naturalize Jefferson's imports and settle them into the communities they will serve. For Alberti they satisfy what the locality, one of his elements of building, demands, and for Quatremère they provide the models for the distinctive character. The Ecole des Beaux Arts perfected the technique of using canonic models, even as single precedents, for composing the interior configuration with its hierarchical arrangement of axes. Its methods, which are akin to emulation, continue to provide fruitful if not essential guidance for Other Modern architects.

The method of the Ecole stops short of imitation, which it mistakenly considered copying and which flourished by serving civil orders that were the latest iterations of national traditions. It belonged to the developments that had rejected beauty and had accepted attractiveness as taste and association as content. As a result its criteria for formal success had more to do with fashion than with beauty as it was understood in the classical tradition, and fashion is a fickle thing. On the Continent the civil orders that used national versions of classicism to express their legitimacy were destroyed in the aftermath of the First World War. The old order was replaced by revolutionary regimes that condemned anything old as impediments to reaching the promised lands present in the future, and architects rushed to their banners. They enlisted the newest ideas among the Fine Arts and the most dramatic offerings of technology to serve the future whose blessings their buildings would presage and whose advent they would hasten. They also invented new methods of training architects in the art of building, and these made the Ecole's program look like cold oatmeal offering old fashioned styles and buildings incapable of serving and expressing the imminent arrival of the modern age. Before long the new method's curriculum and the styles it promoted began to achieve the near total hegemony that the culture of building gives them today.

That culture now knows no other way to think about architecture. It certainly does not acknowledge the central tenet of the classical tradition in architecture: *jus naturale* provides the criteria that *jus civile* must satisfy, civil justice supervises market justice, the civil order exercises control over the architecture that serves and expresses its purposes, and the beautiful provides the standards for buildings that are the counterpart to the justice that the civil order seeks in service to the individual's pursuit of happiness. We find the equivalent relationship between that tenet's pairs when the building idea types and canonic models govern a building's configuration and membrature so that it expresses the purposes of the institution it serves or identifies the institution governing an arrangement. This relationship accepts the commanding role of decorum, it runs all though the history of architecture as a civil art, and it gives the structure to the visible character of cities that we love even if we would not for a moment want to be a citizen in them: even atheists love Rome. That role for decorum and for the buildings serving the civil order is absent from the currently dominant historical narrative and in recent theories, but it often guides Other Modern architects.

In an architecture that builds cities to facilitate the pursuit of happiness decorum must be in command and beauty must be the goal. What follows here is a brief sketch that suggests how the architect in the modern era can use types, models, and imitation to help build that city.

Building idea types are often able to do their work alone and unassisted, for example when a regia generates a residence, which houses an institution. When a type serves an arrangement the resulting building must carry with it the visible presence of its supervising institution. Regias are common supervisors, as when in tabernas that serve commerce and banks and when hypostyle halls become commercial office buildings and sports arena. Types often team up, especially for buildings serving the most important institutions, which makes them composites.

A school is a regia but its auditorium will be a theater and is labs and shops tabernas which, essential as they are in education, do not carry the importance of the institutional purpose of a school. Similarly, a state capitol building normally contains a pair of theater-legislative chambers with a tholos-dome and several taberna-offices for legislators enclosed within a regia whose temple front(s) identify its command in the civil order. How these buildings function is relatively stable compared to those that serve arrangements that adapt to new ways of functioning, but those modifications must not compromise the visible character that identifies their institutional master. This identity is normally expressed with its membrature that finds its canonic model in the relative character of the locality's building tradition. The corruption of historic preservation by requiring that additions and modifications must be "of their time" flies in the face of architecture's role as a civic art.

The Beaux Arts architects who built the still visible urban order in American cities that serve and express the purposes of the civil order's institutions and arrangements illustrate this art very well. Their schools express their role as arenas for training in citizenship, their banks portray their status in the civil order's institutions and their claim on the public's trust, and their commercial skyscrapers decorated the urban order to earn the public's good will. Even municipal waterworks presented themselves as services to the common good. When a courthouse unambiguously looks like a public building, when a bank looks more like a courthouse than a commercial office building, when a school looks like a Carnegie library, and when a pumping plant hides it machinery behind a civic façade decorum is being honored and architecture and urbanism are in service to one another. In a well ordered urban realm a parking garage will exemplify a civic art that decorates the civic realm, and at a university it will look more like a university building than like a place with no greater purpose than providing places to park cars.

This is not the program of Modernism in which form follows function and the architect assures that the building is "of its time," makes sure the building serves the bottom line, and displays the architect's quest for transient fame. It is also beyond the ken of the Ecole's method that taught emulation and depended on precedents. The Ecole's method can carry the architect far but not to a full and robust civic art. Architecture at its best achieves concinnity that produces the synthesis of configuration and membrature and of the three legs of architecture's tripod. This architecture requires skill, knowledge, and judgment. Those requirements can protect against the deficiencies that are all too common in buildings that seek a "contextual" place within traditional settings. It can also rein in tendencies to use abuses rather than skillful invention to give spice to a design. And it offers the only access to the highest standards of beauty in buildings and urban places that enhance the public realm in the interest of the common good and that become canonic for later architects.

One way to think of using imitation can be described as excavation. It supposes that the building to be built already exists in the site it will occupy within metaphoric and physical nature and within the civic, urban, and architectural traditions and traditional building culture of the place. That is, it exists as potentiality in that site and simply needs to be found and made material. The extent of the "site" depends upon the reach of the authority it exercises or the service it renders. The site of a shop is among other shops, that of a house is a street and a block, while that of a state capitol is certainly state-wide but also national.

To find the building requires a careful, long-standing, and penetrating study of the site within a region, as a specific spot on the ground, and as a member of the civil order it will inhabit. The study must draw on broad knowledge and analysis to reach into the nature of the several factors that the architect must address: the exact site, the building idea type(s) it must imitate, the essential and relative character that will express the service it is to render, the customary forms and functions that will make it useable and familiar to its users, the tectonic types that will serve that character, and the natural materials that craftsmanship will make into the membrature as well as the finishing (Quatremère's style), the ornament, and the decoration that will plant the building in its larger rural or urban setting. The descriptive investigations that serve emulation can assist, but reaching the higher standard requires the profounder knowledge achieved with penetrating analytical investigations of the best paradigmatic and canonic models. Either way, through emulation or imitation, the architect seeks to produce a beautifully and marvellously-made building that will always be at home and never be a stranger.

Excavation acknowledges that nature, both as the natural world and as the nature common to all people, offers the materials of the visible qualities of beauty that architecture makes perceptible. Jefferson certainly understood this when, as we saw in the previous chapter, he commented on the ordinary person's capacity to avoid being "led astray by artificial rules."[22] The comment does not come from the engagement with primitivism that was then current on the Continent and was urging people to purge themselves of the corrupting influences of civilization. Instead it points to the classical tradition's recognition that we have encountered, for example when Marsilius of Padua noted that an ordinary person is capable of judging things he is incapable of making such as "the quality of a picture, a house, a ship, and other works of art."[23] Were that not the case there would be no English common law, no quest for just government through the consent of the governed, and no multi-millennia tradition of beauty in architecture and its concomitant art of building cities, all of which vouches for the presence in human nature of *synderesis* or the perception of the connections between the good in acts, the true in things known, and the beautiful in things that are made and in man when he is most unified with nature's order, harmony, and proportionality.

This is a difficult doctrine to promulgate in a culture of architecture that does not hesitate to make courthouses look like banks that themselves look like commercial office buildings or extravagant expressions of the architect's technological prowess and original creativity. This is Modernism, whose rise occurred across the span of a century when the buildings that serve the institutions of the *res publica* come under the sway of the same architectural culture that serves the arrangements in the *res private* or *economica*, when architects become increasingly negligent in fulfilling their obligations to the public good while enjoying the security that the civil order gives them, and when builders are more interested in their bottom line or fame as patrons of the Fine Arts than in the common good that the beauty of urban or rural settings offer.

How can we know to do otherwise when the culture of architecture has divorced itself from its service to the civil order and architecture's service to the common good? To chart a different course in the rapidly changing world of the modern era requires astute navigational skills that are scarcely being taught today. Historians and theorists treat students and practicing architects as passengers on a luxury liner whose captain is the *Zeitgeist*. They plot its course along point-to-point portolans that are intended to legitimate architecture's "progress." New influences and new theories prescribe constantly changed bearings to escape the most recent moment of the wretched past as it steams across uncharted seas to reach Modernism's happy isles that beckon from the horizon where architecture will transform human nature and humankind will enjoy eternal bliss.

A different route, one that serves human nature's enduring pursuit of happiness, has always been with us. It guided Vitruvius, Alberti, Palladio, and Jefferson. It brings the modern discoveries in the world and in the science of politics into the historical narrative and makes the citizen–architect the active protagonist. Vitruvius had viewed his relationship to his present and past through the role that his imperial patron played. Alberti's modernization put the citizen in charge and helped develop the modern navigational charts that began with Brunelleschi's perspective and eventually organized the face of the earth with a geometric order that allowed individuals to locate themselves in an unchanging order. That geometry was eventually extended to the heavens, and Jefferson brought it down to earth as the great American grid that provided the framework for extending the American civil order across the Continent. On its sites where settlers enjoyed the security of their ownership they founded civil orders where the authority of government guaranteed their natural right to pursue their happiness. The modern extension of that geometric control into the third dimension unified architecture and urbanism with traditional architecture becoming the necessary companion of traditional urbanism with the pair joined by concinnity and built on the foundations in nature that they share with the civil order that they serve.

This is the story that could guide the citizen–architect–Argonauts to other times and places that offer them models for their imitation. This story would enable architects to become actors in a narrative whose plot is the interplay between architecture and the civil order, between top-down and bottom-up authority, between tradition and innovation, between the true and the contingent, and between the enduring and the transitory. A few individuals in the current culture of architecture intuitively act within that history, but a properly written historical narrative to guide architects on their way remains a desideratum.

The course traverses the praiseworthy characteristics of earlier forms of civil order and architecture and their renovation within present knowledge and circumstances, a characteristic that Salvatore Settis identified as a distinctive trait of the western, classical tradition.[24] Over the last few decades Other Modern architects have brought a renewed interest in traditional ways of populating cities in America and elsewhere with civic buildings as they restore and adapt the good old ways of building. Unfortunately, only very rarely are they now given the opportunity to work with the principal figures in institutions and arrangements who understand that architecture is a civic art that can serve the common good.[25] Where, then, or when, are we going to muster the will once again to build the good city?

NOTES

1. Michael Carmona, *Haussmann: His Life and Times, and the Making of Modern Paris* (Chicago: Ivan R. Dee, 2002), 149–55; 161.

2. Antoine Chrysostôme Quatremère de Quincy, *An Essay on the Nature, the End, and the Means of Imitation in the Fine Arts*, trans. J.C. Kent (London: Smith, Elder & Co., 1837).

3. Younés, *Quatremère de Quincy*.

4. Younés, "Type, Character, and Style," 33–9. This essay provides a useful digest of this material.

5. Younés, *Quatremère de Quincy*, s.v. character, 107–8; 38–9.

6. For example, Henry Hope Reed, *The Golden City* (Garden City, N.Y.: Doubleday, 1959).

7. For these Other Moderns and these events see especially Younés, "Modern Traditional Architecture," 20–37.

8. Perhaps most comprehensive among his many publications is Léon Krier, *Architecture: Choice or Fate* (Windsor, Berks: Andreas Papadakis, 1998); a useful collection, sanctioned by Krier, is *The Architecture of Community*, 2009. See also Anon., *The Richard H. Driehaus Prize: Inaugural Recipient Léon Krier* (Notre Dame, Indiana: University of Notre Dame School of Architecture, 2003).

9. Jacques Ellul, *The Technological Society*, trans. John Wilkinson (New York: Knopf, 1964). See Léon Krier, "Imitation, Hidden or Declared," in Samir Younés, ed., *Architects and Mimetic Rivalry* (Winterbourne, Berks.: Papadkis, 2012), 52–7; Demetri Porphyrios, "Classicism is not a Style," in Demetri Porphyrios, ed., *Classicism is not a Style* (London: Academy Editions; New York: St. Martin's Press, 1982), 51–7.

10. Nikos Salingaros, *A Theory of Architecture* (n.p.: Nikos A. Salingaros & Umbau, 2006), a work connected with the ideas of the author's mentor and sometime associate, Christopher Alexander.

11. Strauss, *Natural Right*, 35.

12. Samir Younés, "Jacques Ellul and the Eclipse of Artistic Symbolism," *The Empire of Non-Sense: Art in the Technological Society*, trans. Michael Johnson and David Lovekin (Winterbourne, Wilts.: Papadakis, 2014), 12, 17.

13. The same can be said, *mutatis mutandi*, about religious institutions. When architecture is a Fine Art non-public actors control what is built. Some of them collect buildings as examples of the Fine Arts. Whether private collectors or cultural institutions, they confuse the aesthetic life for the ethical life. See Karsten Harries, *The Ethical Function of Architecture* (Cambridge, Mass., and London: MIT Press, 1998). Especially tragic has been the recent program for building federal courthouses. Most are examples of Fine Art rather than civic art. Corporations and speculative commercial builders exploit Modernism's capacity to provide a "brand." Meanwhile, builders and architects are either weak-kneed, ill-informed about alternatives, or both, and simply follow fashion and display their failure as citizens; the others are tyrants.

14 Carroll William Westfall, in Robert Jan van Pelt and Westfall, *Architectural Principles in the Age of Historicism* (New Haven and London: Yale University Press, 1991), Chapter 2, esp. 63–74 for an earlier, fuller discussion.

15 Two citations provide perspective and instruction: Plato's "City of Pig," *Republic*, 369–73e, and Aristotle, *Politics*, 1252b.

16 For an earlier exploration of this material, with six types, see Westfall in van Pelt, *Architectural Principles*, Chapters 2 and 4; see now also Younés, *Imperfect City*, Part 1, Chapter 3. For an assessment of the building idea types as natural symbols see Rafael de Clercq, "Building Plans as Natural Symbols," *Architecture Philosophy*, 1 (2014), 59–80.

17 Gathering and the hypostyle hall are additions made by Samir Younés.

18 Westfall in van Pelt, *Architectural Principles*, 256. For the special case of American wooden stick construction (balloon frame, western platform, and so on) see 266ff.

19 The comment is that of Alvin Holm, "The Buildings We Love," *Clem Labine's Period Homes*, 15:2 (March, 2014), 64. For an excellent short treatment of ornament's banishment and its still essential role in architecture see Kent Bloomer, "The Sacrifice of Ornament in the Twentieth Century," in Samir Younés, ed., *Architects and Mimetic Rivalry* (Winterbourne, Berks: Papadakis, 2012). Essential reading is the risible essay by Adolf Loos, "Ornament and Crime," in Ulrich Conrads, ed., *Programs and Manifestoes on 20th-Century Architecture*, trans. Michael Bullock (Cambridge, Mass., MIT Press, 1970), misdated as 1908. Panayotis Tournikiotis, *Adolf Loos*, trans. Marguerite McGoldrick (New York: Princeton Architectural Press, 1994), 23, states that this essay, which achieved fame quite late, was first given as a lecture in 1910 and then first published in French in 1913, then in 1920, and in German in 1929. For an example of ornament's misuse see Robert Venturi, *Complexity and Contradiction in Architecture* (New York: Museum of Modern Art, 1966).

20 George Hersey, *Pythagorean Palaces: Magic and Architecture in the Italian Renaissance* (Ithaca: Cornell University Press, 1976).

21 Porphyrios, "Classicism is not a Style," 57.

22 TJ to Peter Carr, August 10, 1787, in *Writings*, 902.

23 Marsilius of Padua, *Defender of Peace*, I.xiii.3.

24 Settis, *Future of the 'Classical.'*

25 Two notable exceptions of the former: Jaquelin Robertson, for example in "In Search of an American Urban Order, Part I: The Nagasaki Syndrome," *Modulus 16* (Charlottesville: The University of Virginia School of Architecture, ETC, 1983), 3–15; and "Part II: The House as the City," *Modulus 19* (Charlottesville, 1989); and Greenberg, *Architecture of Democracy*, 138–58. An example of the latter is Joseph Riley, Mayor of Charleston since 1975.

10

The Beautiful and Good City

THE CITY AND CIVIL ARCHITECTURE

The city is the most important thing that we make from nature. We live our lives with others there and in the natural world it modifies. We share our dreams and ambitions there as we seek to live abundantly and well. We pursue our happiness there. The city's service to that pursuit has been a central preoccupation, perhaps the central preoccupation, of the classical, western tradition ever since men recognized that they are responsible for that pursuit. The city is the locus of the government that guides our life in nature, and in *Federalist* # 51 we found James Madison reminding us, "what is government itself but the greatest of all reflections on human nature?"

Madison is writing from within the heart of the classical tradition. He echoes Plato who early in his *Republic* notes that the city is man writ large and proceeds to discover the nature of man by considering how the city seeks justice whose possession is humankind's greatest need. Aristotle, always more down to earth than his tutor, puts humankind as the unique social animal in nature and the city as the instrument that serves the quest for the good life in which a person enjoys the fullness of his nature. In the Hebrew Bible in the beginning there is no city, but it was the second thing the exiles from the Garden made from God's creation. Cain built it after he had murdered his brother Abel, and he named it Enoch, the name of his son, where he could hide from God and find his immorality through the mortal lives of his progeny. The Christian Bible presents God redeeming the blessed and collecting them into the Heavenly City of Jerusalem.[1]

That city had not arrived by the early fifth century when Saint Augustine explained that people had the Church as a surrogate for that City of God and that its earthly home is in the city of man. This doctrine of the two cities had a long future in the western tradition, even into the Founding of the American constitutional order. The Founders recognized that individuals had a natural right to choose the relationship they would have with the City of God and that the city of man had the duty to protect the liberty to exercise that right. To that and similar ends the signers of the Declaration of Independence declared that we "mutually pledge to each other our lives, our Fortunes and our sacred Honor" in our efforts to "assume among the Powers of the earth" what Lincoln would later identify at Gettysburg as "a new nation, conceived in liberty and dedicated to the proposition that all men are created equal." Their compact is to protect the individuals' natural endowment of certain unenumerated inalienable rights in a government that has fitfully but steadily worked to bring the facts of the civic life into correspondence with the nation's founding truths that empower each individual to respond to the classical admonition given at Delphi to each individual, "Know thyself." From their work has grown a prosperous, populous, Continent-spanning civil order, indeed, a city in the broadest meaning of the terms, a city that seeks the good, an imitation of a pattern laid up in heaven, an instrument people use to pursue the happiness of the good life, a city made by "We the People" who seek the concord that is necessary to allow each individual to pursue happiness where a person believes it is to be found. In that city the vehicle for settling differences is in the comity found in reasoned discourse among people of good will.

The animating coherent vision of the good city and comity among its citizens hardly prevails today. We find the city treasured as the market home of *homo economicus*, as the arena for political interest groups, as the hub of the transporting of goods and people, and so on. The classical definition of the city has been replaced by a classic of sociology from 1938 that states, "For sociological purposes a city may be defined as a relatively large, dense, and permanent settlement of socially heterogeneous individuals."[2] Also in 1938 Louis Mumford defined the city as a technologically-based market that is valued as a "generator of culture."[3] Most architects and those who hire them, whether public bodies or private interests, live and build in that 1938 city where they serve the market or exploit its prosperity to make an avant-garde city-as-museum as a cultural artefact. They build buildings that are "of their time" whether on the market's constrained budgets or to indulge the wealthy because, as José Ortega y Gasset explained, their work "helps the elite to recognize themselves and one another in the drab mass of society and to learn their mission which consists of being few and holding their own against the many."[4]

An example of the usurpation of the authority of the avant-garde Fine Arts over the public role of the civic arts is offered by a recent incident in New York City. It illustrates the reduction of the discourse in the American city to Babel where an urban realm based on nonsense prevents people from working together to achieve a common goal.[5] Its buildings are defined as objects of Fine Arts that enjoy First Amendment protection, and although the courts have not tested that claim a recent imperfect consideration reveals how tenuous it is. Richard Serra placed a site-specific slab of Corten steel named *Tilted Arc* in a public plaza. After it became the target of public complaints its owner agreed to remove it. An administrative hearing in a U.S. Court of Appeals did not pass on whether it was an obnoxious nuisance, but the Court's finding is instructive:

> *Those urging removal tended to be federal employees and area residents who complained primarily of the obstruction of Federal Plaza and the sculpture's unappealing aesthetic qualities. Those against removal tended to be artists and others from the art world who pointed to the work's significance in twentieth-century sculpture and the importance of protecting the artist's freedom of expression. [Note the lack of comment about its aesthetic qualities.] But, ruled the court, [T]he First Amendment protects the freedom to express one's views, not the freedom to continue speaking forever.*

Furthermore,

> *Serra is unable to identify any particular message conveyed by Tilted Arc that he believes may have led to its removal. ... Moreover, the Supreme Court has consistently recognized that consideration of aesthetics is a legitimate government function that does not render a decision to restrict expression impermissibly content-based. Finally, several courts have held that the state may regulate the display and location of art based on its aesthetic qualities and suitability for the viewing public without running afoul of First Amendment concerns.*[6]

The entire episode was immersed in emotional assessments that lacked reasoned judgments, and because the basis of the judgment was left in the hands of the Fine Arts community, the comments abrogated a fundamental principle of justice that a person must not be a judge in his own case. In the end it was clear that the work, like the other works of the Fine Arts that it characterized, was Babel with nothing to contribute to civil discourse.

Architecture claims its status as a Fine Art even though two essential characteristics set a building apart from the other members of that club. We noted one of them earlier when we found that a building must address utility. The other is that a building necessarily has a public presence. A painting or sculpture can, and usually does, reside in a semi-private or completely private realm, but a building, or at least its "external," does not. It is a public object, and if it is not expected to "continue speaking forever" it is normally expected to be a public fixture for a very long time. This public aspect of a building raises two points. First, if a person going about his business finds it for whatever reason, or even without a reason, to be a nuisance and cannot conveniently avoid it, as the federal employees in New York City could not avoid *Tilted Arc*, is there a good reason to allow it to have a public presence? Are their reasonable grounds that lie beyond personal taste for identifying it as a nuisance? And second, the land it occupies is ultimately under the control of the civil order. This lends its owner certain rights and duties, although these run with the land and not the owner. Its rights include the protection of its ownership, protection from wonton destruction or fire, guaranteed access from public ways, and so on. The counterpart duties include paying taxes, complying with licensing restrictions, maintaining standards concerning public health, safety, and general welfare, and so on.

Ownership is never absolute. Intrusions run from eminent domain takings to design and zoning restrictions on proposed improvements, preservation restrictions, and so on. These are justified because they contribute to the public good, and they cannot be imposed without due process. This normally requires hearings that are generally peopled by public officials, lay citizens, and experts in the relevant fields. These experts are normally drawn from the clerisy of certified experts in technical matters, self-interested professionals in the building arts, land and property owners, property managers, historians and professionals in preservation, and others who come armed with credentials, facts, and figures. At worst, a building is assessed according to shallow criteria of mere aesthetic delight. At best, that is, in the Supreme Court ruling in *Penn Central v New York* [438 U.S. 104 (1978)] that validated historic preservation, the process invariably treats a building as a Fine Arts object that provides evidence of a now lost past according to the putative rationalist criteria of the historicist narrative of the history of architecture.[7] In line with the diction of Modernism the criteria use the word significant as a synonym for important within the realm of the Fine Arts rather than in its earlier use when architecture was a civic art and a building was significant because it is a sign that points to something that is important, namely, the good that the city seeks. There is no place in the present processes for assessing the role of a building or a district in serving and expressing the purposes of the civic operations whose first purpose is to facilitate the good.

There does exist established law that can bring that assessment into the process. The force of law can be brought to bear when a statute has a "real or substantial relation" to protecting "the public health, the public morals, or the public safety."[8] That is, a civil authority has the power to protect people from insulting, uncivil things and actions such as graffiti, unruly behavior, charged and obscene words, and obscene gestures. By extension it can surely protect them from their equivalents in buildings and the other visible things in the public and private urban and rural realms. While it is not possible to require that beauty be achieved, it can require that it be sought by honoring decorum, which is the principal criterion that elevates a building to a higher service than to that of the market alone, one that is essential in converting a Fine Art object–building into civic architecture, the one that is in command when architecture is a civic art and serves as the capstone for beauty's collection of criteria.

To put decorum in command we might require that all modifications to the natural and built world, whether public or private, be judged by a jury composed of randomly-selected ordinary people, Jefferson's present-day ploughmen, the peers of those that all construction affects and therefore have an interest in what is built. These are the people whose voice is the weakest and most easily dismissed in existing forums. They lack the facts that are required for technical matters, they are normally untrained in articulating views concerning reasoned criteria, and they seldom command the refined diction of those who justify their judgments with aesthetic doctrines. They are not experts, and in the eyes of experts these deficiencies further disqualify them from making judgments about what they will encounter in the urban and rural realms. But they have also most likely "not been led astray by artificial rules." They are unlikely to continence the relativist argument that "One man's vulgarity is another's lyric," and they know that liberty does not justify license that defies common sense, civil decency, and decorum.[9] They understand that decorum must always police offensive acts or obnoxious things in public places. And they also know that some buildings simply do not deserve a place in the urban or rural realms where they and their fellow citizens pursue their happiness.

Imagine, then, reviews of proposed changes to the urban or rural realms in which the new or altered building or other physical component is presented to a panel of (mere) ordinary citizens in an adversarial preceding with a judge presiding as a referee. The thing as seen would be allowed to speak for itself accompanied by reasoned arguments about the reason and nature of the thing and its success or failure in serving the good purposes of the civil order. Aesthetic judgments that are the equivalent of emotivist arguments in moral judgments, that is, subjective, and ideological arguments lacking a reasoned basis in the natural law and common law foundations of the American civil order, would be ruled out of order.[10] Arguments that are based on "artificial rules" or on self-interest at the expense of the public good would be exposed and rejected. Other proposals might be found faulty, and assistance would be found for making improvements before being resubmitted. The issue at hand would always be the effect the proposal would have on the city or the rural countryside, not on the building's merit as a stand-alone object in a city-as-museum or a city-or countryside-as-market where the market establishes the value.

There is abundant evidence that there are such people. They find their way as tourists to the places and districts that they know Disney did not build: Charleston, Boston, Santa Fe, Chicago, Coral Gables, San Francisco, Richmond, Santa Barbara, New York, among others, and to districts that escaped the ravages of more than a half century of work by architects and planners. Ordinary people clearly prefer familiar, traditional places to almost anything that Modernist architects have built except for the tiny handful of currently stylish extravaganzas whose novelty wears out its welcome or becomes a curiosity. When these people are buyers they choose traditional styles that the cognoscenti sneer at as "retro style" and are produced by a building industry that desperately needs the correctives that Jefferson identified. And all the while there is an increasing number of traditional and classical buildings produced by Other Modern architects. Despite a century's effort among the few "elite" who seek to hold their "own against the many" they have not disappeared and are even gaining a broader role, especially among those who refuse to be "led astray by artificial rules."

This procedure that would give authority to ordinary people would make the process of designing and building irksome and time consuming, but while markets can be built quickly cities that people can love take time and care. Add to that love the necessity for the long-term sustainability of a city, which, as the name tells us is the seat of civilization, a necessity that is more important than the short-term return on money spent on transient construction. Here is a rule of thumb that offers guidance: when reviewing the suitability of a building, the more important the purpose of the institution or arrangement it will serve and express and the broader its reach, the more deliberate must be the review, the broader must be the range of voices involved in the review, and the longer the building must be built to last.

Not all buildings are equal, neither when architecture is a Fine Art nor a civic art. When architecture is a civic art buildings ought to be designed by well-trained architects with the buildings that serve the most important purpose entrusted to architects of superior talent and a demonstrable commitment to architecture as a civic art. In any generation such talents are rare, but they have always emerged when architects are trained to practice their art as a civic art and their clients share a commitment to the city's role in facilitating the citizens' aspiration to pursue their happiness and live nobly and well. The classical tradition abounds with these architects and city builders. They produced background buildings, by far the predominant buildings in any city, and the important foreground ones that with their lesser neighbors make beautiful and loveable cities. These buildings were well-built and have been well cared for, often for centuries, by being constantly renewed and adapted. The cities and rural districts they built are far more sustainable than what the modern building culture has been putting on the land. Its clutter of energy-inefficient buildings, both important and merely utilitarian, are not built to last and do not deserve to be adapted to new uses. They are either razed or replaced with both actions having costly environmental consequences, or they remain as unsightly, wasteful, indecorous carcasses testifying to their obsolescence in the present or their unfulfilled promises for the future. Sustainable and loved cities are not built to satisfy leading-edge fashions "of their time" that quickly pall, by using technical innovations that prove to be transient and unrepairable, and within economic and technical parameters that guarantee rapid obsolescence.

People value buildings, cities, and rural districts that express the worthy aspirations of people united in the communal undertaking of city building. They understand that the more important buildings are more expensive and take longer to build in a process that allows adjustments to be made along the way, something that modern practice prevents. Many buildings earn popular opprobrium. They invariably postdate the advent of modern technology, or are presented as products of the Fine Arts, or exhibit a style that was "of its time" but was not of all time or of any later time. Their builders ignored what David Hume wrote, that "amidst all the variety and caprices of taste, there are certain general principles of approbation or blame."[11] Jefferson agreed; the most important buildings need to be taken from models that have "obtained the approbation of fifteen or sixteen centuries, and … [are] therefore, preferable to any design which might be newly contrived."[12]

"We the People" are ordinary people whom nature has endowed with a moral and an aesthetic sense and who in the best of circumstances engage with citizen-experts in law, economics, transportation, commerce, and all the other specialized activities of the modern world. In city building we have become accustomed to deferring to Modernist architects and their enablers who work behind obfuscating screens of procedure, expertise, and superiority in indisputable matters of taste. In the classical tradition that Alberti and Jefferson modernized architects were brought out into full view in the forum to work as citizen–architects engaged in the political life that exercises authority over what is built. We have seen that within the classical tradition the interaction of architecture and the political life it serves has taken a variety of forms and that it has suffered under Modernist architecture. Is it utopian to believe that we can revitalize and revise city building to restore and build the beautiful and good city?

THE GOOD CITY RESTORED

That restoration resides within the classical tradition that includes the American Founding. It was a unique event in history that made a new civic order from the knowledge transmitted by a more than 2,000-year tradition of government and governing. Jefferson drew from that tradition in his architecture and city building. His architecture is part and parcel of the American civil order and shares three characteristics with it. First, it recognizes the reciprocity between buildings and the institutions of the civil order that they serve and that architecture based on nature, reason, and judgment are to the beautiful what nature, reason, and judgment are to the good sought by the civil order. Second, it provides the liberty that is necessary for a person to respond to the admonition "Know thyself," which involves pursuing a happiness that can only be gained as a participant in a civil order. Third, he understood that the blessings of liberty include the blessing of pluralism. It is the antidote to corporatism, tribalism, collectivism, and other threats to the freedom for a person to come to knowledge of himself. Immersed within the complex and often messy synoecism of the American civil order pluralism vastly expands the opportunities for a person to pursue his happiness.

This unique civil order developed a unique urban order to serve is purposes. This urban order and its rural complement were never given the sharp distinction in law that Roman law left on the European Continent. Even there that distinction began to erode in the seventeenth century when nation states began to exert their hegemony over the landscape. Later Romanticism and other forces made more radical changes, but by then the various forces that would be imposed on the putative American wilderness were already in play. The result that we see now is a wide variety of regional urban-rural treatments, although the differences are being eroded by an increasing rate of homogenization. But no matter the region the general divisions that we encountered at Jefferson's University of Virginia are easily identifiable all across the Continent in the landscapes that run from protected wilderness to rural tracts, gardens, civil urban orders, and finally, public commons.

This American urban and rural landscape always exhibits four characteristics. First, the landscape remains visible, even if only as a shrub in a tub in front of a tall apartment building or an almost razor-thin strip of grass between curb and sidewalk. Second, decorum and its tool proportionality are in command. Third, the nation's various regions exhibit their own distinctive regional traditions of architecture, urbanism, and rural landscape. And finally, the same family of forms, the family that Rudolf Wittkower treated as the classical apparatus of forms, provides the members that the art of building uses.[13] More clearly than anywhere else the American urban and rural realms display the intricate balancing and reciprocity of bottom-up and top-down authorities that constantly juggle the claims of public institutions, families, individuals, and the market as they have absorbed the extensive array of infrastructure and improvements to public and private realms.

Here as always residences far outnumber any other buildings, and those serving arrangements are far more numerous than the few that serve the important, non-familial institutions. In America the normative residence is a free-standing house surrounded by a surviving fragment of landscape; a regia surrounded by a fence is the very emblem of the individual's fundamental liberty and role in the civil order. We saw earlier that the house lends its name and shares its formal character with the buildings of other institutions and the arrangements rendering specialized services to the civil order. Whether solitary of collected with others as row houses and apartment houses they are expected to "wear a domestic aspect."[14] Often combined with ground-floor shops, they claim a higher status than the background buildings serving arrangements, but like them they act as soldiers among the institutional buildings that serve as officers in the urban order.

No matter their status all buildings, like all the Athenian soldiers doing battle with Sparta, owe their first obligation to the public good that they serve and that their visible presence expresses.[15] Traditional soldier-buildings will not achieve the level of beauty that buildings serving the most important institutions may, but in the well-tempered city their appearance cannot be neglected, and they can share in the praise of the city's beauty just as the soldier shares in the glory of victory and is memorialized in death.

Cities are dynamic entities undergoing constant change that requires constant review in order to satisfy decorum's criteria. In earlier years of the modern industrial and commercial cities builders of low status commercial buildings decorated rather than defaced cities from Rome to Hamburg and Chicago.[16] Many are being given new life as residences. Although they do not "wear a domestic aspect," they enjoy respect nonetheless because they obey decorum and honor the region's formal and tectonic traditions. But a pig with lipstick is still a pig and belongs in a poke, not in a parlor, and buildings serving tanneries and abattoirs of old and now refineries and rail marshaling yards belong in isolated districts. These can, however, serve the role of the *Vorstadt* of traditional, walled cities where something could be built and then either accepted into the civil order and urban realm or left outside.[17]

More recently Modernist architects and their clients have been building buildings that are notable primarily for shouting, "Look at me!" or "Look at what I do!" even though what they do does not warrant the attention they claim. They are nuisances like *Tilted Arc* or the speeches in a forum that make noise but do not address the public good. Their peers are buildings built by developers using the money of distant others and leave after pocketing their profit.

The good city is built by those who seek the good from and within it. They contribute to a just, elegant, beautiful, and sustainable city, one whose first citizens were founders who stayed and were followed by citizen–successors. They resist the superficial pleasures of fashion and the market's allure and engage as citizens in the top-down and bottom-up reciprocity and synoecism that makes each place unique. When building they offer more than a self-satisfying minimum or the mere delights of the Vitruvian conditions of well-building. They supply more than is required to satisfy public health and safety standards and other legal requirements, and certainly more than mere short-term personal, financial, partisan, or professional advantage. The best of them seek congruence with nature's order, harmony, and proportionality.

THE NECESSITY OF PROPORTIONALITY

Proportionality is the condition necessary for the good and the beautiful.[18] Proportionality is not simply the presence of dimensional ratios or proportions identified with the beautiful. Today architects in the main stream of Modernism occasionally mention beauty and proportions in the same sentence. When pressed where they are to be found they point to geometric constructions that yield the golden section, or to ratios between whole numbers in various dimensions, or to diagrams showing parallel lines falling on important parts of the composition, or other numerical and geometric propositions. When asked why those yield beauty they normally point to the authority of pre modern buildings or texts that play no other role in their designs. Others who are devoted to the classical columnar orders praise the integrated, proportioned dimensioning of their many parts that exhibit numerical ratios traditionally cited as their source of beauty. None of this is to be faulted, but neither is it adequate for proportionality, which depends more on reasoned judgment than on canonic proportions alone.

Proportions guide judgment to reach the proportionality that makes beauty perceptible in what we recognize as shapeliness. Vitruvius wrote: "Eurhythmy (shapeliness) is an attractive appearance and a coherent aspect in the composition of the elements"[19] (1.2.3). Indra Kagis McEwen commented,

> *The built analogue for a man's well-shapedness, the appearance of symmetry, is what Vitruvius called eurhythmy, "the beautiful appearance and fitting aspect of the parts once they have been put together"; (1.4.5) the utterly convincing visible coherence of form that an architect must strive for by adjusting or 'tempering' proportions so as to flatter the eye of the beholder.*[20]

Vitruvius' eurhythmy and Alberti's concinnity stressed the adjustments that had to be made to the dimensions to make the canonic proportions convincingly present and perceptible. To achieve proportionality required judgment based on experience, talent and reason and not only a measuring rod.

The proportionality of proportions has assisted buildings in making the beautiful perceptible ever since architecture emerged from the art of building.[21] Pythagoras (c.570–c.490BC) is said to have discovered proportions, which he explicated as establishing the mean between extremes, blending opposites into a relationship, and producing thereby a pleasing harmony. This role became a pervasive element in the thought of the western tradition.[22] Without it there is mere random chaos. Proportion's ratios establish an orderly congruence between two things of different kinds such as a well-formed human body and a building, and judgment then tempers the proportions to produce the proportionality. Therein lies the difference between measurements and things that have a measured order. Polyclitus embodied proportions in the proportionality that allowed his two canon figures to imitate the well-formed human figure. And Socrates found proportionality between diverse things to be the essential content of justice in the good city in the "City of Pigs" passage in Plato's *The Republic* (370c–372d).

In classical thought, proportionality conjoins the good and the beautiful, but seeking that conjunction is no longer central in discussions of architecture, of cities, of justice, or of beauty. It began to be shown the door when writers on the Continent began to dissociate the moral and the natural sciences, narrow the role for reason, and abandon the Great Chain of Being that put man at its pinnacle. Lost in the scuffle of that renovation of intellectual culture was the central premise of the western tradition, that we are endowed with reason and free will, burdened with the charge, "Know thyself!" and in possession of a human nature that seeks to know the true, do the good, and make the beautiful with the doctrine of imitation serving as our instrument for doing so.

But as we saw, west of the Channel the fate of classical thought was quite different. In Britain mathematics, geometry, and proportions resisted having no life outside Newton's mathematics. Palladio carried concinnity from Alberti to Britain and America. And Jefferson founded an architecture that would use reason, judgment, and nature to make the buildings that would serve and express the purposes of the civil order's authoritative institutions and establish a just, proportionate, reciprocal relationship between the beautiful and the good that was founded on natural law.

Proportionality's principal role is to bring unity to diverse things. In classical architecture it melds tradition and innovations necessitated by new contingencies. An institution seeks proportionality between its ends and its means, between it and other institutions of the civil order, between purposive institutions and the functional arrangements serving them, and between the civil order and the people who make it and whom it governs. A building requires proportionality as it serves and expresses the purposes of the institution that builds or uses it and in the place it occupies among other buildings in the rural and urban order.

Proportionality masters the synthesis of the three legs of the tripod that supports architecture and serves each of them. In the tectonic leg it makes perceptible the resistance to the laws of nature that threaten stability and deterioration. It reins in monstrous oversizing or anorexic insubstantiality. It provides convincing evidence that supporting elements are robust enough to support their loads. It puts hard or rough materials below, not above, less hard, smooth, or transparent materials and gives them convincing support. It uses the art of building and architecture to elevate humble materials to the rank that decorum demands of them. Note that at the University of Virginia Jefferson's brick columns are sheathed with stucco and sand painted to present them as if they are stone and therefore appropriate for their task and place. We can add that pilasters add little if any actual strength to a wall but their scansion evinces regularity and thereby a more convincing perception of stability. In these and many other instances the art of building provides facts that fiction elevates to the truth that proportionality demands of architecture.

The formal leg begins with the building in which the type and character of the configuration find their completion and style in the membrature that the tectonic leg supplies. The proportionality between the configuration and membrature reaches down to the formal qualities of the membrature's parts and extends upward to the elements, motifs, and collocations that make the building's integument and is under the command of the urban leg's agent, decorum. Now, finally, the imitation of nature's beauty becomes visible in the beauty of the buildings and the urban and rural settings that serve the civil order that imitates nature's moral content as it facilitates the citizens' pursuit of happiness.

The happiness first takes the form of the pleasure that the aesthetic sense furnishes, and is perceived perhaps in the moral sense as well, a statement that requires careful scrutiny. Recall that the moral sense finds its happiness in good acts while beauty resides in things that are made. Beauty is certainly the complement of the good, but the qualities of the one are not to be transferred to the other, although there is a strong tendency to do so. The moral sense causes us to avert our gaze from evil, and the aesthetic sense draws us to things whose beauty is revealed by our sensory apparatus, which in architecture is primarily that of sight. Conflating judgments about the one with the other has led some people to condemn classical architecture because it has been the favored architecture of tyrants, dictators and enemies of liberty, a conflation that calls for two observations.

First, in the western tradition the architecture that we now identify as classical, a tradition that includes what we now call the Gothic style, was not a style but simply the best outcome of the art of building, and the judgments made about the appearance of buildings concerned imitation's success in achieving beauty. The assault on traditional architecture that began in the late seventeenth century led to assessing a building according to how well it emulated the visual qualities of the precedents drawn from historical styles that associated the building with the reason for choosing that style, which led to a series of revival styles. French precedents served to legitimate he authority of French governments. To provide an antidote for Americans who studied at the Ecole des Beaux Arts and tilt them toward ancient and Renaissance Rome, Charles Follen McKim helped found the American Academy in Rome. In England toward the middle of the nineteenth-century variations of medieval styles were called on to support the Anglo-Catholic movement in the Church of England. The United States followed suit after Jefferson's American architecture gave way to Romanticism. Ralph Adams Cram, the great American architect who is most known as a Gothic Revivalist ecclesiastical architect, tutored his office's fledglings by sending them to England to measure churches.[23]

It is obvious that buildings are built by those who have the power to build them, that they build with a particular purpose in mind, and that they can control what the building expresses. It should come as no surprise that public building will express what Hamilton called the vigor of government. The tradition that Modernism assaulted associated what is now called classical architecture with the authoritative institutions of civil orders, and its program was intent on revolutionary changes in both the civil orders and their architecture serving and expressing them. This program was too late to affect the program that the United States government undertook in 1902 for the restoration, revision, expansion, and modernization of the original classical program for Washington, D.C. The project stretched into the Presidency of Franklin Delano Roosevelt who, with others in the government, equated the nation's *tradition* of classical architecture with their vigorous protection of American liberty against threats from abroad.[24] Meanwhile, Hitler was beginning to use the classical *style* to express the authority of his vicious, tyrannical assault on liberty. Hitler's program did not corrupt or delegitimize the classical tradition in architecture and urbanism. He used classical building to serve the evil and immoral acts of his Nazi government, and their classicism was to express the respectability of the Nazi civil order and mask his evil program. For his machinery of war and death he used Modernist buildings.[25] The classical style was to express the legitimacy of his authority; his national ambitions; the continuity between ancient Roman emperors, earlier leaders in Germany, and himself; and his program to elevate Germany to the capital of world domination. This program depended on the connection between style and content that had been part of the program in the Ecole des Beaux Arts and had become solidified in the then-current narrative of the history of architecture. It attested to the aesthetic power of classical architecture, but it was unconnected to the moral content of the acts they were to facilitate. It is fallacious to believe that the formal properties of a building can be identified with the moral content of acts committed in them. The beautiful presents the criteria for things made such as buildings, and the good provides the criteria for acts. Were it not so we could condemn the materials used to build Hitler's buildings and burden Volkswagen drivers with responsibility for Nazi atrocities.

Beauty can be congruent with the good, and beautiful buildings can be the counterpart to the good intended by the purposes they serve and express, but as Hitler demonstrated, beauty can also be a mask that hides evil. The opposites are also true: good deeds can be done in ugly buildings; acts that are good do not make the unbeautiful beautiful; bad people can make beautiful buildings; and being a good person does not assure the capacity to make a beautiful building.

We repeatedly exercise this separation of aesthetic and moral judgments without thinking, but not consistently. For example, when we encounter places where a heinous crime has been committed we either avoid it or we indulge our ghoulish curiosity. We are normally quite able to understand that beautiful buildings can serve tyranny and other positions we do not endorse. Consider the Pantheon in Rome. It was built to express the governing authority of divine ancient emperors, it was converted to a Christian Church, and it became a shrine to "sanctified" individuals as different from one another as Raphael and the first two kings of modern Italy. It is highly unlikely that the throng of tourists from throughout the world who find aesthetic pleasure in this "must-see" attraction know that history, and it they were told it is more than likely that the pleasure felt by the democrats, atheists, or philistines among them would not be the least bit diminished.

Ordinary people are moved by beauty; the richer its presence, the deeper and longer lasting the pleasure and the happiness of its enjoyment. The capacity to present that richer presence is the valued property of classical architecture, and so is the proportionality between the extent of the richness and the importance of the building's service to human happiness. The man from Mars visiting the United States does not need to be told that the purpose of the Supreme Court Building is more important than the whiskey company that had Mies van der Rohe build the Seagram's Building in New York City. A well-tuned proportionality between the claims on attention that the buildings of the civil and urban realms make attests to the well-ordered arrangement of the authorities in the civil order they serve. In a culture that endorses the diversity that pluralism sanctions proportionality is especially important. It is also essential in establishing the relationships between the three legs of architecture that embrace constructions as different as bicycle sheds are from cathedrals. Each can have an aesthetic appeal that is appropriate for it, but only if the decorum whose end is proportionality is in command can the appeal reside in the beautiful. A bicycle shed that pretends to be a cathedral or a courthouse can no more be beautiful than can a cathedral or a courthouse that looks like a bicycle shed. Their character would be disproportionate to their purpose, and each would evoke a tradition that is alien to the other: the machine analogy is as wrong for a cathedral as the traditions that serve religion are to a bicycle shed, and no good purpose is served by denying this.

Proportionality is the defense against a building's or an urban realm's falling into chaos or kitsch at one extreme and banality, bombast, meanness, or triviality at the other. It recognizes that justice sought in a bar is barroom justice and that a courthouse that looks little better than a bar or resembles a bicycle shed demeans justice. Those who work to build the good city know that the justice that is found in a place that has been built to serve a market is market justice and does not reach the justice that people need to enjoy their happiness, a happiness that the beautiful and good city seeks to make accessible.

And finally, proportionality describes how we are to live with our island home, the earth. We are the stewards of this wonderful garden and the fullness thereof, and a well-tended garden repays us with what we need for our sustenance and for the happiness of ourselves and our posterity. The great cosmos can tell us how to live abundantly and well within it. In how we live together and in how we build to serve that life we merely need to imitate its order, harmony, and proportionality, these three, and the greatest of these is proportionality.

Proportionality's loss in our political life, in architecture, in city building, and in our life with the earth was accompanied by the abandonment of the beautiful as architecture's authoritative content. As heirs of Claude Perrault, Julien Guadet and the others at the Ecole des Beaux Arts were perhaps not off the mark when they dismissed proportions as "Pures chimères," their "cabalistic combinations, mysterious properties of numbers" lacking validity, their analogies with music bogus, and their sanction by a supposedly inviolable antiquity spurious.[26] After proportions were detached from the metaphysical cosmos and converted to numerical ratios they quickly become quackery or absurd, idiosyncratic "discoveries" such as Le Corbusier's in *The Modulor*.[27] In general, proportions became meaningless.

In the American civil order and its architecture proportions can assist in finding the proportionality necessary for the beautiful in architecture that serves as the complement to the good. Proportionality is the quality that architecture shares with the civil order when they both imitate nature and make perceptible the "nature and the reason of the thing," to use Hamilton's language once again. Here natural law holds sway in marshalling diversity into unity and a beautiful order and in fending off chaos from disorder in governing to protect and promote the public good. And here proportionality retains its fundamental role of guiding judgment to separate opinion from truth, fabrication from fact, hearsay from knowledge, and copying from inventing.

When a building's beauty can be explicated in reasonable speech it can also make visible the otherwise invisible analogy between the good and the beautiful. That analogy is imbedded in the traditions of architecture as a civil art and its sources in the beautiful and the good in nature. A building is a symbol of the good, one that makes visible the invisible quality of justice, the quality that is perceptible to those who have eyes that see. Those who seek justice for themselves and their fellow citizens will seek those buildings, and those who have the talent and training to imitate nature as they make new buildings will be able to furnish them to the city's urban and rural settings as they participate with the other citizens in restoring the *città felice*, the good city that fulfills the needs of men.

NOTES

1   Jacques Ellul, *The Meaning of the City*, trans. Dennis Pardee (Grand Rapids: Eerdmans, 1970).

2   Louis Wirth, "Urbanism as a Way of Life," *The American Journal of Sociology*, 44 (1938), reprinted in Paul K. Hatt and Albert J. Reiss, Jr, *Cities and Society* (New York: The Free Press, 1951; 1957), 50.

3   Lewis Mumford, *The Culture of Cities* (New York: Harcourt, Brace and Company, 1938), expanded and published as *The City in History: its Origins and Transformations, and its Prospects* (New York: Harcourt, Brace & World, 1961).

4   José Ortega y Gasset, "The Unpopularity of the New Art," (1948) in *The Dehumanization of Art and other Writings on Art and Culture* (Garden City, N.Y.: Doubleday Anchor Books, n.d.), 7.

5   Jacques Ellul, *The Empire of Non-Sense: Art in the Technological Society*, trans. Michael Johnson and David Lovekin (Winterbourne, Wilts.: Papadakis, 2014).

6   "United States Court of Appeals for the Second Circuit, Nos. 822–823—August term, 1987," in Clara Weyergraf-Serra and Martha Buskirk, *The Destruction of* Tilted-Arc: *Documents* (Cambridge, Mass., and London: MIT, 1991), 248, 249, 250, 252.

7   The criteria include no role for beauty or for civic value. Instead, they follow the various classificatory categories developed by historians and theorists in the nineteenth century: "type, period, or method of construction, or that represent the work of a master, or that possess high artistic values." This last criterion avoids beauty and instead puts the judgment in the lap of the Fine Arts that long ago foreswore a commitment to civic value. For more on this topic see Carroll William Westfall, "Historians, Testimony, and Designation Criteria," "The Forum: Bulletin of the Committee on Preservation (Society of Architectural Historians)," no. 16, August, 1987. The National Trust for Historic Preservation now advocates preserving modernist

buildings, which are not easily "loveable," and are an "acquired taste." See for example *Preservation: People Saving Places*, 66:1, (winter, 2014), 6, 22, 25.

8   *Mugler v Kansas*, 123 U.S. 623 (1887), cited in Hadley Arkes, The Philosopher in the City: The Moral Dimensions of Urban Politics (Princeton: Princeton University Press, 1981), 18.

9   *Cohen v California*, 403 U.S. (1971) at 25; discussed in Arkes, *Philosopher in the City*, 66.

10 For emotivism see Alasdair MacIntyre, *After Virtue: A Study in Moral Theory* (Notre Dame, Indiana: University of Notre Dame Press, 1981).

11 Hume, *Four Dissertations*, 214.

12 TJ to James Madison, Paris, September 1, 1785, *Writings*, 822.

13 Wittkower, *Architectural Principles*.

14 See Carroll William Westfall, "From Homes to Towers: A Century of Chicago's Best Hotels and Tall Apartments Buildings," in John Zukowsky, ed., *Chicago Architecture 1872–1922: Birth of a Metropolis* (Munich: Prestel-Verlag and The Art Institute of Chicago, 1987), 267–89; and "Chicago's Better Tall Apartment Buildings: 1871–1923," *Architectura*, 21:2 (1991), 177–208.

15 Thucydides, *History of the Peloponnesian War*, trans. Rex Warner, rev. edn (Harmondsworth: Penguin Books, 1972), 148.

16 For Chicago, see Carroll William Westfall, "Buildings Serving Commerce," in John Zukowsky. ed., *Chicago Architecture 1872–1922: Birth of a Metropolis* (Munich: Prestel-Verlag and The Art Institute of Chicago, 1987), 77–89. The building recently refitted to serve as the University of Notre Dame's center in Rome began life in the 1920s as a factory.

17 I owe this insight to the sculptor Richard S. Schubert who in a railroad yard in Seattle opened for me the pleasure that can be found in an artistically-designed pedestrian bridge.

18 An earlier version of the rest of this chapter appeared in "Beauty and Proportionality in Architecture," *American Arts Quarterly*, 30:1 (2013), 32–42.

19 The passage continues directly: "It is achieved when the elements of the project are proportionate in height to width, length to breadth, and every element corresponds in its dimensions to the total measure of the whole."

20 McEwen, *Vitruvius*, quoting p. 198 (original emphasis); see also 210–12.

21 Indra Kagis McEwan, *Socrates Ancestor: An Essay on Architectural Beginnings* (Cambridge, Mass.: MIT, 1993).

22 This point is clearly presented and richly developed in Keith Critchlow, "The Platonic Tradition on the Nature of Proportion," in Christopher Bamford, ed., *Homage to Pythagoras: Rediscovering Sacred Science* (Hudson New York: Lindisfarne, 1994), 133–68.

23 See the interesting recollections of his experience in Ralph Adam Cram's office in the accounts by Chester Anderson Brown, *My Best Years in Architecture with Ralph Adams Cram, F.A.I.A.: Architect, Author, Crusader*, (photocopy of typescript: University of Notre Dame Architecture Library, 1971); and *My Finest Holiday: An Account of my Trip to England in 1923*, (photocopy of typescript: University of Notre Dame Architecture Library, 1977).

24 See Carroll William Westfall, "The Jefferson Memorial: A Pyrrhic Victory for American Architecture," in Thomas S. Luebke, ed., *Civic Art: A Centennial History of the U. S. Commission of Fine Arts* (Washington: U.S. Commission of Fine Arts, 2013), 154–63.

25 See among others especially Léon Krier, *Alberti Speer: Architecture, 1932–1942*, facsimile of 1985 edn with additional material (New York: Monacelli Press, 2013).

26 Julien Guadet, *Éléments et théorie de l'architeture*, 4 vols, (Paris: Librairie de la construction modern, 1901), 1: 137–9.

27 Le Corbusier, *The Modulor: A Harmonious Measure to the Human Scale Universally Applicable to Architecture and Mechanics*, trans. Peter de Francia and Anna Bostock, 2nd edn (Cambridge, Mass.: Harvard University Press, 1954); and *Modulor 2: 1955, (Let the User Speak next)*, trans. Peter de Francia and Anna Bostock (Cambridge, Mass.: Harvard University Press, 1958).

Bibliography

Ackerman, James S., *Palladio*, Harmondsworth: Penguin, 1966.

Ackerman, James S., "Imitation," in *Origins, Imitation, Conventions*, 125–41, Cambridge, Mass. and London: MIT Press, 2002.

Adam, Robert, *Ruins of the Palace of the Emperor Diocletian at Spalatro in Dalmatia*, London: for the author, 1764.

Alberti, Leon Battista, *L'Architettura*. Translated by Cosimo Bartoli, Florence: Lorenzo Torrentino, 1550.

Alberti, Leon Battista, *Ten Books on Architecture*, edited by Joseph Rykwert, a republication of the edition of London, Edward Owen, for Robert Alfray, 1755, itself a translation of James Leoni, 3 vols in 1, London: Thomas Edlin, 1726, London: Alec Tiranti, 1955.

Alberti Leon Battista, "I Libri della famiglia," in *Opere Volgari*, edited by Cecil Grayson, vol. 1, Bari: Gius. Laterza & Figli: Scrittori d'Italia, no. 218, 1960.

Alberti, Leon Battista, "Villa," in *Opere Volgari*, edited by Cecil Grayson, vol. I, 359–63, Bari: Gius. Laterza & Figli: Scrittori d'Italia, no. 218, 1960.

Alberti, Leon Battista, *L'Architettura (de re aedificatoria)*, Latin text and Italian translation by Giovanni Orlandi, 2 vols, Milan: Polifilo, 1966.

Alberti, Leon Battista, "Fate and Fortune." Translated by Arturo B. Fallico and Herman Shapiro, in *Renaissance Philosophy: The Italian Philosophers*, 33–40, New York: The Modern Library, 1967.

Alberti, Leon Battista Alberti, *The Family in Renaissance Florence*. Translated by Renée Watkins, Columbia: University of South Carolina Press, 1969.

Alberti, Leon Battista, *On the Art of Building in Ten Books*. Translated by Joseph Rykwert, Neil Leach, and Robert Travenor, Cambridge, Mass. and London: MIT Press, 1988.

Alberti, Leon Battista, *Momus*. Translated by Sarah Knight, Cambridge, Mass.: Harvard University Press, 2003.

Alberti, Leon Battista, *Il Nuovo* de pictura *di Leon Battista Alberti/The New* de pictura *of Leon Battista Alberti*. Edited by Rocco Sinisgalli, Rome: Kappa, 2006.

Allen, William C., *History of the United States Capitol: A Chronicle of Design, Construction, and Politics*, Washington: U.S. Government Printing Office, 2001.

Anon, *The Richard H. Driehaus Prize: Inaugural Recipient Léon Krier*, Notre Dame, Indiana: University of Notre Dame School of Architecture, 2003.

Aquinas, St Thomas, *Treatise on Law*. Introduction by Stanley Parry, Washington, D.C.: Regnery Gateway, n.d. [1987 printing].

Argan, Giulio Carlo and Nesca A. Robb, "The Architecture of Brunelleschi and the Origins of Perspective Theory in the Fifteenth Century," *Journal of the Warburg and Courtauld Institutes*, 9 (1946): 96–121.

Aristotle, *Rhetorica*. Translated by W. Rys Roberts. In *The Basic Works of Aristotle*, edited by Richard McKeon, 1317–1451, New York: Random House, 1941.

Aristotle, *Nicomachean Ethics*. Translated by W.D. Ross. In *The Basic Works of Aristotle*, edited by Richard McKeon, 927–1112, New York: Random House, 1941.

Aristotle, *Nicomachean Ethics*. Translated by R.C. Bartlett and Susan D. Collins, Chicago: University of Chicago Press, 2011.

Arkes, Hadley, *The Philosopher in the City: The Moral Dimensions of Urban Politics*, Princeton: Princeton University Press, 1981.

Arkes, Hadley, *First Things: An Inquiry into the First Principles of Morals and Justice*, Princeton: Princeton University Press, 1986.

Arkes, Hadley, *Beyond the Constitution*, Princeton: Princeton University Press, 1990.

Arkes, Hadley, *Constitutional Illusions and Anchoring Truths: The Touchstone of the Natural Law*, Cambridge: Cambridge University Press, 2010.

Augustine of Hippo, *Confessions*. Translated by R.S. Pine-Coffin, Harmondsworth: Penguin, 1961.

Baron, Hans, "Leon Battista Alberti as an Heir and Critic of Florentine Civic Humanism," in *In Search of Florentine Humanism*, 258–88, Princeton: Princeton University Press, 1988, vol. 1.

Barzman, Karen-edis, *The Florentine Academy and the Early Modern State*, Cambridge: Cambridge University Press, 2000.

Bellomo, Manlio, *The Common Legal Past of Europe, 1000–1800*. Translated by Lydia G. Cochrane, Washington: Catholic University Press of America, 1995.

Berg, Scott W., *Grand Avenues: The Story of the French Visionary who Designed Washington, D. C.*, New York: Pantheon Book, 2007.

Berger, Robert W., *The Palace of the Sun King: The Louvre of Louis XIV*, University Park: Pennsylvania State University Press, 1993.

Białostocki, Jan, "The Renaissance Concept of Nature and Antiquity," in *The Renaissance and Mannerism: Studies in Western Art, Acts of the Twentieth International Congress of the History of Art*, vol. 2, edited by Millard Meiss, 19–30, Princeton: Princeton University Press, 1963.

Biondo, Flavio, *Italy Illuminated*. Edited and translated by Jeffrey A. White, vol. 1 Cambridge, Mass., and London: The I Tatti Renaissance Library and Harvard University Press, 2005.

Black, Antony, *Monarchy and Community: Political Ideas in the Later Conciliar Controversy 1430–50*, Cambridge: Cambridge University Press, 1970.

Black, Antony, *Council and Commune: The Conciliar Movement and the Fifteenth-Century Heritage*, London: Burns & Oats, and Shephardstown: Patmos Press, 1979.

Black, Antony, *Political Thought in Europe, 1250–1450*, Cambridge: Cambridge University Press, 1992.

Blondel, Jacques-François, *Cours d'architecture, ou traité de la décoration, distribution & construction des bâtiments; Contenant les leçons données en 1750, & les années suivantes*, 8 vols, Paris: Desaint, 1771–77.

Blondel, Jacques-François, *L'Architecture français*, Paris: Librairie centrale des beaux-arts, É. Lévy, 1904.

Bloomer, Kent, "The Sacrifice of Ornament in the Twentieth Century," in *Architects and Mimetic Rivalry*, edited by Samir Younés, 77–95, Winterbourne, Berks: Papadakis, 2012.

Blunt, Anthony, *Artistic Theory in Italy, 1450–1600* (1940), 8th impression, Oxford and New York: Oxford University Press, 1985.

Bosanquet, Bernard, *A History of Aesthetic*, 2nd edn, London: George Allen & Unwin, 1904.

Boullée, Étienne-Louis, *Treatise on Architecture, A Complete Presentation of the Architecture, Essai sur l'art*. Edited by Helen Rosenau, London: Alec Tiranti, 1953.

Boullée, Étienne-Louis, *Architecture, Essai sur l'art*. Edited by Jean-Marie Pérouse de Montclos, Paris: Hermann, 1968.

Braunfels, Wolfgang, *Mittelalterliche Stadtbaukunst in der Toskana*, 3rd edn, Berlin: Mann, 1966.

Brown, C. Allan, "Thomas Jefferson's Poplar Forest: the Mathematics of an Ideal Villa," *Journal of Garden History* 10 (1990): 117–39.

Brown, Chester Anderson, *My Best Years in Architecture with Ralph Adams Cram, F.A.I.A.: Architect, Author, Crusader*, photocopy of typescript, University of Notre Dame Architecture Library, 1971.

Brown, Chester Anderson, *My Finest Holiday: An Account of my Trip to England in 1923*, photocopy of typescript, University of Notre Dame Architecture Library, 1977.

Brownell, Charles E. et al., *The Making of Virginia Architecture*, Charlottesville and London: University Press of Virginia, 1992.

Brownell, Charles, "Thomas Jefferson's Architectural Models and the United States Capitol," in *A Republic for the Ages: The United States Capitol and the Political Culture of the Early Republic*, edited by Donald R. Kennon, 316–401, Charlottesville and London: University Press of Virginia, 1999.

Brucker, Gene, *Renaissance Florence*, New York et al.: John Wiley, 1969.

Brucker, Gene, *The Civic World of Early Renaissance Florence*, Princeton: Princeton University Press, 1977.

Bruni, Leonardo, "Panegyric to the City of Florence," in *The Earthly Republic: Italian Humanists on Government and Society*, edited by B.G. Kohl and translated by Ronald G. Witt, 135–73, n.p.: Benjamin G. Kohl, University of Pennsylvania Press, 1978.

Burckhardt, Jacob, *The Civilization of the Renaissance in Italy* (1860). Translated by S.G.C. Middlemore, 2 vols, New York, et al.: Harper Torchbook, 1958.

Burke, Edmund, *A Philosophical Enquiry into the Origin of our Ideas of the Sublime and Beautiful*, 2nd edn, 1759. Edited by Adam Phillips, Oxford: Oxford University Press, 1990.

Campbell, Colen, *Vitruvius Britannicus*, 3 vols. London: printed by the author, 1715–25.

Caniggia, Gianfranco and Gian Luigi Maffei, *Interpreting Basic Building: Architectural Composition and Building Typology*. Translated by Susan Jane Faser, Florence: Alinea, 2001.

Canning, L.P., "Law, Sovereignty and Corporation Theory, 1300–1450," in *The Cambridge History of Medieval Political Thought c.350–1450*, edited by J.H. Burns, 454–77, Cambridge et al.: Cambridge University Press, 1988.

Carmona, Michael, *Haussmann: His Life and Times, and the Making of Modern Paris*, Chicago: Ivan R. Dee, 2002.

Cassirer, Ernst, *The Individual and the Cosmos in Renaissance Philosophy*. Translated by Mario Domandi, New York: Harper and Row, 1964.

Chambers, S. Allen, *Poplar Forest and Thomas Jefferson*, Forest, Virginia: The Corporation for Jefferson's Poplar Forest, 1993.

Choay, Françoise, *The Rule and the Model: On the Theory of Architecture and Urbanism*. Edited by Denise Bratton, Cambridge, Mass. and London: MIT, 1997.

Christian, Lynda Gregorian, "The Figure of Socrates in Erasmus' Works," *The Sixteenth Century Journal*, 3:2 (1972): 1–10.

Cicero, *De officiis*. Translated by Walter Miller, Loeb Classical Library, Cambridge, Mass., and London: Harvard University Press and William Heinemann, 1925.

Cicero, *De oratore*. Translated by H. Rackham, 2 vols, Loeb Classical Library, Cambridge, Mass. and London: Harvard University Press, 1942.

Cicero, *Academica*. Translated by H. Rackham, Loeb Classical Library, revised edn, Cambridge, Mass. and London: Harvard University Press, 1951.

Cicero, *Pro Milone*. Translated by N.H. Watts, Loeb Classical Library, revised edn, Cambridge, Mass. and London: Harvard University Press, 1953.

Cicero, *Orator*. Translated by H.M. Hubbell, Loeb Classical Library, revised edn, Cambridge, Mass., and London: Harvard University Press, 1962.

Cicero, *De inventione*. Translated by H.M. Hubbell, Cambridge, Mass. and London: Harvard University Press, 1976.

Cicero, *De natura deorum*. Translated by H. Rackham, Loeb Classical Library, Cambridge, Mass.: Harvard University Press, 1979.

Cohen, Jeffrey A., "Forms into Architecture: Reform Ideals and the Gauntlet of the Real in Latrobe's Surveyorships at the U. S. Capitol, 1803–1817," in *The United States Capitol: Designing and Decorating a National Icon*, edited by Donald R. Kennon, 23–55, Athens, Ohio: Ohio University Press, 2000.

Cohen, Jeffrey A. and Charles E. Brownell, *The Architectural Drawings of Benjamin Henry Latrobe*, Part 1, New Haven and London: Yale University Press, 1994.

Collins, Peter, *Changing Ideals in Modern Architecture 1750–1950*, 2nd edn, Montreal & Kingston, etc.: McGill-Queen's University Press, 1998.

Cooper, Anthony Ashley 3rd Earl of Shaftsbury, "Soliloquy: or Advice to an Author," in *Characteristicks of Men, Manners, Opinions, Times*, 5th edition, 1: 151–364, London: [no publisher listed], 1732.

Cooper, Anthony Ashley 3rd Earl of Shaftsbury, "The Moralist, a Philosophical Rhapsody," in *Characteristicks of Men, Manners, Opinions, Times*, 5th edition, 2: 175–443, London: [no publisher listed], 1732.

Cooper, Anthony Ashley 3rd Earl of Shaftsbury, "Sensus Communis: an Essay on the Freedom of Wit and Humour," in *Characteristicks of Men, Manners, Opinions, Times*, 5th edition, 1: 58–150, London: [no publisher listed], 1732.

Cooper, Anthony Ashley, Lord Shaftsbury, "A Letter concerning Design," *Characteristicks of Men, Manners, Opinions, Times*, 5th edition, 3: 394–410, London: [no publisher listed], 1732.

Critchlow, Keith, "The Platonic Tradition on the Nature of Proportion," in *Homage to Pythagoras: Rediscovering Sacred Science*, edited by Christopher Bamford, 133–68, Hudson, New York: Lindisfarne, 1994.

Crowe, Norman, *Nature and the Idea of a Man-Made World* Cambridge, Mass.: MIT Press, 1995.

De Clercq, Rafael, "Building Plans as Natural Symbols," *Architecture Philosophy*, 1:1 (2014): 59–80.

Deming, Mark, *La Halle au Blé de Paris, 1762–1813*, Brussels: Archives d'Architecture Moderne, 1984.

d'Entrèves, A.P, *Natural Law: An Historical Survey*, London: Hutchinson, 1951; reprinted New York: Harper Torchbook, 1965.

Desmond, William, *Art and the Absolute: A Study of Hegel's Aesthetics*, Albany: State University of New York Press, 1986.

D'Evelyn, Margaret Muther, *Venice and Vitruvius: Reading Venice with Daniele Barbaro and Andrea Palladio*, New Haven and London: Yale University Press, 2012.

du Prey, Pierre de la Ruffinière, *Hawksmoor's London Churches: Architecture and Theology*, Chicago and London: University of Chicago, 2000.

Dupré, Louis, *The Enlightenment and the Intellectual Foundations of Modern Culture*, New Haven and London: Yale University Press, 2004.

Durand, Nicolas-Louis, *Précis des Leçons d'Architecture*, Brussels: Meline, Cans, 1840.

Durand, Nicolas-Louis, *Précis des Leçons d'Architecture*, 2 vols, Paris: Didot, 1819; republished Nördlingen: Uhl, 1981.

Durand, Nicolas-Louis, *Précis of the Lectures of Architecture*. Translated by David Britt, Los Angeles: Getty Research Institute, 2000.

Eco, Umberto, *Art and Beauty in the Middle Ages*. Translated by Hugh Bredin, New Haven and London: Yale University Press, 1986.

Economacis, Richard M., "From Apologia to Praxis," in *Architecture: Timeless Building for the Twentieth-Century*, edited by Alireza Sagharchi and Lucien Steil, 310–15, New York et al.: Rizzoli, 2013.

Ellul, Jacques, *The Technological Society*. Translated by John Wilkinson, New York: Knopf, 1964.

Ellul, Jacques, *The Meaning of the City*. Translated by Dennis Pardee, Grand Rapids: Eerdmans, 1970.

Ellul, Jacques, *The Empire of Non-Sense: Art in the Technological Society*. Translated by Michael Johnson and David Lovekin, Winterbourne, Wilts.: Papadakis, 2014.

Filarete, *Treatise on Architecture, Being the Treatise by Antonio di Piero Averlino, Known as Filarete*. Facsimile and transion with notes by John R. Spencer, 2 vols, New Haven and London: Yale University Press, 1965.

Filarete, *Trattato di architettura*. Edited by Anna Maria Finoli and Liliana Grassi, 2 vols, Milan: Polifilo, 1972.

Fletcher, Sir Banister and Banister F[light] Fletcher, *A History of Architecture for the Student, Craftsman, and Amateur being a Comparative View of the Historical Styles from the Earliest Period*, London: B.T. Batsford; New York: Charles Scribner's Sons, 1896.

Freart, Sieur de Chambray Roland, *The Whole Body of Ancient and Modern Architecture Comprehending ... Ten Principal Authors Who Have Written upon the Five Orders*. Translated by John Evelyn, London: J. Wilkinson et al., 1680.

Friedman, David, "'Fiorenza': Geography and Representation in a Fifteenth Century City View," *Zeitschrift für Kunstgeschichte*, 64 (2001): 56–77.

Friedman, Lawrence M., *A History of American Law*, New York: Simon and Schuster: A Touchstone Book, 1973.

Gadol, Joan, *Leon Battista Alberti: Universal Man of the Early Renaissance*, Chicago and London: University of Chicago Press, 1969.

Geertman, Herman, "Teoria e attualità della progettistica architettonica di Vitruvio," in *Le project de Viturve, Actes du colloque internationale ... 1993*, 7–30, Rome: Ecole Française de Rome, Palais Farnèse, 1994.

Gerbino, Anthony, *Françoise Blondel: Architecture, Erudition, and the Scientific Revolution*, London and New York: Routledge, 2010.

Gibbs, James, *Rules for Drawing the Several Parts of Architecture*, 3rd edn, London: W. Innes, et al., 1753.

Giordano, Ralph G., *The Architectural Ideology of Thomas Jefferson*, Jefferson, North Carolina, and London: McFarland & Company, 2012.

Grafton, Anthony, *Leon Battista Alberti: Master Builder of the Italian Renaissance*, New York: Hill and Wang, 2000.

Green, Bryan Clark, *In Jefferson's Shadow: The Architecture of Thomas R. Blackburn*, Richmond: Virginia Historical Society and New York: Princeton Architectural Press, 2006.

Greenberg, Allan, *George Washington Architect*, London: Andres Papadakis, 1999.

Greenberg, Allan, *The Architecture of Democracy*, New York: Rizzoli, 2006.

Gregory, Brad S., *The Unintended Reformation: How a Religious Revolution Secularized Society*, Cambridge, Mass., and London: Harvard University Press, 2012.

Guadet, Julien, *Éléments et théorie de l'architeture*, 4 vols, Paris: Librairie de la construction modern, 1901.

Hafertepe, Kenneth, "An Inquiry into Thomas Jefferson's Ideas of Beauty," *Journal of the Society of Architectural Historians*, 59 (2000): 216–31.

Hanneford-Smith, W., *The Architectural Work of Sir Banister Fletcher*, London: Batsford, 1934.

Harries, Karsten, *The Ethical Function of Architecture*, Cambridge, Mass., and London: MIT Press, 1998.

Hart, Vaughan, "Serlio and the Representation of Architecture," in *Paper Palaces: The Rise of the Renaissance Architectural Treatise*, edited by Hart and Peter Hicks, 170–85, New Haven and London: Yale University Press, 1998.

Hernandez, Jorge. "Palladio in Contemporary Academy and Practice." Paper presented at symposium, *From Vernacular to Classical: The Perpetual Modernity of Palladio*, School of Architecture, University of Notre Dame, June 10–12, 2011.

Herrmann, Wolfgang, *The Theory of Claude Perrault*, London: A. Zwemmer, 1973.

Hersey, George L., *High Victorian Gothic: A Study in Associationism*, Baltimore and London: Johns Hopkins University Press, 1972.

Hersey, George, *Pythagorean Palaces: Magic and Architecture in the Italian Renaissance*, Ithaca: Cornell University Press, 1976.

Hersey George and Richard Freedman, *Possible Palladian Villa (Plus a Few Instructively Impossible Ones)*, Cambridge, Mass.: MIT, 1992.

Holm, Alvin, "The Buildings We Love," *Clem Labine's Period Homes*, 15:2 (March, 2014): 64.

Home, Henry, Lord Kames, *Elements of Criticism*, 6th edn, (1785), vol. 2. Edited by Peter Jones, Indianapolis: Liberty Fund, 2005.

Hon, Giora and Bernard R. Goldstein, *From* Summetria *to Symmetry: The Making of a Revolutionary Scientific Concept*, n.p.: Springer, 2008.

Howard, Hugh, *Dr. Kimball and Mr. Jefferson: Rediscovering the Founding Fathers of American Architecture*, New York: Bloomsbury, 2006.

Hume, David, "Of the Standard of Taste," in *Four Dissertations*, 203–40, London: Millar, 1757.

Huppert, Ann C., "Envisioning New St. Peter's: Perspectival Drawings and the Process of Design," *Journal of the Society of Architectural Historians*, 68 (2009): 158–77.

Hutcheson, Francis, *An Inquiry into the Original of Our Ideas of Beauty and Virtue in Two Treatises*, revised edn. Edited by Wolfgang Leidhold, Indianapolis: Liberty Fund, 2008.

Jacks, Philip, *The Antiquarian and the Myth of Antiquity*, Cambridge and New York: Cambridge University Press, 1993.

Jefferson, Thomas, *The Writings of Thomas Jefferson*. Edited by Paul Leicester Ford, New York and London: G.P. Putman's Sons, 1899.

Jefferson, Thomas, "An Account of the Capitol in Virginia," in *The Writings of Thomas Jefferson*, edited by Albert Ellery Bergh, vol. 17, 353–4, Washington: The Thomas Jefferson Memorial Association, 1904.

Jefferson, Thomas, *The Papers of Thomas Jefferson*. Edited by Julian P. Bond, Princeton: Princeton University Press, 1950 ongoing.

Jefferson, Thomas, *Notes on the State of Virginia*. Edited by William Peden, New York and London: W. W. Norton, 1954.

Jefferson, Thomas, *The Portable Thomas Jefferson*. Edited by Merrill D. Peterson, New York and London: Penguin, 1977.

Jefferson, Thomas, *Writings*. Edited by Merrill D. Peterson, New York: Library of America, 1984.

Jenkins, Frank, *Architect and Patron*, London: Oxford University Press, 1961.

Johnson, Samuel, in George B.N. Hill, *Johnson Miscellanies*, Oxford: Oxford University Press, 1897.

Jones, Mark Wilson, *Principles of Roman Architecture*, New Haven and London: Yale University Press, 2000.

Kant, Immanuel, *Critique of Judgment*. Translated by James Creed Meredith, Oxford: Clarendon Press, 1928.

Kant, Immanuel, *Observations on the Feeling of the Beautiful and Sublime*. Translated by John T. Goldthwait, Berkeley, Los Angeles, and London: University of California Press, 1960.

Kauffmann, Emil, *Architecture in the Age of Reason: Baroque and Post-Baroque in England, Italy, and France*, Cambridge, Mass.: Harvard University Press, 1955.

Kemp, Martin, "From 'Mimesis' to 'Fantasia': The Quattrocento Vocabulary of Creation, Inspiration and Genius in the Visual Arts," *Viator*, 8 (1977): 347–98.

Kennedy, Roger G., *Orders from France: The Americans and the French in a Revolutionary World, 1780–1820*, New York: Alfred A. Knopf, 1989.

Kimball, Fiske, "Thomas Jefferson and the First Monument of the Classical Revival in America," *Journal of the American Institute of Architects*, 3 (1915): 375–6.

Kimball, Fiske, *Domestic Architecture of the American Colonies and of the Early Republic*, New York: Charles Scribner's Sons, 1922.

Kimball, Fiske, *American Architecture*, Indianapolis and New York: Bobbs-Merrill, 1928.

Kimball, Fiske, "Jefferson and the Public Buildings of Virginia, II. Richmond, 1779–1780," *Huntington Library Quarterly*, 12 (1949): 303–10.

Kimball, Fiske, *Thomas Jefferson, Architect*, Boston: Riverside Press for Private Distribution, 1916; reprinted New York: Da Capo Press, 1968.

Kimball, Fiske, *The Capitol of Virginia: A Landmark of American Architecture*. Revised and expanded from a 1989 republication edited by Jon Kukla, with a new introduction by Charles Brownell, Richmond: Library of Virginia, 2001.

Kipp, David, "Alberti's 'Hidden' Theory of Visual Art," *British Journal of Aesthetics*, 24 (1984): 231–40.

Kirker, Harold, *The Architecture of Charles Bulfinch*, Cambridge, Mass.: Harvard University Press, 1969.

Kirker, Harold, "Charles Bulfinch," in *Macmillan Encyclopedia of Architects*, edited by Adolph K. Placzek, 4 vols, New York: The Free Press, 1982.

Kirker, Harold and James Kirker, *Bulfinch's Boston, 1787–1817*, New York: Oxford University Press, 1964.

Knight, Richard Payne, *An Analytical Inquiry into the Principles of Taste*, 2nd edn, London: Luke Howard, 1805.

Krier, Léon, *Architecture: Choice or Fate*, Windsor, Berks: Andreas Papadakis, 1998.

Krier, Léon, *The Architecture of Community*. Edited by Dhiru A. Thadani and Peter J. Hetzel, Washington, etc.: Island Press, 2009.

Krier, Léon, "Imitation, Hidden or Declared," in *Architects and Mimetic Rivalry*, edited by Samir Younés, 52–7, Winterbourne, Berks.: Papadkis, 2012.

Krier, Léon, *Albert Speer: Architecture, 1932–1942*, facsimile of 1985 edn with additional material, New York: Monacelli Press, 2013.

Kristeller, Paul Oskar, "The Modern System of the Arts," in *Renaissance Thought II: Papers on Humanism and the Arts*, New York, Evanston, and London: Harper Torchbooks, 1965; originally published in *Journal of the History of Ideas*, 12:4 (1951): 496–527, and 13:1 (1952): 17–46; 163–227.

Kristeller, Paul Oscar, *Eight Philosophers of the Italian Renaissance*, Stanford: Stanford University Press, 1964.

Kristeller, Paul Oskar, *Renaissance Thought and Its Sources*. Edited by Michael Mooney, New York: Columbia University Press, 1979.

Kristeller, Paul Oskar, "Afterword: 'Creativity' and 'Tradition,'" in *Renaissance Thought and the Arts*, Princeton: Princeton University Press, 1990: 247–58.

Kruft, Hanno-Walter, *A History of Architectural Theory from Vitruvius to the Present*. Translated by Ronald Taylor, Elsie Callander, and Antony Wood, London and New York: Zwemmer and Princeton Architectural Press, 1994.

Latrobe, Benjamin Henry, *The Correspondence and Miscellaneous Papers of Benjamin Henry Latrobe*. Edited by John C. Van Horne, 3 vols, New Haven and London: Yale University Press, 1984–88.

Laugier, Marc-Antoine, *An Essay on Architecture*, 2nd edn. Translated by Wolfgang and Anni Herrmann, Los Angeles: Hennessey & Ingalls, 1977.

Lavin, Sylvia, *Quatremère de Quincy and the Invention of a Modern Language of Architecture*, Cambridge, Mass., and London: MIT Press, 1992.

Le Corbusier, *The Modulor: A Harmonious Measure to the Human Scale Universally applicable to Architecture and Mechanics*. Translated by Peter de Francia and Anna Bostock, 2nd edn, Cambridge, Mass.: Harvard University Press, 1954.

Le Corbusier, *Modulor 2: 1955, (Let the User Speak next)*. Translated by Peter de Francia and Anna Bostock, Cambridge, Mass.: Harvard University Press, 1958.

Leidhold, Wolfgang, introduction to *An Inquiry into the Original of Our Ideas of Beauty and Virtue in Two Treatises*, by Francis Hutcheson, ix–xviii, revised edn, edited by Wolfgang Leidhold, Indianapolis: Liberty Fund, 2008.

LeRoy, Julien-David, *Les ruines des plus beaux monuments de la Grèce*, Paris: Guerin & Delatour, 1758.

Loos, Adolf, "Ornament and Crime," in *Programs and Manifestoes on 20th-Century Architecture*, edited and translated by Michael Bullock, 19–24, Cambridge, Mass.: MIT Press, 1970.

l'Orme, Philibert de, *Architecture*, Rouen: David Ferrand, 1648.

Lowic, Lawrence "The Meaning and Significance of the Human Analogy in Francesco di Giorgio's Trattato," *Journal of the Society of Architectural Historians*, 42 (1983): 360–70.

Lovejoy, Arthur, "'Nature' as Aesthetic Norm," *Modern Language Notes*, 42 (1927): 444–50; republished in *Essays in the History of Ideas*, New York: Capricorn Books, G.P. Putnam's Sons: 1960.

Lovejoy, Arthur O., *The Great Chain of Being: A Study in the History of an Idea*, Cambridge, Mass.: Harvard University Press, 1936.

Lucks, Henry A., "Natura Naturans—Natura Naturata," *The New Scholasticism* 9 (1935): 1–24.

Niccolò, Machiavelli, *The Prince*. Translated by Harvey C. Mansfield, Jr, Chicago and London: University of Chicago Press, 1985.

MacCulloch, Diarmaid, *Christianity: The First Three Thousand Years*, New York: Viking Penguin, 2010.

MacIntyre, Alasdair, *After Virtue: A Study in Moral Theory*, Notre Dame, Indiana: University of Notre Dame Press, 1981.

Mallgrave, Henry Francis, *Modern Architectural Theory: A Historical Survey, 1673–1968*, Cambridge et al.: Cambridge University Press, 2005.

McCormick, Thomas J., *Charles-Louis Clérisseau and the Genesis of Neo-Classicism*, Cambridge, Mass., and London: MIT Press, 1990.

McEwan, Indra Kagis, *Socrates Ancestor: An Essay on Architectural Beginnings*, Cambridge, Mass.: MIT, 1993.

McEwen, Indra Kagis, "On Claude Perrault: Modernizing Vitruvius," in *Paper Palaces: The Rise of the Renaissance Architectural Treatise*, edited by Vaughan Hart and Peter Hicks, 320–37, New Haven and London: Yale University Press, 1998.

McEwen, Indra Kagis, *Vitruvius: Writing the Body of Architecture*, Cambridge, Mass., and London: MIT, 2003.

McNamara, Denis R., *Catholic Church Architecture and the Spirit of Liturgy*, Chicago and Mundelein: Hillenbrand Books, 2009.

Major, Thomas, *Ruins of Paestum*, London: T. Major, 1768.

Mancini, Girolamo, *Vita di Leon Battista Alberti*, 2nd edn, 1911; reprint, Rome: Bardi, 1971.

Manetti, Giannozzo, "On Famous Men of Great Age," in *Biographical Writings*, edited and translated by Stefano U. Baldassarri and Rolf Bagemihl, 106–31, Cambridge, Mass., and London: Harvard University Press, 2003.

Marchi, Alessandro and Maria Rosaria Valazzi, eds. *La città ideale: l'utopia del rinascimento a urbino tra Piero della Francesca e Raffaello*. Milan: Electra, 2012.

Maritain, Jacques, *Art and Scholasticism*. Revised edition and translation by J.F. Scanlan, New York: Charles Scribner's Sons, 1947.

Marsilius of Padua, *The Defensor Pacis*. Edited by C.W. Previté-Orton, Cambridge: Cambridge University Press, 1928.

Marsilius of Padua, *The Defender of Peace: The* Defensor pacis. Translated by Alan Gewirth, 2 vols, New York: Columbia University Press, 1951–6, reprint of vol. 2, New York: Harper & Row, 1967.

Marsilius of Padua, *The Defender of the Peace*. Edited and translated by Annabel Brett, Cambridge: Cambridge University Press, 2005.

Martini, Francesco di Giorgio, *Trattati di architettura ingegneria e art militare*. Edited by Corrado Maltese, Milan: Il Polifilo, 1967.

Mayernik, David, *The Challenge of Emulation in Art and Architecture*, Burlington, Vermont: Ashgate, 2013.

Maynard, W. Barksdale, *Architecture in the United States, 1800–1850*, New Haven and London: Yale University Press, 2002.

Metrović, Branko, *Serene Greed of the Eye: Leon Battista Alberti and the Philosophical Foundations of Renaissance Architectural Theory*, Munich and Berlin: Deutscher Kunstverlag, 2005.

Mumford, Lewis, *The Culture of Cities*, New York: Harcourt, Brace and Company, 1938.

Mumford, Lewis, *The City in History: Its Origins and Transformations, and its Prospects*, New York: Harcourt, Brace & World, 1961.

Nelson, Louis P., *The Beauty of Holiness: Anglicanism and Architecture in Colonial South Carolina*, Chapel Hill: University of North Carolina Press, 2008.

Nichols, Frederick D. "Jefferson: The Making of an Architect," in *Jefferson and the Arts: An Extended View*, edited by William Howard Adams, 159–85, Washington: National Gallery of Art, 1976.

Norton, Paul, "Latrobe's Ceiling for the Hall of Representatives," *Journal of the Society of Architectural Historians*, 10 (1951): 5–10.

Nye, David E., "Energy," in *Rethinking the American City*, edited by Miles Orvell and Klaus Benesch, 1–27, Philadelphia: University of Pennsylvania Press, 2014.

O'Neal, William Bainter, *Jefferson's Fine Arts Library: His Selections for the University of Virginia Together with His Own Architectural Books*, 2nd edn, Charlottesville: University Press of Virginia, 1976.

Onians, John, *Bearers of Meaning*, Princeton: Princeton University Press, 1988.

Ortega y Gasset, José, "The Unpopularity of the New Art," (1948) in *The Dehumanization of Art and other Writings on Art and Culture*, 1–50, Garden City, N.Y.: Doubleday Anchor Books, n.d.

O'Sullivan, Richard, "The Philosophy of the Common Law," (1949) in *The Spirit of the Common Law*, edited by B.A. Wortley, 63–86, Tenbury Wells, Worcs.: Fowler Wright Books, 1965.

Palladio, Andrea, *I Quattro libri dell'architettura*, Venice: Domenico de'Franceschi, 1570.

Palladio Andrea, *The Four Books of Architecture*. Translated by Isaac Ware, London: Isaac Ware, 1738.

Palladio, Andrea, *The Four Books on Architecture*. Translated by Robert Tavernor and Richard Schofield, Cambridge, Mass., and London: MIT, 1997.

Panofsky, Erwin, "Artist, Scientist, Genius: Notes on the 'Renaissance-Dämmerung,'" in *The Renaissance: Six Essays*, 121–82, New York and Evanston: Harper Torchbooks, 1962.

Panofsky, Erwin, *Idea: A Concept in Art Theory*. Translated by Joseph J.S. Peake, Columbia: University of South Carolina Press, 1968.

Paul, Jürgen, *Il Palazzo Vecchio in Florenz*, Florence: Leo S. Olscki, 1969.

Payne, Alina A., "Rudolf Wittkower and Architectural Principles in the Age of Modernism," *Journal of the Society of Architectural Historians*, 53 (1994): 322–42.

Payne, Alina A., *The Architectural Treatise in the Italian Renaissance*, Cambridge: Cambridge University Press, 1999.

Pearson, Caspar, *Humanism and the Urban World: Leon Battista Alberti and the Renaissance City*, University Park: Pennsylvania State University Press, 2011.

Pérez-Gómez, Alberto, "Introduction," to Claude Perrault, *Ordonnance for the Five Kinds of Columns after the Method of the Ancients*. Translated by Indra Kagis McEwen, 1–44, Santa Monica: Getty Center, 1993.

Perrault, Claude, *Dix livres d'architecture de Vitruve, corrigex et tradvits nouvellement en françois, avec des notes & des figures*, Paris: J.B. Coignard, 1673.

Perrault, Claude, *Abregé des dix livres d'architecture de Vitruve*, Paris: J.B. Coignard, 1674.

Perrault, Claude, *Ordonnance des cinq especes des colonnes selon la methode des anciens*, Paris: J.B. Coignard, 1683.

Perrault, Claude, *Dix livres d'architecture de Vitruve, corrigex et tradvits nouvellement en françois, avec des notes & des figures*, 2nd revised and enlarged edn, Paris: J.B. Coignard, 1684.

Perrault, Claude, *A Treatise on the Five Orders of Architecture*. Translated by John James, London: Benj. Motte, 1708.

Perrault, Claude, *Ordonnance for the Five Kinds of Columns after the Method of the Ancients*. Translated by Indra Kagis McEwen, Santa Monica: Getty Center, 1993.

Petrarch, Francesco, "On his own Ignorance and that of many Others," in *The Renaissance Philosophy of Man*, edited by Ernest Cassirer et al. Translated by Hans Nachod, 49–133, Chicago and London: University of Chicago Press, 1948.

Pevsner, Nikolaus, *Academies of Art Past and Present*, Cambridge: Cambridge University Press, 1940.

Phelan, G.B., "The Concept of Beauty in St. Thomas Aquinas," in *Selected Papers*, edited by Arthur G. Kirn, 155–80, Toronto: Pontifical Institute of Mediaeval Studies, 1967.

Pickens, Buford, "Mr. Jefferson as Revolutionary Architect," *Journal of the Society of Architectural Historians*, 34 (1975): 257–79.

Plucknett, Theodore F.T., *A Concise History of the Common Law*, 5th edn, London: Butterworth & Co., 1956.

Porphyrios, Demetri, "Classicism is not a Style," in *Classicism is not a Style*, edited by Demetri Porphyrios, 51–7, London: Academy Editions; New York: St. Martin's Press, 1982.

Porphyrios, Demetri, *Classical Architecture*, London: Academy Editions, 1991.

Porphyrios, Demetri, "The Relevance of Classical Architecture," *Architectural Design* 59:9–10 (1989), 53–6; reprinted in *Theorizing a New Agenda for Architecture*, edited by Kate Nesbitt, 91–6, New York: Princeton Architectural Press, 1996.

Powers, Alan, "John Summerson and Modernism," in *Twentieth-Century Architecture and its Histories*, edited by Louise Campbell, 153–75, n.p.: Society of Architectural Historians of Great Britain, 2000.

Preservation: People Saving Places, 66:1, (winter, 2014).

Proctor. Robert E., "Beauty as Symmetry: The Education of Vitruvius' Architect," *American Arts Quarterly*, 27:1 (2010): 8–16.

Quatremère de Quincy, Antoine Chrysostôme, *An Essay on the Nature, the End, and the Means of Imitation in the Fine Arts*. Translated by J.C. Kent, London: Smith, Elder & Co., 1837.

Quatremère de Quincy: *The Historical Dictionary of Architecture*: See Younés, 1999.

Reed, Henry Hope, *The Golden City*, Garden City, N.Y.: Doubleday, 1959.

Reps, John W., "Thomas Jefferson's Checkerboard Towns," *Journal of the Society of Architectural Historians*, 20 (1961): 108–14.

Reps, John, *Monumental Washington: The Planning and Development of the Capital Center*, Princeton: Princeton University Press, 1967.

Reynolds, Sir Joshua, *Discourses on Art*. Edited by Stephen O. Mitchell from the definitive 1797 edition, Indianapolis et al.: Bobbs-Merrill, the Library of Liberal Arts, 1965.

Robertson, Jaquelin, "In Search of an American Urban Order, Part I: The Nagasaki Syndrome," *Modulus 16* (Charlottesville, 1983): 3–15; and "Part II: The House as the City," *Modulus 19* (Charlottesville, 1989): 138–59.

Robinson, Daniel N., *An Intellectual History of Psychology*, revised edn, New York: Macmillan; London: Collier Macmillan, 1981.

Robinson, Daniel N., "The Scottish Enlightenment and the American Founding," *The Monist*, 90 (2007): 170–81.

Robinson, Daniel N., "Aesthetics, Phantasia and the Theistic," in *Turning Images in Philosophy, Science, and Religion: A New Book of Nature*, edited by Charles Taliaferro and Jil Evans, 133–55, Oxford and New York: Oxford University Press, 2011.

Roskill, Mark W., *Dolce's "Aretino" and Venetian Art Theory in the Cinqecento*, New York: New York University Press, 1968.

Rowland, Ingrid, "The Fra Giocondo Vitruvius at 500 (1511–2011)," *Journal of the Society of Architectural Historians*, 70 (2011): 285–9.

Rowland, Ingrid, "From Vitruvian Scholarship to Vitruvian Practice," *Memoirs of the American Academy in Rome*, 50 (2005): 15–40.

Rowe, Colin, "The Mathematics of the Ideal Villa," *Architectural Review* (1949) and in *The Mathematics of the Ideal Villa and Other Essays*, Cambridge, Mass., and London: MIT, 1976; paperback 1982.

Rusk, David, *Cities without Suburbs: Fourth Edition: A Census 2010 Perspective*, Washington, D.C.: Woodrow Wilson Center Press, 2013.

Ryan, Alan, *On Politics: A History of Political Thought from Herodotus to the Present*, 2 vols, New York and London: Liveright Publishing, W.W. Norton, 2012.

Rykwert, Joseph, *The Idea of a Town: The Anthropology of Urban Form in Rome, Italy and the Ancient World*, Princeton: Princeton University Press, 1976.

Rykwert, Joseph, "Theory as Rhetoric: Leon Battista Alberti in Theory and in Practice," in *Paper Palaces: The Rise of the Renaissance Architectural Treatise*, edited by Vaughan Hart and Peter Hicks, 32–50, New Haven and London: Yale University Press, 1998.

Saisselin, Rémy G., "Architecture and Language: The Sensationalism of Le Camus de Mézière," *The British Journal of Aesthetics*, 15 (1975): 239–54.

Salingaros, Nikos, *A Theory of Architecture*, n.p.: Nikos A. Salingaros & Umbau, 2006.

Savile, Anthony, "The Sirens' Serenade," in *Philosophy, the Good, the True and the Beautiful, Royal Institute of Philosophy Supplement: 47*, edited by Anthony O'Hear, 237–55, Cambridge: Cambridge University Press, 2000.

Scamozzi, Vincenzo, *L'Idea della architecttura universal*, Venice: self-published, 1615.

Schulz, Juergen, "Jacopo de'Barbari's View of Venice: Map Making, City Views, and Moralized Geography before the Year 1500," *The Art Bulletin*, 60 (1978): 425–74.

Scruton, Roger, *The Aesthetics of Architecture*, Princeton: Princeton University Press, 1979.

Serlio, Sebastiano, *Sebastiano Serlio on Architecture*. Translated and comments by Vaughan Hart and Peter Hicks, 2 vols, New Haven and London: Yale University Press, 1996–2001.

Settis, Salvatore, *The Future of the 'Classical.'* Translated by Allan Cameron, Cambridge, U.K., and Malden, Mass.: Polity Press, 2006.

Sinisgalli, Rocco, *The New* de picture *of Leon Battista Alberti*, Rome: Edizione Kappa, 2006.

Skinner, Quentin, *The Foundations of Modern Political Theory*, 2 vols, Cambridge, London, et al.: Cambridge University Press, 1978.

Skinner, Quentin, "Political Philosophy," in *The Cambridge History of Renaissance Philosophy*, edited by Skinner and Eckhard Kessler, 387–452, Cambridge: Cambridge University Press, 1988.

Smith, Christine, "Originality and Cultural Progress: Brunelleschi's Dome and a Letter by Alberti," in *Architecture in the Culture of Early Humanism*, 19–39, New York and Oxford: Oxford University Press, 1992.

Smith, Christine, "Alberti's Description of Florence Cathedral as Architectural Criticism," in *Architecture in the Culture of Early Humanism*, 80–97, New York and Oxford: Oxford University Press, 1992.

Smith, Norris Kelly, *Here I Stand: Perspective from Another Point of View*, New York: Columbia University Press, 1994.

Stillman, Damie, "From the Ancient Roman Republic to the New American One: Architecture for a New Nation," in *A Republic for the Ages: The United States Capitol and the Political Culture of the Early Republic*, edited by Donald R. Kennon, 271–315, Charlottesville and London: University Press of Virginia, 1999.

Strauss, Leo, *Natural Right and History*, Chicago and London: University of Chicago Press, 1953.

Strauss, Leo, *The City and Man*, Chicago: Rand McNally, 1964.

Strauss, Leo, "Marsilius of Padua," in *A History of Political Philosophy*, 3rd edn, edited by Leo Strauss and Joseph Cropsey, 276–95, Chicago and London: University of Chicago Press, 1987.

Stuart, James and Nicholas Revett, *The Antiquities of Athens*, 5 vols, London: J. Haberkorn, 1762–1830.

Summers, David, *Michelangelo and the Language of Art*, Princeton: Princeton University Press, 1981.

Summers, David, *The Judgment of Sense: Renaissance Naturalism and the Rise of Aesthetics*, Cambridge: Cambridge University Press, 1987.

Summerson, John, *The Classical Language of Architecture*, London: Methuen, 1964.

Tafuri, Manfredo, *Interpreting the Renaissance: Princes, Cities, Architects*. Translated by Daniel Sherer, New Haven and London: Yale University Press, 2006.

Tanner, Marie, *Jerusalem on the Hill: Rome and the Vision of St. Peter's in the Renaissance*, Turnhout, Belgium: Harvey Miller, 2010.

Tatarkiewicz, Władysław, *History of Aesthetics*. Edited by J Harrell and translated by Adam and Ann Czerniawski, 3 vols, Mouton: The Hague and Paris; and Warsaw: PWN—Polish Scientific Publishers, 1970–74

Tatarkiewicz, Władysław, *A History of Six Ideas: An Essay on Aesthetics*. Translated by Christopher Kasparek, The Hague, Boston, London: Martinus Nijhoff and Warsaw: PWN—Polish Scientific Publishers, 1980.

Taub, Liba Chia, *Ptolemy's Universe: The Natural Philosophical and Ethical Foundations of Ptolemy's Astronomy*, Chicago and LaSalle, Illinois: Open Court, 1993.

Temple, William, *Readings in St. John's Gospel* (first and second series), London: Macmillan and Co., 1952.

Terzoglou, Nikolaos-Ion, "The Human Mind and Design Creativity: Leon Battisa Alberti and *lineamenta*," in *The Humanities in Architectural Design: A Contemporary and Historical Perspective*, edited by Soumyen Bandyopadhyay, Jane Lombolt, et al., 136–46, London and New York: Routledge, 2010.

Thucydides, *History of the Peloponnesian War*. Translated by Rex Warner, rev. edn, Harmondsworth: Penguin Books, 1972.

Tournikiotis, Panayotis, *Adolf Loos*. Translated by Marguerite McGoldrick, New York: Princeton Architectural Press, 1994.

Townsend, Dabney, "Shaftsbury's Aesthetic Theory," *Journal of Aesthetics and Art Criticism*, 41 (1982): 205–13.

Townsend, Dabney, "From Shaftsbury to Kant," *Journal of the History of Ideas*, 48 (1987): 287–305.

Townsend, Dabney, "Lockean Aesthetics," *Journal of Aesthetics and At Criticism*, 49 (1991): 349–61.

Trachtenberg, Marvin, "What Brunelleschi Saw: Monument and Site at the Palazzo Vecchio in Florence," *Journal of the Society of Architectural Historians*, 47 (1988): 14–44.

Trachtenberg Marvin, "Scénographie urbaine et identité civique: réflexion sur la Florence du Trecento," *Revue de l'Art*, 102 (1993): 11–31.

Travernor, Robert, *Palladio and Palladianism*, London: Thames and Hudson, 1991.

Travernor, Robert, *On Alberti and the Art of Building*, New Haven and London: Yale University Press, 1998.

Trinkaus, Charles, *In Our Image and Likeness: Humanity and Divinity in Italian Humanist Thought*, 2 vols, London: Constable, 1970.

Trussell, Timothy, "A Landscape for Mr. Jefferson's Retreat," in, *Jefferson's Poplar Forest: Unearthing a Virginia Plantation*, edited by Barbara J. Heath and Jack Gary, 69–84, Gainsville et al.: University Press of Florida, 2012.

Turner, Frederick, *Beauty: The Value of Values*, Charlottesville, and London: University Press of Virginia, 1991.

Tzonis. Alexander and Liane Lefaivre, *Classical Architecture: The Poetics of Order*, Cambridge, Mass.: MIT Press, 1986.

Ullmann, Walter, *A History of Political Thought: the Middle Ages*, Harmondsworth: Penguin Books, 1965.

van Eck, Caroline, "The Structure of *De re aedificatoria* Reconsidered," *Journal of the Society of Architectural Historians*, 57 (1998): 280–97.

van Eck, Caroline, ed., *British Architectural Theory, 1540–1750: An Anthology of Texts*, Aldershot, Hants; and Burlington, Vermont: Ashgate, 2003.

van Pelt, Robert Jan and Carroll William Westfall, *Architectural Principles in the Age of Historicism*, New Haven and London: Yale University Press, 1991.

Varro, *On the Latin Language*. Translated by Roland G. Kent, Loeb Classical Library, Cambridge, Mass. and London: Harvard University Press, 1951.

Vasari, Giorgio, *The Lives of the Most Excellent Painters, Sculptors, and Architects*. Translated by Gaston du C. de Vere, edited by Philip Jacks, New York: Modern Library, 2006.

Venturi, Robert, *Complexity and Contradiction in Architecture*, New York: Museum of Modern Art, 1966.

Vidler, Anthony, *Histories of the Immediate Present: Inventing Architectural Modernism*, Cambridge, Mass., and London: MIT Press, 2008.

Vignola, Giacomo Barrozzi da, *Canon of the Five Orders of Architecture*. Translated with an introduction by Branko Mitrović, New York: Acanthus Press, 1999.

Vincent of Beauvais, *Speculum Doctrinale*, Graz: Akademische Druk- und Verlagsanstalt, 1965, reproduction of *Biblioteca Mundi seu Speculum Maioris*, Douai: Baltazaris Belieri, 1524, vol. II: *Speculum Doctrinale*.

Vitruvius, Marcus Pollio, *Ten Books on Architecture*. Translated by Fra Giocondo, Venice: Joannis de Tridino, 1511.

Vitruvius, *De architectura*. Translated and comments by Caesare Cesariano, Como: Gotardo da Ponte, 1521.

Vitruvius, Marcus Pollio, *I Dieci libri dell'architettura*. Translated and comments by Danielle Barbaro, Venice: Francesco de'Franceschi Senese, 1567.

Vitruvius, Marcus Pollio, *Ten Books on Architecture*. Translated by Morris Hicky Morgan, Cambridge, Mass: Harvard University Press, 1914.

Vitruvius, Marcus Pollio, *Ten Books on Architecture*. Edited and Translated by Frank Granger, 2 vols, Loeb Classical Library, revised edn, Cambridge, Mass. and London: Harvard University Press, 1933–35.

Vitruvius, *I Dieci libri dell'architettura*. Translated and comments by Danielle Barbaro, Venice: Francesco de'Franceschi Senese, 1567, republished and edited by Manfredo Tafuri, Milan: Polifilo, 1987.

Vitruvius, Marcus Pollio, *Ten Books on Architecture*. Translated by Ingrid D. Rowland, Cambridge: Cambridge University Press, 1999.

Vitruvius, Marcus Pollio, *Vitruvius on Architecture*. Edited by Thomas Gordon Smith, "Emendation by Stephen Kellogg of the English translation of the *Ten Books on Architecture*" by Morris Hicky Morgan, New York: Monacelli, 2003.

Vitruvius, Marcus Pollio, *On Architecture*. Translated by Richard Schofield, London: Penguin, 2009.

Waley. Daniel, *The Italian City-Republics*, New York and Toronto: McGraw-Hill, 1969.

Watkin, David, *Morality and Architecture: The Development of a Theme in Architectural History and Theory from the Gothic Revival to the Modern Movement*, Chicago: University of Chicago Press, 1977.

Watkin, David, *The Rise of Architectural History*, Chicago: University of Chicago Press, 1980.

Wenger, Mark R., "Thomas Jefferson and the Virginia State Capitol," *Virginia Magazine of History and Biography*, 101 (1993): 77–102.

Westfall, Carroll William, "Society, Beauty, and the Humanist Architect in Alberti's *de re aedificatoria*," *Studies in the Renaissance*, 16 (1969): 61–79.

Westfall, Carroll William, "Biblical Typology in the *Vita Nicolai V* by G. Manetti," in *Acta Conventus Neo-Latini Lovaniensis*, Louvain, 1971, edited by J. IJsewijn and E. Kessler, 701–9, Leuven: Leuven University Press, 1973.

Westfall, Carroll William, *In This Most Perfect Paradise: Alberti, Nicholas V, and the Invention of Conscious Urban Planning in Rome, 1447–44*, University Park and London: Pennsylvania State University Press, 1974.

Westfall, Carroll William, "Historians, Testimony, and Designation Criteria," *The Forum: Bulletin of the Committee on Preservation (Society of Architectural Historians)*, 16 (August, 1987).

Westfall, Carroll William, "Buildings Serving Commerce," in *Chicago Architecture 1872–1922: Birth of a Metropolis*, edited by John Zukowsky, 77–89, Munich: Prestel-Verlag and The Art Institute of Chicago, 1987.

Westfall, Carroll William, "From Homes to Towers: A Century of Chicago's Best Hotels and Tall Apartments Buildings," in *Chicago Architecture 1872–1922: Birth of a Metropolis*, edited by John Zukowsky, 267–89, Munich: Prestel-Verlag and The Art Institute of Chicago, 1987.

Westfall, Carroll William, "Classical American Urbanism," in *New Classicism: Omnibus Volume*, edited by Andreas Papadakis and Harriet Watson, 73–5, New York: Rizzoli, and London: Academy Editions, 1990.

Westfall, Carroll William, "Chicago's Better Tall Apartment Buildings: 1871–1923," *Architectura*, 21 (1991): 177–208.

Westfall, Carroll William, "Painting and the Liberal Arts: Alberti's View," *Journal of the History of Ideas*, 30 (1969): 487–506; reprinted in *Renaissance Essays II*, edited by William J. Connell, 130–49, Rochester: University of Rochester Press, 1993.

Westfall, Carroll William, "Making Man's Dignity Visible in Buildings: The Foundations in Leon Battista Alberti's *de re aedificatoria*," in *Human Nature in its Wholeness: A Roman Catholic Perspective*, edited by Daniel N. Robinson, Gladys M. Sweeney, and Richard Gill, 144–59, Washington, D.C.: Catholic University of America Press, 2006.

Westfall, Carroll William, "Classicism and Language in Architecture," *American Arts Quarterly*, 27:1 (2010): 17–27.

Westfall, Carroll William, "Toward the End of Architecture," *Journal of Architectural Education*, 64:2 (2011): 149–57.

Westfall, Carroll William, "Beauty and Proportionality in Architecture," *American Arts Quarterly*, 30:1 (2013): 32–42.

Westfall, Carroll William, "The Jefferson Memorial: A Pyrrhic Victory for American Architecture," in *Civic Art: A Centennial History of the U. S. Commission of Fine Arts*, edited by Thomas S. Luebke, 154–63, Washington: U.S. Commission of Fine Arts, 2013.

Weyergraf-Serra, Clara and Martha Buskirk, *The Destruction of* Tilted-Arc: *Documents*, Cambridge, Mass., and London: MIT, 1991.

Whiffen, Marcus, *The Public Buildings of Williamsburg, Colonial Capital of Virginia*, Williamsburg: Colonial Williamsburg, 1958.

Wiebenson, Dora, *Sources of Greek Revival Architecture*, London: A. Zwimmer, 1969.

Wilson, Douglas L., "Dating Jefferson's Early Architectural Drawings," *Virginia Magazine of History and Biography*, 101 (1993): 56–60.

Wilson, James, *Lectures on Law* in *The Works of the Honourable James Wilson, L.L.D.* Edited by Bird Wilson, 3 vols, Philadelphia: Bronson and Chauncey, 1804.

Wilson, Richard Guy, "Jefferson's Lawn: Perceptions, Interpretations, Meanings," in *Thomas Jefferson's Academical Village: The Creation of an Architectural Masterpiece*, edited by R.G. Wilson, 47–83; 86–90, Charlottesville and London: University Press of Virginia, 1993.

Wilson, Richard Guy, "Thomas Jefferson's 'Bibliomanie' and Architecture," in *American Architects and their Books*, edited by Kenneth Hafertepe and James F. O'Gorman, 59–72, Amherst: University of Massachusetts Press, 2001.

Wirth, Louis, "Urbanism as a Way of Life," *The American Journal of Sociology*, 44 (1938), reprinted in *Cities and Society*, edited by Paul K. Hatt and Albert J. Reiss, Jr., 46–63, New York: The Free Press, 1951; 1957.

Wittkower, Rudolf, "Brunelleschi and 'Proportion in Perspective,'" *Journal of the Warburg and Courtauld Institutes* 16 (1953): 275–91.

Wittkower, Rudolf, "Individualism in Art and Artists: A Renaissance Problem," *Journal of the History of Ideas*, 22 (1961): 291–302.

Wittkower, Rudolf, *Architectural Principles in the Age of Humanism*, 3rd edn, London: Tiranti, 1962.

Wittkower, Rudolf and Margot Wittkower, *Born Under Saturn: The Character and Conduct of Artists: A Documentary History from Antiquity to the French Revolution*, London: Weidenfeld and Nicolson, 1963.

Wittkower, Rudolf, "Imitation, Eclecticism, and Genius," in *Aspects of the Eighteenth Century*, edited by Earl R. Wasserman, Baltimore: Johns Hopkins Press, 1965: 143–61.

Wittkower, Rudolf, "English Neo-Palladianism, the Landscape Garden, China and the Enlightenment," (1969), in *Palladio and Palladianism*, 176–90, 143–61, New York: George Braziller, 1974.

Wotton, Henry, *The Elements of Architecture* (1624) facsimile, Charlottesville: University Press of Virginia, 1968.

Wren, Christopher, "Tracts on Architecture," in *Wren's "Tracts" on Architecture and Other Writings*, Lydia M. Soo, 119–95, Cambridge: Cambridge University Press, 1998.

Wright, Gwendolyn, "History for Architects," in *The History of History in American Schools of Architecture 1865–1975*, edited by Gwendolyn Wright and Janet Parks, 13–52, New York: Temple Hoyne Buell Center for the Study of American Architecture and Princeton Architectural Press, 1990.

Wulfram, Hartmut, *Literische Vitruvrezeption in Leon Battista Albertis* De re aedificatoria, Munich and Leipzig: K.G. Saur, 2001.

Younés, Samir, *The True, the Fictive, and the Real: The Historical Dictionary of Architecture of Quatremère de Quincy*, London: Andreas Papadakis, 1999.

Younés, Samir, "Type, Character, and Style," in *New Palladians: Modernity and Sustainability for 21st Century Architecture*, edited by Alireza Sagharchi and Lucien Steil, 33–9, London: Artmedia, 2010.

Younés Samir, *The Imperfect City: On Architectural Judgment*, Farnham, Surrey, and Burlington, Vermont: Ashgate, 2012.

Younés, Samir, "Modern Traditional Architecture," in *Architecture: Timeless Building for the Twentieth-Century*, edited by Alireza Sagharchi and Lucien Steil, 20–37, New York et al.: Rizzoli, 2013.

Younés, Samir, "Jacques Ellul and the Eclipse of Artistic Symbolism," in *The Empire of Non-Sense: Art in the Technological Society*, translated by Michael Johnson and David Lovekin, 7–20, Winterbourne, Wilts.: Papadakis, 2014.

Zubov, Vasilij Pavlovič, "Léon Battista Alberti et les Auteurs du Moyen Age," *Medieval and Renaissance Studies* (University of London: The Warburg Institute), 4 (1958): 245–66.

Zubov, Vasilij Pavlovič, "La théorie architecturale d'Alberti," translated by Rénata Feldman, in *Albertiana*, 3 (2000): 11–62.

Index

academies
　Accademia del disegno, Florence, 78–81
　Accademia di San Luca, Rome 79
　American Academy in Rome 148, 177
　École des Beaux Arts 80, 91, 147, 160, 177, 178, 179
　French Royal Academy of Architecture 82
Adam, Robert 112, 127
Addison, James 86
Alberti, Leon Battista 6, 61, 69, 70, 71, 72, 77, 79, 119, 155, 164
　ancient buildings 26, 34
　art of architecture 27, 30–34, 43, 52
　art of building 26–9, 33–4, 45, 51, 52, 112
　beauty 27–32, 35, 39, 46–51, 52–4, 63
　content of architecture 30, 54
　defined 28, 50
　buildings by 44–5, **45**
　civil orders 41–2, 43–5, 51
　columnar orders 27–9, 31, 46–7
　concinnity 47–50
　de re aedificatoria translations 48, 49, 61, 112
　Florentine 40–41
　hierarchy of buildings 33–4, 52–4; *see also* decorum (*decore*)
　imitation 27, 31–2, 45–7, 50–51, 54
　life of 25–6
　lineaments 26, 33, 46–9, 51
　medieval sources 30, 41–2, 49, 51
　ornament 64, 70, 72, 160
　　church in city as 53, 54
　　column as 28, 29, 70
　　compartition as 33
　　urban plan as 54
　role of architect 39–40, 43, 44, 54

theory of painting 46, 63, 79, 81, 82
urbanism 51–4
Vitruvius 26, 27, 29
analogy, role of in architectural form
　anthropomorphic 8, 129, 176
　　Alberti 32
　　Barbaro, Danielle 69
　　Palladio 72
　　Perrault 82–3
　　Vitruvius 16, 17–18
　linguistic 88–9
　machine 89, 160, 179
architecture
　art of 7, 8, 80, 90, 103, 159, 175–7; *see also* Alberti, Leon Battista
　　Vitruvius 13–16, 19
　civic art x, 34, 39, 54, 120, 131
　　Jefferson 120, 131
　Fine Art 81, 169,
　styles of 1–3, 7, 90–91
　treatises 5–6, 61–9
architecture's tripod 149–60, 177–8
Aquinas, Saint Thomas 30, 50, 98
Aristotle 1, 4–5, 7, 20, 41–2, 48, 98, 100, 150, 153, 167
Augustus, Emperor 13, 18–19, 32, 77
Augustine, Saint 25, 29, 32, 41, 48, 49, 50, 53, 98, 167

Bacon, Francis 100
Barbaro, Danielle 69
Bartolus of Sassoferrato 41–2
beauty 63, 77, 91–2, 105, 125, 131, 149, 150, 152, 161–2, 163–4, 170, 174–8, 180; *see also* Alberti, Leon Battista; delight (*venustas*)
　British and early American authors 86–8, 101–6, 125

classical tradition (*pulcher*, pulchritude) 7–10, 17–18, 22, 27, 74, 77, 82, 92, 101–2, 105, 124–5, 149–50, 152, 170 180
   assault on 82, 176–7
   beauty and the good ix–x, 7, 9, 104, 177–8, 180
   beauty and the True 8, 10, 103
   Jefferson 119, 124–5, 127, 128–9, 130
   Kant 86, 91
   medieval authors 29–30, 49
   medieval trilogy 30
   Palladio 69–72, 74
   portrayal of 5
   relative (customary) 82, 89, 91–2, 101, 105, 108, 161, 175
      Alberti 29
      Perrault 82–5
      Vassari 80
      Vitruvius 17
Bernini, Gianlorenzo 78, 81, 111
Białostocki, Jan 4, 6–7
Blondel, Jacques-François 87
Blondel Françoise 82, 85
Boethius 29
Borromini, Francesco 81, 111
Boullée, Étienne-Louis 88, **88**
Boyle, Robert, Lord Burlington 111–12
Bramante, 63, 64, **66**, 71, 77, 81
Brunelleschi, Filippo 33, 41, 46, 80, 164
Bruni, Leonardo 40–41
building, art of 7–8, 121, 148, 150, 158, 159, 161, 173, 175–7; *see also* Alberti, Leon Battista
   Palladio 112
   Serlio 63
   Vitruvius 13–14, 18–19, 23, 27, 52
Bullfinch, Charles 127, 130
Burckhardt, Jacob 25
Burke, Edmund 86
Burnham, Daniel H. 107

Campbell, Colen 111, 112
Camus, Nicolas de Mézière Le 87
Chambers, William 127–8
character 4, 15, 21–2, 34, 54, 71–2, 87, 89, 101, 128–30, 134, 138, 148–9, 155–63, 174, 177, 179
Cicero 5, 7, 9, 20, 22, 29, 42, 53, 77, 78
city 32, 168; *see also* urban, urbanism
   American civil order 167–8
   doctrine of two cities 25, 41, 167–8
classical tradition 1, 5, 9, 17, 20–23, 26, 29, 32, 34, 45, 51–2, 72, 74, 77, 101, 119–20, 125–8, 130, 134, 138, 140, 147, 150–53, 155, 161, 163, 164, 167, 172–3, 178
   in Britain and America 100, 106–8, 112
   Modernism's demolition of 89, 91–2, 131, 155
   Perrault's assault on 82
classical triplet 27, 28, 46, 176
Clérisseau Charles-Louis 123, 138
Conciliarism 43
columnar orders 9, 46, 64, **67, 68**, 69, 70, 80, **84**, 85, 88, 89, 103, 105, 108, 112, 128, 131, 140, 148, 159, 160, 175, 177; *see also* Alberti, Leon Battista
concinnity , 47–50, 54, 63, 80, 124, 126, 152, 162, 164, 175–6
configuration 27, 33, 48, 53, 61, 72, 155, 158, 160–62
   and membrature 177, 34, 46, 48, 53, 140, 147, 151, 158, 160–62, 177
copy, copying 1, 2, 7, 8, 51, 79–80, 83, 103, 149, 161, 180
cosmos (universe) as model 9, 17, 20–21, 69
Cram, Ralph Adams 177

decorum (*decore*) 131, 160–61, 170–73, 179
   Alberti 33–4, 53–4
   Aquinas 30
   Jefferson 122, 129
   Palladio 71, 72
   Quatremère 149
   Vitruvius 14, 21–3
delight (*venustas*) 13–14, 17–18, 22, 27, 30, 33, 34, 39, 49, 51–2, 63, 71, 81, 83, 152, 170, 175
Descartes, René 100, 104
disegno 79–80
Donne, John 101
Dupré, Louis 90, 102
Durand, Claude-Nicolas-Louis 88

Ellul, Jacques 151
emulation 79–80, 81, 149
Erasmus 51, 81, 98
eurhythmy (*eurythmia*) 71, 82 175; *see also* concinnity
   in Vitruvius 14, 16, 17–18

Federalist Papers 109–10, 167
Ficino, Marsilio 78
fiction 7, 149, 159–60, 176
Filerete, Anionio Averlino called 61
Fine Arts 81, 89, 90, 103, 106, 120, 127, 131, 148, 161, 164, 168–70, 172

Fletcher, Sir Banister 1, 90
 Tree of Architecture **2**, 3, 91, 107
Freart Sieur de Chambray, Roland 112, **113**
Frederico da Montefeltro 42

Gibbs, James 112
Great Chain of Being 6, 10, 50, 99, 176
Greenberg, Allan 129
Guadet, Julien 179

Hamilton, Alexander 109, 134, 177, 180
Haussmann, Baron 148
Hegel, G.W.F. 1, 91–2
Hernandez, Jorge 72
Hitler 178
Hobbes, Thomas 104
Home, Henry, Lord Kames 105, 111
Hume, David 104, 111, 120, 172
Hutcheson, Francis 86, 102–5, 106, 111

imitation 1, 3–8, 20–21, 25, 103, 160
 Alberti 6–7, 31–5, 45–51, 54
 as excavation 162–3
 Jefferson 127, 129
 natura naturans and *natura naturata* 31–2, 48, 50, 110, 150, 155, 158–9
 Palladio 70
 Platonizing 78
 Perrault 83
 Shaftsbury 102
 Vitruvius 16, 17, 19, 70
influence 1, 3
innovation xi, 6, 27, 32, 81, 90, 98, 107, 109, 119, 125–6, 140, 159, 164, 176
institutions and functional arrangements 153–8, 176

Jefferson, Thomas 98, 107, 108, 109, 120–28, 134, 138, 147, 148, 160, 163, 164
 Alberti 119, 124
 cubic and spherical 124–5, 137–8
 models 121–2, 124, 125–7, 129–31, 138, 172
 Monticello 124, 130, 135, 138
 natural law 120
 Palladio 119, 122, 124, 125, 126, 130, 140
 Parisian buildings 130
 Poplar Forest 135–8, **136**, **137**, 140
 standing as architect 119
 training in architecture 112, 121
 urban schemes 135, 137–8, 139–40
  Jackson, Mississippi 135

Washington, D.C., involvement in 130–35, **132**, **133**
 University of Virginia 124, 129, 138–40, **139**, 176
 Virginia Capitol 122, **125**, 127, **128**, 129
 Virginia capital 122, 131
 Vitruvius 119
Jeffersonianism 147
Johnson, Samuel 87
Jones, Inigo 111
Julius Caesar 13
Julius II, Pope 61, 63, 77, 78, 81
jus natural, *see* law

Kant, Emmanuel, 86, 90–91, 102, 104
Kent, William 111
Kimball, Fiske 121, 122
kitsch 7, 179
Knight, Richard Payne 106
Krier, Leon 150, **151**, 159

Latrobe, Benjamin Henry 130, 131, 136, 138
Laugier, Marc-Antoine 70, 87
law
 common 97–100, 107, 120, 153
 laws of nature 7–8, 158–9, 176
 natural
  and architecture 7, 20, 49, 149–50, 161
  jus civile 20–21, 49, 109, 149–50, 161
  jus naturale 20, 49, 99–100, 106–9, 149–50, 161
Le Corbusier 89, 179
Ledoux, Claude-Nicolas 87–8, **88**
L'Enfant, Pierre Charles 131, 133, **133**, 134, 135
Leonardo da Vinci 78, 79
Leoni, Giacomo (James) 48, 111, 112, 121
Lincoln, Abraham 3, 168
lineaments
 Alberti 26–8, 32–5, 46–7, 70, 79
 and *structura* 26, 70
 Danielle Barbaro 70
 Palladio 70, 72
Locke, John 100, 102, 106
Louis XIV 78, 81, 85, 89, 90, 111

McEwan, Indra Kagis 17, 18, 175
Machiavelli 43, 64
McKim, Charles Follen 148, 177
Madison, James 107, 109, 122, 127, 128, 167
Maison Carrée, Nîmes 122, **123**, 124, 129–30, 160

Manetti, Giannozzo 43
Maritain, Jacques 51
Marsilius of Padua 41–2, 163
Martini, Francesco di Giorgio 61, **62**, 63
membrature, *see* configuration
Michelangelo 71, 78, 79, 81, 159
mimesis, *see* imitation
models 2, 4, 5–9, **8**, 13, 17, 19, 27, 31–4, 41, 61, 63–4, 69–72, 77, 78, 79–81, 82, 89–91, 105, 107, 112, 121–2, 124, 125–7, 129–31, 138, 140, 148–9, 160–64, 172
More, Thomas 81, 98
Mumford, Lewis 168

nature 7, 17, 31, 48, 72, 98, 124
Newton, Sir Isaac 100, 101, 176
Nicholas V, Pope 77

Onians, John 22
ordering (*ordinatione*) in Vitruvius 14–17
Orme, Philibert de l' 64, 82, 130
ornament 27, 29, 34, 46, 47, 50, 64, 70, 72, 160
orders, *see* columnar orders
Ortega y Gasset, José 168
O'Sullivan, Richard 99
Other Modern xi, 13, 150, 160, 161, 164, 171

painting 1, 5, 46, 79–80, 82, 103–6, 121, 169
Palladio, Andrea 69–**73**, **160**, 164
  Alberti 69
  images of modern and ancient buildings in 69–72, 90
  in Britain and America 69, 111–12, 176
  I Quattro libri, translations and editions of 111, 112, 126
Panofsky, Erwin 5
Pantheon, Rome 63, 78, 124, 138, 140, 160, 178
Perrault, Claude 82–5, **84**, 101, 102, 105, 124, 179
picturesque 86, 121
Piranesi, Giovanni Battista 86, **87**
Plato 4–5, 17, 44, 51, 78, 150, 152, 167, 176
Porphyrios, Demetri 7–8, 10, 148, 150, 158, 160
Ptolemy, Claudius 9

precedent(s)
  architecture 6, 31–4, 42, 53, 63–4, 71, 80–81, 91, 105, 123, 125–7, 134, 149, 160–62, 177
  common law 98–9, 126
Pythagoras 175

Quatremère de Quincy, Antoine Chrysostôme 88, 148–50, 155, 160
  fictive image 149
  imitation 149
  models 149
  representation 149
  type, character, and style 149–50, 163

Raphael 64, 78, 79, 81, 178
Reed, Henry Hope 150
representation 4–8, 63, 149
  arts of 32, 79–80, 103, 106
Reynolds, Sir Joshua 106, 111
rhetoric 22, 40–41, 53, 89, 107, 109
Richmond 122, 127, **128**, 129, 131, 171
Robinson, Daniel N. 100
Rohe, Mies van der 179
Romanticism 78, 86, 89, 106, 121, 173, 177
Ruskin, John 8, 89

Salingaros, Nikos 151–2
Scamozzi, Vincenzo 69, 82, **113**, 123
sculpture, 1, 79–82, 101, 106, 121, 169
Serlio, Sebastiano 63–7, 70, 79
  columnar orders **67**
  images of modern and ancient buildings in 63–4, **65**, **66**, 71, 90
Serra, Richard *Tilted Arc* 168–9, 174
Settis, Salvatore 164
Shaftsbury, Anthony Ashley Cooper, Third Earl of 101, 102, 104, 105, 111, 112, 120
Soane, Sir John 127, 133
style, in art and architecture 4, 81, 90, 177, 178; *see also* Quatremère de Quincy, Antoine Chrysostôme
sublime 86, 87, 106, 130
Summerson, Sir John 88–9
symmetry (*symmetria*)
  in Vitruvius 14, 16, 17
  in Palladio 71
  in Perrault, as proportions 82–5
  lacking in Alberti 46
synoecism 110, 138, 153–4, 173–4

Tanner, Marie 77
taste 29, 79, 83–5, 86, 111, 127, 131, 160–61, 169, 172
   Hume 104–5, 172
   Jefferson 126–8, 130
Tatarkiewicz, Władyslaw 22
tectonics 7, 26, 148
Thornton, William 138
tradition xi, 6, 27, 34, 90, 106, 125, 155, 159, 164, 176
Tzonis, Alexander 64

universal law, see law, natural
urban, urbanism 20–21, 77, 92, 134–5, 164, 174; see also city; Jefferson, urban schemes
   Alberti, 34, 39, 45, 51–4
   Palladio 71–2
   Vitruvius 19, 20–21

Vanbrugh, Sir John 106, 111
venustas, see delight (*venustas*)
Vasari, Giorgio 71, 78–81, 85
vernacular 7, 159
   Alberti 29, 34
   Krier, 150
   Porphyrios 7, 158
Vignola, Giacomo Barozzi da 64, **68**, 82

Vitruvius 6, 9, 13, 26, 39–40, 43, 46, 54, 105, 152, 164; see also imitation
   appearance, aspect (*aspectus*) 15, 17–18, 26
   editions and translations of treatise 26, 61
   fabrica and ratiocination 14–15, 26
   Vitruvian man, see analogy, role of in architectural form, anthropomorphic
   Vitruvian trilogy 13–14, 16, 22, 175
      Alberrti 30, 48, 52
      Palladio 71
Vitruvianism 61, 64, 69, 77, 126
Voltaire 90

Washington, D.C. 128, 129–34, **133**, 178, 176
Washington, George 129, 131, 133, 134
Watkin, David 1
Webb, John 111
Williamsburg 121, 122, 126–7, 134
Wilson, James 127
Winckelmann, Johan Joachim 90
Wittkower, Rudolf 101, 173
Wooton, Sir Henry 13, 82
Wren, Sir Christopher 101, 111, 112, 120

Zeuxis 5–6